A PRIMER ON THE TAGUCHI METHOD

Ranjit K. Roy

COMPETITIVE
Manufacturing
SERIES

VNR VAN NOSTRAND REINHOLD
New York

Copyright © 1990 by Van Nostrand Reinhold

Library of Congress Catalog Card Number 89-14736
ISBN 0-442-23729-4

Printed in the United States of America

Van Nostrand Reinhold
115 Fifth Avenue
New York, NY 10003

Van Nostrand Reinhold International Company Limited
11 New Fetter Lane
London EC4P 4EE, England

Van Nostrand Reinhold
480 La Trobe Street
Melbourne, Victoria 3000, Australia

Nelson Canada
1120 Birchmount Road
Scarborough, Ontario M1K 5G4, Canada

16 15 14 13 12 11 10 9 8 7 6 5 4 3 2 1

Library of Congress Cataloging-in-Publication Data

Roy, Ranjit.
    A primer on the Taguchi method / Ranjit Roy.
        p.   cm. -- (Competitive manufacturing series)
    Bibliography: p.
    Includes index.
    ISBN 0-442-23729-4
    1. Taguchi methods (Quality control)   2. Taguchi, Gen 'ichi, 1924–
        I. Title.   II. Series.
    TS156.R69   1990
    658.5'62--dc20   89-14736
                                                         CIP

*To my wife Krishna and
my daughters Purba and Paula.*

People don't use their eyes. They never see a bird, they see a sparrow. They never see a tree, they see a birch. They see concepts.

—Joyce Cary

— VNR COMPETITIVE MANUFACTURING SERIES —

Product and Process Design

PRACTICAL EXPERIMENT DESIGN by William J. Diamond
VALUE ANALYSIS IN DESIGN by Theodore C. Fowler
A PRIMER ON THE TAGUCHI METHOD by Ranjit Roy
MANAGING NEW-PRODUCT DEVELOPMENT by Geoff Vincent
ART AND SCIENCE OF INVENTING by Gilbert Kivenson
RELIABILITY ENGINEERING IN SYSTEMS DESIGN AND OPERATION by
Balbir S. Dhillon
RELIABILITY AND MAINTAINABILITY MANAGEMENT by
Balbir S. Dhillon and Hans Reiche
APPLIED RELIABILITY by Paul A. Tobias and David C. Trindad

Manufacturing (hard)

INDUSTRIAL ROBOT HANDBOOK:
CASE HISTORIES OF EFFECTIVE ROBOT USE IN 70 INDUSTRIES by Richard K. Miller
ROBOTIC TECHNOLOGY: PRINCIPLES AND PRACTICE by Werner G. Holzbock
MACHINE VISION by Nello Zuech and Richard K. Miller
DESIGN OF AUTOMATIC MACHINERY by Kendrick W. Lentz, Jr.
TRANSDUCERS FOR AUTOMATION by Michael Hordeski
MICROPROCESSORS IN INDUSTRY by Michael Hordeski
DISTRIBUTED CONTROL SYSTEMS by Michael P. Lukas
BULK MATERIALS HANDLING HANDBOOK by Jacob Fruchtbaum
MICROCOMPUTER SOFTWARE FOR MECHANICAL ENGINEERS by Howard Falk

Manufacturing (soft)

WORKING TOWARDS JUST-IN-TIME by Anthony Dear
GROUP TECHNOLOGY: FOUNDATION FOR COMPETITIVE MANUFACTURING by
Charles S. Snead
FROM IDEA TO PROFIT: MANAGING ADVANCED MANUFACTURING TECHNOLOGY
by Jule A. Miller
COMPETITIVE MANUFACTURING by Stanley Miller
STRATEGIC PLANNING FOR THE INDUSTRIAL ENGINEERING FUNCTION by
Jack Byrd and L. Ted Moore

SUCCESSFUL COST REDUCTION PROGRAMS FOR ENGINEERS AND MANAGERS by
E. A. Criner
MATERIAL REQUIREMENTS OF MANUFACTURING by Donald P. Smolik
PRODUCTS LIABILITY by Warren Freedman
LABORATORY MANAGEMENT: PRINCIPLES & PRACTICE by
Homer Black, Ronald Hart, Orrin Peterson

Materials Management

TOTAL MATERIALS MANAGEMENT: THE FRONTIER FOR COST-CUTTING
IN THE 1990S by Eugene L. Magad and John Amos
MATERIALS HANDLING: PRINCIPLES AND PRACTICE by Theodore H. Allegri, Sr.
PRACTICAL STOCK AND INVENTORY TECHNIQUES THAT CUT COSTS AND
IMPROVE PROFITS by C. Louis Hohenstein

Contents

Preface /xi
Abbreviations /xii

1. **Quality Through Product and Process Optimization** /1
   1-1 Background /1
   1-2 Design of Experiments—The Conventional Approach /1
       Exercises /5

2. **The Taguchi Approach to Quality and Cost Improvement** /7
   2-1 Background /7
   2-2 Taguchi Philosophy /8
   2-3 The Concept of the Loss Function /10
   2-4 Experiment Design Strategy /14
   2-5 Analysis of Results /16
   2-6 Areas of Application /17
   2-7 The New Approach—Its Appeal and Limitations /17
       Exercises /18

3. **Measurement of Quality** /19
   3-1 The Quality Characteristic /19
   3-2 Variation as a Quality Yardstick /20
   3-3 Cost of Variation /22
   3-4 Quality and Variation /22
   3-5 The Quality We Are After /22
   3-6 The Taguchi Quality Strategy /23
   3-7 Selecting Design Parameters for Reduced Variation /24
   3-8 Common Terminology /27
       Exercises /28

4. **Procedures of the Taguchi Method and Its Benefits** /29
   4-1 The New Discipline /29
   4-2 Up-Front Thinking /31
   4-3 Experimental Efficiency /31
   4-4 Effective Use of Statistical Process Control /32
   4-5 Long Term Benefits /32
   4-6 Quantifying Cost Benefits—Taguchi Loss Function /33
   4-7 Specifying Tolerance Levels /37
       Exercises /39

5. Working Mechanics of the Taguchi Design of Experiments   /40
   5-1 Formulas for Experiment Layout   /40
   5-2 Basic Methodology   /40
   5-3 Designing the Experiment   /44
      5-3-1 Order of Running the Experiments   /46
      5-3-2 Analysis of Results   /47
      5-3-3 Quality Characteristics   /49
      5-3-4 ANOVA Terms and Notations   /50
      5-3-5 Variation Computation—Examples   /51
      5-3-6 Degrees of Freedom (DOF)   /52
      5-3-7 Projecting of the Optimum Performance   /55
   5-4 Designing with More than Three Variables   /56
      5-4-1 Designs with 2-Level Variables   /56
      5-4-2 Designs with 3-Level Variables   /58
      5-4-3 Designs with Mixed Levels Using Standard Arrays   /58
   5-5 Designs with Interactions   /58
      5-5-1 Steps in the Design and Analysis   /62
      5-5-2 Interaction Effects   /68
      5-5-3 Key Observations   /71
      5-5-4 More Designs with Interactions   /72
   5-6 Designs with Mixed Factor Levels   /75
      5-6-1 Preparation of a 4 Level Column   /77
      5-6-2 Preparation of an 8 Level Column   /79
   5-7 Dummy Treatment (Column Degrading)   /82
   5-8 Combination Design   /87
   5-9 Designing Experiments to Investigate Noise Factors   /90
   5-10 Benefiting from Repetitions   /91
   5-11 Definition of *S/N* Ratio   /92
   5-12 Repetitions under Controlled Noise Conditions   /94
   5-13 Design and Analysis Summary   /96
      Exercises   /98

6. Analysis of Variance (ANOVA)   /100
   6-1 The Role of ANOVA   /100
   6-2 ANOVA Terms, Notations and Development   /100
   6-3 One Way ANOVA   /106
   6-4 One Factor Two Level Experiments (One Way ANOVA)   /112
      6-4-1 Confidence Intervals   /116
   6-5 Two Way ANOVA   /117
   6-6 Experiments with Replications   /121
      6-6-1 Procedures for Pooling   /124

6-7 Standard Analysis with Single and Multiple Runs   /126
    6-7-1 Analysis Using Single Run   /126
    6-7-2 Pooling   /134
    6-7-3 Confidence Interval of Factor Effect   /138
    6-7-4 Estimated Result at Optimum Condition   /139
    6-7-5 Confidence Interval of the Result at the Optimum
        Condition   /140
    6-7-6 Analysis with Multiple Runs   /142
6-8 Application of the S/N Ratio   /145
    6-8-1 Conversion of Results into S/N Ratios   /145
    6-8-2 Advantage of S/N Ratio over Average   /146
    6-8-3 Computation of the S/N Ratio   /148
    6-8-4 Effect of the S/N Ratio on the Analysis   /150
    6-8-5 When to Use the S/N Ratio for Analysis   /154
    Exercises 155

7. Loss Function   /156
7-1 Derivation of Loss Function   /156
7-2 Average Loss Function for Product Population   /160
7-3 Application of Loss Function Concepts   /160
    Exercises   /172

8. Brainstorming—An Integral Part of the Taguchi Philosophy   /173
8-1 The Necessity of Brainstorming   /173
8-2 The Nature of the Session   /173
8-3 Topics of the Discussions   /175
8-4 Typical Discussions in the Session   /176
    Exercises   /179

9. Examples of Taguchi Case Studies   /181
9-1 Application Benchmarks   /181
9-2 Application Examples Including Design and Analysis   /182
    Example 9-1 Engine Valve-Train Noise Study   /182
    Example 9-2 Study of Crankshaft Surface Finishing Process   /186
    Example 9-3 Automobile Generator Noise Study   /190
    Example 9-4 Engine Idle Stability Study   /193
    Example 9-5 Instrument Panel Structure Design Optimization   /195
    Example 9-6 Study Leading to the Selection of the Worst Case
               Barrier Test Vehicle   /198
    Example 9-7 Airbag Design Study   /203
    Example 9-8 Transmission Control Cable Adjustment
               Parameters   /204

Example 9-9 Front Structure Crush Characteristics   /208

References   /210

Appendix A Orthogonal Arrays, Triangular Tables and
            Linear Graphs   /211
Appendix B F-Tables   /231
Appendix C Glossary   /243

Index   /245

Preface

Since the late 1940s Dr. Genichi Taguchi has introduced several new statistical concepts which have proven to be valuable tools in the subject of quality improvement. Many Japanese manufacturers have used his approach for improving product and process quality with unprecedented success. The quality of Japanese automobiles is attributable largely to the widespread application of the Taguchi Method.* This book introduces the basic concepts of the Taguchi methods through application examples and special case studies.

Taguchi's method is based upon an approach which is completely different from the conventional practices of quality engineering. His methodology emphasizes designing the quality into the products and processes, whereas the more usual practice relies upon inspection. In his quality improvement practices Taguchi essentially utilizes the conventional statistical tools, but he simplifies them by identifying a set of stringent guidelines for experiment layout and the analysis of results. Taguchi's approach has been extremely effective in improving the quality of Japanese products. Recently Western industries have begun to recognize Taguchi's method as a simple but highly effective approach to improving product and process quality.

Taguchi's experimental design approach is suitable for a wide range of applications. But his techniques have commonly been applied to what he classifies as "off-line" quality control. He distinguishes three phases of off-line quality control: system design, parameter design, and tolerance design. Parameter design is primarily the subject of this book.

This book is intended for practicing engineers and managers who are interested in developing a basic understanding and basic skill in utilizing the Taguchi concepts and methodologies. Common application methods and simple analysis techniques are discussed in detail. More complex analysis and application techniques are beyond the scope of this work.

---

*The term *Taguchi Method*™ is a trademark of the American Supplier Institute, Inc., Dearborn, Michigan, and is used by permission.

ACKNOWLEDGMENT

I would like to express my gratitude to Ron Gaizer, Ellen Menzies and Doug Carr of Technicomp, Cleveland, Ohio, who approached me to prepare a manual to be used to develop a video training program on the subject. My thanks also to a group of reviewers whom Technicomp employed to review the text materials during the video production.

I am also grateful to the hundreds of practicing engineers at General Motors, my former place of employment, who have unknowingly served as guinea pigs as I preached and practiced the application methodologies outlined in this book. I thank all the lead engineers who sought my advice in carrying out their Taguchi case studies and asked me to facilitate the brainstorming sessions. These application exercises provided much of the material in this book.

I am also indebted to my colleagues at Nutek, Inc., Girish Bapu and Roxanne Lawrence for their help in putting together the original report on the subject. A large portion of the early versions of this manuscript were distributed in summary form to my seminar attendees and returned to me with suggestions for improvement. I thank Ayenul Haque, Scott Taylor, Marcel Beauregard, Brad Hammer, Gary Engel, William Howell, Avi Shah, Phil Ross and Viswas Bowele for innumerable suggestions for improvements. I would also like to express my thanks to Dr. R. Roychoudhury and Dr. S. Khashnabis, who have given me advice and suggestions for this book that only close personal friends can give. Their criticism has been invaluable. I am also deeply grateful to two members of Van Nostrand Reinhold: Gene Dallaire for finding me and for providing encouragement to undertake this endeavor, and George M. Kaplan for editing the manuscript and for making a number of suggestions toward improving the presentation of the material.

Finally, thanks to all members of my family for their kind understanding of my frequent absence from family activities and for help preparing the manuscript.

ABBREVIATIONS AND SYMBOLS

A, B . . . Variables used in the design of an experiment
A_i The sum of observations under condition A_i ($i = 1,2,3$, etc.)
A_i The average of observations under condition A_i
C.I.   The confidence interval
DOE   Design of experiment
e Experimental error
f, n Degrees of freedom
F Variance ratio
k A constant used in the expression for the loss function
L The Taguchi loss function
L_8 An orthogonal array that has 8 experiments
MSD   Mean square deviation
N The number of experiments
OA   Orthogonal array, L_4, L_8, L_{16}, etc.
P The percent contribution of a variable
S The sum of squares
S' The net/pure sum of squares
S/N The signal to noise ratio
T The sum of all observations
V The variance (mean square, S/f)
Y Results measured in terms of quality characteristics.
          Examples: cost, weight, length, surface finish.
α Alpha
μ Population mean
σ Population standard deviation
σ^2 Population variance

1

Quality Through Product and Process Optimization

1-1 BACKGROUND

Mankind has always had a fascination with quality. Today's technology bears testimony to man's incessant desire to provide a higher level of quality in products and services to increase market share and profits. Sometimes, quality is essential. A pacemaker that controls heart action must operate continuously and precisely. An erratic pacemaker is valueless, useless, and dangerous.

Driven by the need to compete on price and performance and to maintain profitability, quality conscious manufacturers are increasingly aware of the need to optimize products and processes. Quality achieved by means of design optimization is found by many manufacturers to be cost effective in gaining and maintaining a competitive position in the world market.

1-2 DESIGN OF EXPERIMENTS—THE CONVENTIONAL APPROACH

The technique of defining and investigating all possible conditions in an experiment involving multiple factors is known as the design of experiments. In the literature this technique is also referred to as factorial design. The concepts of design of experiments have been in use since Fisher's work in agricultural experimentation, approximately half a century ago. Fisher (Ref. 12) successfully designed experiments to determining optimum treatments for land to achieve maximum yield. Numerous applications of this approach, especially in the chemical and pharmaceutical industries, are cited in the literature. A thorough coverage of this subject is beyond the scope of this study, but the method and its advantages and disadvantages from an engineering point of view, is illustrated by a simple example.

Consider a snack food company planning to introduce a new chocolate chip cookie in the market. The product designers have standardized all other ingredients except the amount of sugar and chocolate chips. Two levels of chips, C_1 and C_2 and two levels of sugar, S_1 and S_2 were selected. (Subscripts 1 and 2, respectively refer to the low and high levels of each factor.) In order to select the best combination of these ingredients that appeal most to potential customers, the market research group decided to conduct a market survey of customer preference.

This is one of the simplest cases of design of experiments. It involves two factors (chips and sugar) at two different levels (high and low) that affect the taste of cookies. Such an experiment is described as a 2×2 factorial experiment. There are four (2^2) possible treatments or combinations. The responses to these factors, as obtained by a taste test, are given in Table 1-1.

Examination of customer response shows a 10% (55-45) increase in preference for the sugar level S_2 at the low level (C_1) of chocolate chips but the response increases to 15% (80-65) when more chips C_2 are used. These increases are called the simple effect of sugar. On the other hand, for the higher amount of chips, the taste preference increased from 45% to 65% at sugar level S_1 and further increased to 80% with the higher sugar level S_2. The mean response, i.e., the difference between the av-

Table 1-1. Taste Survey with Preference in Percent

LEVEL OF CHOCOLATE CHIPS	SUGAR LEVEL		MEAN	MEAN RESPONSE (CHOCOLATE CHIPS) ($C_2 - C_1$)
	S_1	S_2		
C_1	45	55	50.0	22.5
C_1	65	80	72.5	
Mean	55.0	67.5	Grand mean 61.25	
Mean response (sugar) ($S_2 - S_1$)	12.5			

erage effects at two levels of sugar (12.5%), is called the main effect of sugar. Similarly, the main effect for chocolate chips is 22.5%. It is important to note that in this example, only the main effects are analyzed; no attempt is made to analyze the interactions between the factors. These interactions may or may not be present. The interactions between various factors of an experiment can be quantitatively determined by using the analysis of variance (ANOVA). This procedure is described in Chapter 6.

For the present, the degree of the interactions for a 2 × 2 experiment can be determined from Figure 1-1 which graphs the response against one factor (C) for two levels of the second factor (S). Since the lines for the two levels, S_1 and S_2 are almost parallel, the factors (S and C) are said to be independent and little or no interaction is assumed to exist. Nonparallel lines would indicate the presence of some interaction. Highly skewed or intersecting lines would indicate strong interaction between the two factors. Figure 1-1 indicates a slight interaction between the two factors (sugar and chocolate chips).

In the above example there were only two factors, each at two different levels. It would be rather easy to manufacture four types of cookies reflecting all possible combinations of the factors under study and to subject them to a market survey.

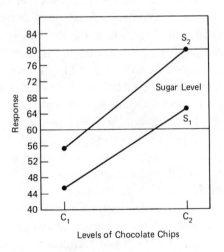

Figure 1-1. Factor effects.

Table 1-2. Test Matrix with Three Factors at Two Levels

	A_1		A_2		
	B_1	B_2	B_1	B_2	AVERAGE
C_1					
C_2		Cell			
Average					

For a full factorial design the number of possible designs N is

$$N = L^m \tag{1.1}$$

where L = Number of levels for each factor
and m = Number of factors

Thus, if the qualities of a given product depends on three factors A, B, and C and each factor is to be tested at two levels then, Eq. (1-1) indicates 2^3 (8) possible design configurations. This three factor, two level experiment is represented by Table 1-2.

The size of the test matrix is still easily managed and every combination can be investigated. Each box in the table is called a cell. In order to improve accuracy several observations are made per cell and the significance of the results are determined by statistical analysis (ANOVA).

Now let us consider the case where the cookies under consideration have 15 different ingredients, at two levels of each. In this case, 2^{15} (32,768) possible varieties of cookies need to be investigated before the most desirable recipe can be established. A market research program of this magnitude would be exorbitant in cost and time. Techniques such as fractional factorial experiments are used to simplify the experiment. Fractional factorial experiments investigate only a fraction of all the possible combinations. This approach saves considerable time and money but requires rigorous mathematical treatment, both in the design of the experiment and in the analysis of the results. Each experimenter may design a different set of fractional factorial experiments. Herein lies Taguchi's contribution to the science of the design of experiments. He simplified and standardized the fractional factorial designs in such a manner that two engineers conducting tests thousands of miles apart, will always use similar designs and tend to obtain similar results. Therefore, to summarize, factorial and fractional factorial designs of experiments are widely and effectively used. However, they suffer the following limitations:

1. The experiments become unwieldy in cost and time when the number of variables is large.
2. Two designs for the same experiment may yield different results.
3. The designs normally do not permit determination of the contribution of each factor.
4. The interpretation of experiments with a large number of factors may be quite difficult.

Taguchi contributed discipline and structure to the design of experiments. The result is a standardized design methodology that can easily be applied by investigators. Furthermore, designs for the same experiment by two different investigators will yield similar data and will lead to similar conclusions. Taguchi overcame the limitations of factorial and fractional factorial experiments.

EXERCISES

1-1. What are the three main disadvantages of the conventional design of experiment approach as compared with Taguchi's method?

1-2. Which one of the following two "Factor Effect" graphs (Fig. 1-2) indicate the existence of an interaction between the two factors of an experiment?

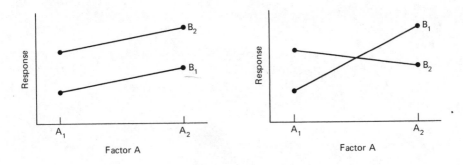

Figure 1-2. Factor effect plots.

Table 1-3. Two Factor Experiment Data

	A		AVERAGE	RESPONSE TO B $(B_1 - B_2)$
	A_1	A_2		
B_1	40	70	$B_1 = 55$	
B_2	65	45	$B_2 = 55$	0
Average	$A_1 = 52.5$	$A_2 = 57.5$		
Response $(A_2 - A_1)$	5			

1-3. A product involves three primary parameters at three different levels of each. In order to optimize the product, a full factorial design is planned for experimental evaluations. How many possible design configurations need to be tested to achieve the objective? $3^3 = 27$

1-4. Draw a factor graph for the experiment shown in Table 1-3 and discuss the results.

An interaction is present.

2

The Taguchi Approach to Quality
and Cost Improvement

2-1 BACKGROUND

After the Second World War the allied forces found that the quality of
the Japanese telephone system was extremely poor and totally unsuitable
for long term communication purposes. To improve the system the allied
command recommended that Japan establish research facilities similar to
the Bell Laboratories in the United States in order to develop a state-of-
the-art communication system. The Japanese founded the Electrical Communication Laboratories (ECL) with Dr. Taguchi in charge of improving
the R&D productivity and enhancing product quality. He observed that
a great deal of time and money was expended in engineering experimentation and testing. Little emphasis was given to the process of creative
brainstorming to minimize the expenditure of resources.

Dr. Taguchi started to develop new methods to optimize the process
of engineering experimentation. He developed techniques which are now
known as the Taguchi Methods. His greatest contribution lies not in the
mathematical formulation of the design of experiments, but rather in the
accompanying philosophy. His approach is more than a method to lay
out experiments. His is a concept that has produced a unique and powerful
quality improvement discipline that differs from traditional practices.

Two completely opposing points of views are commonly held about
Taguchi's contribution to the statistical design of experiments. One view
holds that Dr. Taguchi's contribution to the field of quality control is one
of the most significant developments of the last few decades. The other
view maintains that many of the ideas proposed in his approach are neither
new nor were they developed by Dr. Taguchi. This text will not resolve
this controversy but will document successful case studies using Taguchi's
methods. These new techniques were transplanted to the United States
and created significant changes in quality engineering methods in this
country. The Taguchi approach has been successfully applied in several

7

industrial organizations and has completely changed their outlook on quality control.

2-2 TAGUCHI PHILOSOPHY

Taguchi espoused an excellent philosophy for quality control in the manufacturing industries. Indeed, his doctrine is creating an entirely different breed of engineers who think, breathe and live quality. He has, in fact, given birth to a new quality culture in this country. Ford Motor Company, for example, has decreed that all Ford Motor and suppliers' engineers be trained in Taguchi methodology and that these principles be used to resolve their quality issues. His philosophy has far reaching consequences, yet it is founded on three very simple and fundamental concepts. The whole of the technology and techniques arise entirely out of these three ideas. These concepts are:

1. Quality should be designed into the product and not inspected into it.
2. Quality is best achieved by minimizing the deviation from a target. The product should be so designed that it is immune to uncontrollable environmental factors.
3. The cost of quality should be measured as a function of deviation from the standard and the losses should be measured system-wide.

Taguchi built upon W. E. Deming's observation that 85% of poor quality is attributable to the manufacturing process and only 15% to the worker. Hence he developed manufacturing systems that were "robust" or insensitive to daily and seasonal variations of environment, machine wear, and other external factors. The three principles were his guides in developing these systems, testing the factors affecting quality production and specifying product parameters.

Taguchi believed that the better way to improve quality was to design and build it into the product. Quality improvement starts at the very beginning, i.e., during the design stages of a product or a process, and continues through the production phase. He proposed an "off-line" strategy for developing quality improvement in place of an attempt to inspect quality into a product on the production line. He observed that poor quality cannot be improved by the process of inspection, screening and salvaging. No amount of inspection can put quality back into the product;

it merely treats a symptom. Therefore, quality concepts should be based upon, and developed around, the philosophy of prevention. The product design must be so robust that it is immune to the influence of uncontrolled environmental factors on the manufacturing processes. He emphasizes that quality is what one designs into a product.

His second concept deals with actual methods of effecting quality. He contended that quality is directly related to deviation of a design parameter from the target value, not to conformance to some fixed specifications. A product may be produced with properties skewed towards one end of an acceptance range yet show shorter life expectancy. However, by specifying a target value for the critical property and developing manufacturing processes to meet the target value with little deviation, the life expectancy may be much improved.

His third concept calls for measuring deviations from a given design parameter in terms of the overall life cycle costs of the product. These costs would include the cost of scrap, rework, inspection, returns, warranty service calls and/or product replacement. These costs provide guidance regarding the major parameters to be controlled.

Taguchi views quality improvement as an ongoing effort. He continually strives to reduce variation around the target value. A product under investigation may exhibit a distribution that has a mean value different from the target value. The first step towards improving quality is to achieve the population distribution as close to the target value as possible. To accomplish this, Taguchi designs experiments using especially constructed tables known as "orthogonal arrays" (OA). The use of these tables makes the design of experiments very easy and consistent.

A second objective of manufacturing products to conform to an ideal value is to reduce the variation or scatter around the target. To accomplish this objective, Dr. Taguchi cleverly incorporates a unique way to treat noise factors. Noise factors, according to his terminology, are factors which influence the response of a process, but cannot be economically controlled. The noise factors such as weather conditions, machinery wear, etc., are usually the prime sources for variations. Through the use of what he calls the "outer arrays," Taguchi devised an effective way to study their influence with the least number of repetitions. The end result is a "robust" design affected minimally by noise, i.e., with a high signal to noise value.

To achieve desirable product quality by design, Dr. Taguchi recommends a three stage process.

1. Systems design
2. Parameter design
3. Tolerance design

The focus of the system design phase is on determining the suitable working levels of design factors. It includes designing and testing a system based on the engineer's judgment of selected materials, parts, and nominal product/process parameters based on current technology. Most often it involves innovation and knowledge from the applicable fields of science and technology.

While system design helps to identify the working levels of the design factors, parameter design seeks to determine the factor levels that produce the best performance of the product/process under study. The optimum condition is selected so that the influence of the uncontrolled factors (noise factors) causes minimum variation of system performance. This text deals solely with parameter design.

Tolerance design is a step used to fine tune the results of parameter design by tightening the tolerance of factors with significant influence on the product. Such steps will normally lead to identifying the need for better materials, buying newer equipment, spending more money for inspection, etc.

2-3 THE CONCEPT OF THE LOSS FUNCTION

The concept of the "total loss function" employed by Dr. Taguchi has forced engineers and cost accountants to take a serious look at the quality control practices of the past. The concept is simple but effective. He defines quality as "the total loss imparted to the society from the time a product is shipped to the customer." The loss is measured in monetary terms and includes all costs in excess of the cost of a perfect product. The definition can be expanded to include the development and manufacturing phases of a product.

A poorly conceived and designed product begins to impart losses to society from the embryonic stage and continues to do so until steps are taken to improve its functional performance. There are two major categories of loss to society with respect to the product quality. The first category relates to the losses incurred as a result of harmful effects to society (e.g., pollution) and the second relates to the losses arising because of excessive variation in functional performance. In this book, the total loss function refers essentially to the second category.

The conventional method of computing the cost of quality is based on the number of parts rejected and reworked. This method of quality evaluation is incapable of distinguishing between two samples, both within the specification limits, but with different distributions of targeted properties. Figure 2-1 shows the conventional method and Taguchi's view of loss function. This graph depicts the loss function as a function of deviation from an ideal or the target value of a given design parameter. Here T represents the target value or the most desirable value of the parameter under consideration. This parameter may be a critical dimension, color of the product, surface finish or any other characteristic that contributes to the customer's conception of quality. How this ideal value of the parameter was arrived at and how significant this value is in achieving our quality goals, will be evident later.

UAL and LAL in Figure 2-1, represent upper and lower acceptable limits of a design parameter, respectively. Normally the product is functionally acceptable if the value of the specified parameter is within the range between the UAL and LAL limits. No societal loss is assumed to occur; the product is shipped to the consumer. However outside these limits, as shown by the crosshatched region, 100% functional deterioration occurs and the product is either discarded or subjected to salvage operations. Every attempt is made to control the manufacturing process to maintain the product within these limits.

However, according to Taguchi, there is no sharp cutoff in the real world. Performance begins to gradually deteriorate as the design parameter deviates from its optimum value. Therefore he proposed that the loss function be measured by the deviation from the ideal value. This function is continuous as shown by the dotted line in Figure 2-1. Product perfor-

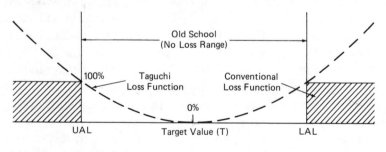

LAL = Lower allowable limit
UAL = Upper allowable limit

Figure 2-1. Taguchi and conventional loss functions.

mance begins to suffer when the design parameters deviate from the ideal or the target value. Taguchi's definition clearly puts more emphasis on customer satisfaction, whereas previously all definitions were related to the producer. Optimum customer satisfaction can be achieved by developing the products which meet the target value on a consistent basis. It may be worthwhile to mention that Taguchi allows for more than 100% loss imparted by a product. Such cases can occur when a subsystem results in a failure of the entire system or when a system fails catastrophically. Thus the single most important aspect of Taguchi's quality control philosophy is the minimization of variation around the target value.

A case study conducted by SONY makes it abundantly clear that these two schools of thought are significantly different from each other, and indeed affect customer satisfaction. SONY manufactures color TVs in Japan and in the U.S. The TVs from both sources are intended for the U.S. market and have identical design and system tolerances. Yet American consumers consistently preferred the color characteristics of the TV sets manufactured overseas.

A study was conducted to determine a cause for the difference in customer preference. The results indicated that the frequency distributions for the sets manufactured in U.S. and those manufactured in Japan were significantly different as shown in Figure 2-2. Plants in both countries produced TVs with color density within tolerance range. No TVs with out-of-tolerance color characteristics were shipped to the consumer. However, the U.S. built sets followed a somewhat flat distribution consistent with a go/nogo philosophy, while the product manufactured in Japan followed a normal distribution with small deviation from the target value. The large scatter, observed in the performance characteristics of the product manufactured in the U.S., as is evident from Figure 2-2, was responsible for significantly lower customer preference for these sets. Once the process in the U.S. plant was brought under control and began to produce the frequency distribution similar to the TVs produced in Japan, customer satisfaction with the U.S. product achieved the level of satisfaction seen with the imported sets. The Sony case demonstrated that quality is more than just producing between upper and lower limits— quality is achieving the target as much as possible and limiting deviations from the target.

Consider another example which will further support this concept of quality. Two batches of main bearings for an internal combustion engine were received from two different sources, *A* and *B*, for a new engine development program. Under laboratory conditions, bearings from source

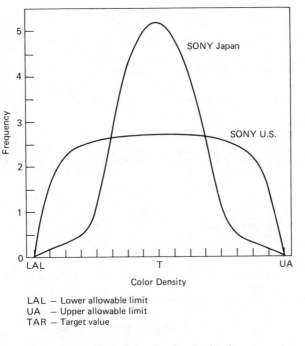

LAL — Lower allowable limit
UA — Upper allowable limit
TAR — Target value

Figure 2-2. Color density distributions.

B wore much faster than those from source *A*. To pinpoint the cause of unequal wear, selected performance characteristics of the bearings were measured and posted. Both batches of bearings were within the design specifications. However, the source *B* bearings consistently measured a mean diameter on the larger side of the tolerance limits as depicted in Figure 2-3. Although within the tolerance band the larger diameter resulted in excessive clearance. Bearing analysis later revealed that excessive clearance adversely effected the oil film thickness, causing the poor wear properties of this batch. The problem was solved by adjusting the manufacturing process to maintain bearing diameter near the target value.

The loss function and its implications are discussed in detail in later sections. At present, it is important to note that:

- The quality loss function is a continuous function and is a measure of deviation from the target value. The conformance to specification limits LAL and UAL is an inadequate measure to define the quality loss function.
- Quality loss is related to product performance characteristics and can

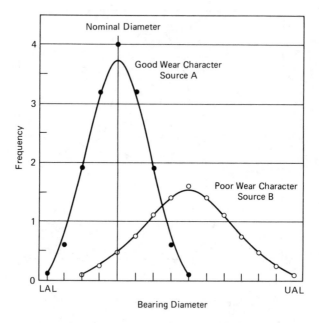

Figure 2-3. Bearing diameter distribution.

best be minimized by designing quality into the product. Prevention of poor quality is less costly than rework, and yields far better returns.
- Quality loss results from customer dissatisfaction and should be measured system-wide rather than at a discrete point in the manufacturing process.
- Quality loss is a financial and social loss.
- Minimization of quality loss is the only way to be competitive and survive in today's international business environment.

2-4 EXPERIMENT DESIGN STRATEGY

Taguchi constructed a special set of orthogonal arrays (OAs) to lay out his experiments. The use of latin squares orthogonal arrays for experiment designs dates back to the time of World War II. By combining the orthogonal latin squares in a unique manner, Taguchi prepared a new set of standard OAs to be used for a number of experimental situations. A common OA for 2 level factors is shown in Table 2-1. This array, designated by the symbol L_8, is used to design experiments involving up to seven 2 level factors. The array has 8 rows and 7 columns. Each row represents a trial condition with factor levels indicated by the numbers

Table 2-1. Orthogonal Array $L_8(2^7)$

				FACTORS			
TRIAL NUMBER	A	B	C	D	E	F	G
1	1	1	1	1	1	1	1
2	1	1	1	2	2	2	2
3	1	2	2	1	1	2	2
4	1	2	2	2	2	1	1
5	2	1	2	1	2	1	2
6	2	1	2	2	1	2	1
7	2	2	1	1	2	2	1
8	2	2	1	2	1	1	2

in the row. The vertical columns correspond to the factors specified in the study.

Each column contains four level 1 and four level 2 conditions for the factor assigned to the column. Two 2 level factors combine in four possible ways, such as (1,1), (1,2), (2,1), and (2,2). When two columns of an array form these combinations the same number of times, the columns are said to be balanced or orthogonal. Note that any two columns of an L_8 (2^7) have the same number of combinations of (1,1), (1,2), (2,1), and (2,2). Thus, all seven columns of an L are orthogonal to each other.

The OA facilitates the experiment design process. To design an experiment is to select the most suitable orthogonal array, assign the factors to the appropriate columns, and finally, describe the combinations of the individual experiments called the trial conditions. Let us assume that there are at most seven 2 level factors in the study. Call these factors A, B, C, D, E, F and G, and assign them to columns 1, 2, 3, 4, 5, 6, and 7 respectively of L_8. The table identifies the eight trials needed to complete the experiment and the level of each factor for each trial run. The experiment descriptions are determined by reading numerals 1 and 2 appearing in the rows of the trial runs. A factorial experiment would require 2^7 or 128 runs, but would not provide appreciably more information.

The array forces all experimenters to design almost identical experiments. Experimenters may select different designations for the columns but the eight trial runs will include all combinations independent of column definition. Thus the OA assures consistency of design by different experimenters.

2-5 ANALYSIS OF RESULTS

In the Taguchi method the results of the experiments are analyzed to achieve one or more of the following three objectives:

1. To establish the best or the optimum condition for a product or a process
2. To estimate the contribution of individual factors
3. To estimate the response under the optimum conditions

The optimum condition is identified by studying the main effects of each of the factors. The process involves minor arithmetic manipulation of the numerical results and usually can be done with the help of a simple calculator. The main effects indicate the general trend of the influence of the factors. Knowing the characteristic, i.e., whether a higher or lower value produces the preferred result, the levels of the factors which are expected to produce the best results can be predicted.

The knowledge of the contribution of individual factors is a key to deciding the nature of the control to be established on a production process. The analysis of variance (ANOVA) is the statistical treatment most commonly applied to the results of the experiment to determine the percent contribution of each factor. Study of the ANOVA table for a given analysis helps to determine which of the factors need control and which do not.

Once the optimum condition is determined, it is usually a good practice to run a confirmation experiment. It is, however, possible to estimate performance at the optimum condition from the results of experiments conducted at a non-optimum condition. It should be noted that the optimum condition may not necessarily be among the many experiments already carried out, as the OA represents only a small fraction of all the possibilities.

Taguchi suggests two different routes to carry out the complete analysis. First, the standard approach, where the result of a single run, or the average of repetitive runs, are processed through main effect and ANOVA analyses as identified above. The second approach, which he strongly recommends for multiple runs, is to use signal to noise ratio (*S/N*) for the same steps in the analysis. *S/N* analysis determines the most robust set of operating conditions from variations within the results.

2-6 AREAS OF APPLICATION

Analysis
In the design of engineering products and processes, analytical simulation plays an important role, transforming a concept into the final product design. The Taguchi approach can be utilized to arrive at the best parameters for the optimum design configuration with the least number of analytical investigations. Although there are several methods available for optimization, using such simulations when the factors are continuous, the Taguchi method is the method that treats factors at discrete levels. Frequently this approach significantly reduces computer time.

Test and Development
Testing with prototypes is an efficient way to see how the concepts work when they are put into a design. Since experimental hardware is costly, the need to accomplish the objectives with the least number of tests is a top priority. The Taguchi approach of laying out the experimental conditions significantly reduces the number of tests and the overall testing time.

Process Development
Manufacturing processes typically have a large number of factors that influence the final outcome. Identification of their individual contributions and their intricate interrelationships is essential in the development of such processes. The Taguchi concepts used in such projects has helped many U.S. and Japanese companies realize significant cost savings in recent times.

2-7 THE NEW APPROACH—ITS APPEAL AND LIMITATIONS

The Appeal

- Upfront improvement of quality by design and process development.
- Measurement of quality in terms of deviation from the target (loss function).
- Problem solution by team approach and brainstorming.
- Consistency in experimental design and analysis.
- Reduction of time and cost of experiments.
- Design of robustness into product/process.

- Reduction of variation without removing its causes.
- Reduction of product warranty and service costs by addressing them with the loss function.

Taguchi's design methodology has wide ranging applications. Generally speaking, experimental design using OAs can be applied where there are a large number of design factors. Taguchi's OAs for the design of experiments, signal/noise analysis, and cost guidance based on the loss function has made his approach increasingly popular among practicing engineers. The items listed above are common features of the Taguchi approach. The team approach to problem solving resulted from Taguchi's extension of loss beyond the production line.

Limitations

The most severe limitation of the Taguchi method is the need for timing with respect to product/process development. The technique can only be effective when applied early in the design of the product/process system. After the design variables are determined and their nominal values are specified, experimental design may not be cost effective. Also, though the method has wide ranging applications, there are situations in which classical techniques are better suited; in simulation studies involving factors that vary in a continuous manner, such as the torsional strength of a shaft as a function of its diameter, the Taguchi method may not be a proper choice.

EXERCISES

2-1. There are two types of losses that society incurs because of the poor quality of a product. What are these losses?

2-2. Explain why the old definition of cost of quality is inadequate.

2-3. What is the most important idea of Taguchi's concept of achieving higher product quality?

2-4. Name three stages in the process of achieving desirable quality by design.

2-5. List some areas in your field where the Taguchi approach can be used to improve a product or the efficiency of a manufacturing process.

2-6. A manufacturer of hi-fi speakers uses a gluing operation at the last stage in the manufacturing process. Recently because of a change in the bonding agent, the quality of the bond has been observed to be below specifications. Some engineers maintain that the poor quality of the bond is attributable not to the change of glue but rather to the accompanying application temperature. A 2×2 factorial experiment including two different glues at two application temperatures is planned. List at least three noise factors which may influence the outcome of the test.

3

Measurement of Quality

3-1 THE QUALITY CHARACTERISTIC

Every product is designed to perform some intended function. Some measurable characteristic, generally referred to as the quality characteristic is used to express how well a product performs the function. Consider a light bulb; its quality can be measured in terms of its hours of life. For a machine automatically producing 2.00 inch diameter shafts, the deviation from this target dimension may be a quality characteristic. In a majority of the cases, the quality characteristic may be a single measurable quantity such as weight, length, hours, etc. For some products subjective measurements like "good," "bad," "low," and "high" may be used. In other instances, subjective and objective evaluations may be combined into an Overall Evaluation Criteria (OEC).

No matter how the quality of the product is measured, by a single criterion, or by a combination of multiple criteria, the measure will possess one of the following three characteristics:

- the bigger the better
- the smaller the better
- the nominal the best

Suppose that we are investigating a pump to determine the best design parameters which produce the maximum flow rate. In this case, the quality of the design is judged by the flow rate measured in units of cubic feet per minute and therefore will be of the characteristic "the bigger the better."

If on the other hand, the purpose of the study is to determine the least noisy pump, the noise measured in units of say, decibels, will be of the type described by "the smaller the better." When the object or process under study has a target value, as for a battery of 9.0 volts or a process to machine a cylinder with a 3.00 inch inside diameter, the measure of quality will possess "the nominal the best" characteristic.

3-2   VARIATION AS A QUALITY YARDSTICK

Variation is the law of nature. In nature no two objects are absolutely alike. They could be very similar, but hardly identical. No two people are exactly alike. No two apples have precisely the same weight. Mother Nature likes variety. Consider man/machine made items. Superficially parts look and function alike. However, when examined closely, machine made products also exhibit variation. Variations in nature are often obvious to the human eye. This may not always be the case for manufactured products. Two ball point pens of the same brand do not write in the same way; two light bulbs do not last the same length of time; two appliances do not function in exactly the same manner; two engines of similar specifications do not perform identically. This is because products made for the same purpose will show factor influences.

Generally speaking, the quality characteristic of a product varies in two ways. First, it differs from another of the same kind, and second, it differs from the desired (target) value. Consider five 9 volt transistor batteries. When their voltages are measured accurately with a voltmeter, they may display a range of 8.90, 8.95, 8.99, 9.20, and 9.20 volts. All of the batteries may work well for radios with a range of acceptance of 8.5 to 9.5 volts, exceeding the variation in these batteries. But for a sophisticated instrument, only batteries which exhibit a voltage very close to the target value, say 8.95 to 9.05 volts, will operate the instrument properly. Batteries with excessive deviations from the target value may produce unreliable readings or may even damage the instrument.

The first kind of variation can be displayed by comparing one item to another. The maximum voltage variation among the batteries is 0.3 (9.2 to 8.9) volts. Although all of the batteries are nominally rated at 9 volts, most of them will deviate from this value. The deviation from this target or nominal value, constitutes the other type of variation. These variations are shown in Figure 3-1. In Figure 3-1(a), the average value of the parameter deviates from the target value; the range of value (variation) is also excessive. Figure 3-1(b) shows the average on target but the variation is still excessive. Figure 3-1(c) illustrates the desired characteristic—on target and with narrow variation.

Average value off target.
Too much variation around average value.

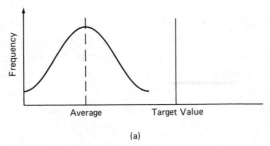

(a)

Average value on target.
Too much variation around target value.

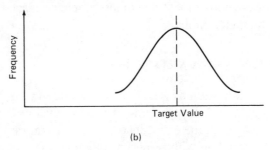

(b)

Average value on target.
Little variation around target value.

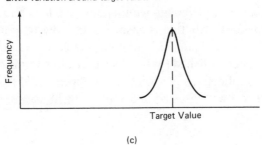

(c)

Figure 3-1. Typical quality distributions.

3-3 COST OF VARIATION

Early in his research, Taguchi observed that variation is common to all manufacturing processes and that variation was the primary cause for rejection of parts. Parts were rejected upon inspection when they did not conform to a predefined specification. Rejection increases the cost of production. Often 100 percent inspection is excessively costly or impractical, thus a defective part may reach a customer and lead to warranty costs and customer dissatisfaction. Taguchi held that variation is costly even beyond the immediate factory production cost and that excessive variation causes loss of quality. He contended that the cure of quality loss is reduction of variation. Thus he recommended that effort should be directed toward zero variation with less emphasis placed on production within fixed tolerance limits.

3-4 QUALITY AND VARIATION

Taguchi viewed variation as a lack of consistency in the product giving rise to poor quality. With this view, Taguchi developed methodologies aimed at reducing both the elements of variation—(a) deviation from the target, and (b) variation with respect to others in the group. In Figure 3-2, a typical quality measure of a product is compared to the desired state. Note that the product mean value is off target and that the variation around the mean is large though within upper and lower acceptance limits. A much narrower distribution is desired with more frequent achievement of the target value and smaller variation around the target value.

How is this accomplished? What does it mean in terms of cost savings? The financial implications of variation will be covered in a later chapter. In this chapter we will discuss, in detail, Taguchi's approach to variation reduction.

3-5 THE QUALITY WE ARE AFTER

The quality of a product or a process may be difficult to define in quantitative terms. Quality is what the customers perceive it to be, thus quality varies from product to product and from customer to customer. The criteria customers use to judge the quality of a product are related to the satisfaction derived from the product and are numerous and often difficult to quantify. Research has shown that a lack of product consistency is a

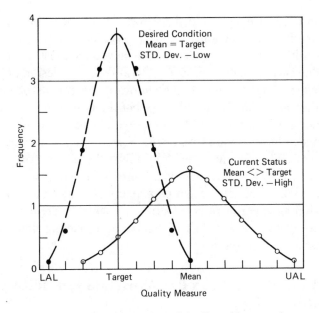

Figure 3-2. Representation of the Taguchi approach.

major factor in the perception of poor quality. Consistency (reduced level of variation) favorably affects most common elements of quality. To customers, quality may include service after delivery, ease of assembly, product performance, frequency of maintenance, etc. Our focus is that element of quality reflected by the performance of a product. The Taguchi approach for reducing variation in performance is a two-step process.

1. Make the product/process perform in the best manner most of the time (less deviation from the target).
2. Make all products perform as identically as possible (less variation between the products).

3-6 THE TAGUCHI QUALITY STRATEGY

Taguchi's approach to enhance quality in the design phase involves two steps:

1. Optimizing the design of the product/process (system approach).
2. Making the design insensitive to the influence of uncontrollable factors (robustness).

When a product is optimum, it performs best under the available operating conditions. Depending upon the specified performance, the optimum will imply that the product has achieved the most, the least or the target value of the quality measure. Optimizing the design of a product means determining the right combination of ingredients or making the proper adjustments to the machine so that the best results are obtained.

Consider a baking process. Assume several bakers are given the same ingredients to bake a pound cake, the object being to produce the best tasting cake. Within limits, they can adjust the amount of ingredients, but they can only use the ingredients provided. They are to make the best cake within available design parameters. Taguchi's approach would be to design an experiment considering all baking ingredients and other influencing factors such as baking temperature, baking time, oven type (if a variable) and so on.

3-7   SELECTING DESIGN PARAMETERS FOR REDUCED VARIATION

In the last section quality according to Taguchi's methodology was defined. Taguchi strives to attain quality by reducing the variation around the target. In an effort to reduce variations, he searched for techniques that allow variability to be reduced without necessarily eliminating the causes of variation. Often in an industrial setting, totally removing the causes of variation can be expensive. A no cost or low cost solution may be achieved by adjusting the levels and controlling the variation of other factors. This is what Taguchi tries to do through his *Parameter Design* approach. There is no cost or low cost in reducing variability in parameter design. Furthermore, the cost savings realized far exceed the cost of additional experiments needed to reduce variations.

The Taguchi method is most effective when applied to experiments with multiple factors. But the concept of selecting the proper levels of design factors, and reducing the variation of performance around the optimum/target value, can be easily illustrated through an example involving only one factor. An electronic circuit which controlled the color characteristics of a television set, was significantly influenced by the line voltage. The experimenter, wishing to select the right voltage, investigated the color quality at several input voltages. The influence of voltage variation on color quality is shown in Figure 3-3. If the desirable range of voltage for circuit design is between V_C and V_D, then what voltage

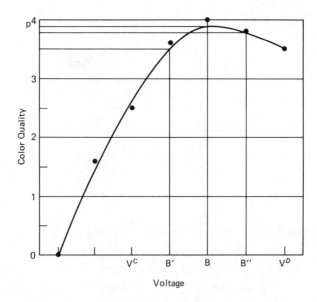

Figure 3-3. Color quality response curve.

should be specified for the circuit? Obviously, the choice should be a point within working voltage range V_C and V_D that provides stable color quality. In Taguchi terminology, look for the input voltage that reduces variation of the color quality. The experimenter would initially select a voltage at point B, so the variation around B, say to B' or B'', would minimally affect the output i.e., the color quality. Voltage B is highly attractive because small fluctuations in the line voltage (B' to B'') will not significantly affect the color quality of the TV as perceived by the customer-user.

Figure 3-4. Cake baking experiment.

The best pound cake
I have ever tasted!

Figure 3-5. The desirable result of an optimized baking process.

The objective for products involving multiple factors is similar but slightly more complex. The idea is to combine the factors at appropriate levels, each within the respective acceptable range, to produce the best result and yet exhibit minimum variation around the optimum result. To see how the Taguchi technique is used for many factors, consider once again the process of determining the best recipe for a pound cake (Figure 3-4). Our objective is to determine the right proportions of the five major ingredients, eggs, butter, milk, flour and sugar, so that the recipe will

Ingredients	How much/many		
A. Egg	A_1		A_2
B. Butter	B_1		B_2
C. Milk	C_1		C_2
D. Flour	D_1		D_2
E. Sugar	E_1		E_2

Figure 3-6. Factors and levels for a pound cake experiment.

produce the best cake most of the time (Figure 3-5). Based upon past experience the working ranges of these factors are established at the levels as shown in Figure 3-6. At this point we face the following questions. How do we do determine the right combination? How many experiments do we need to run and in what combination?

3-8   COMMON TERMINOLOGY

The technique for laying out the conditions of experiments when multiple factors are involved, has been known to statisticians for a long time. It was first introduced by R. A. Fisher in England, in the 1920s and is popularly known as the *Factorial Design of Experiments*. The method helps an experimenter determine the possible combinations of factors and to identify the best combination. To determine the optimum combination Taguchi prescribes carrying out a number of experiments under the conditions defined by the rules he has developed. In experimental layout he uses the same principles as that of factorial design, except that his methods are much simplified and standardized.

In the case of the cake example, with five factors each at two levels there are 32 (2^5) combinations of all possible factors and levels. If we could bake 32 cakes, we would surely find the best tasting cake among these 32 cakes and we would know the impact of each ingredient level on taste. For most industrial situations, carrying out a large number of experiments is not feasible.

Taguchi accomplishes the same objective with a smaller number of tests. He selects a particular 8 trial fractional factorial design (orthogonal array) that produces the most information regarding the best tasting cake. The factor/level combinations for these 8 experiments are defined by using the L_B (2^7) Orthogonal Arrays. An OA is a table developed for two level factors such that columns contain two sets of all possible combinations of levels. OAs are amenable to statistical analysis with a high degree of confidence. Thus, an experiment planned to be consistent with the array design, provides statistically meaningful results.

An OA experiment design leads to reduction of variation because of controllable factors. Uncontrollable factors (noise, dust, etc.) can be handled in two ways. First, the experiment trial can be repeated at different noise conditions. Second, the noise factors can be included in a second OA which is used in conjunction with the array of controllable factors. This is clarified in Chapter 5.

Because OAs are used to define the unique experimental conditions as well as the noise factors, Taguchi calls the former design *Inner Array* and the latter *Outer Array*. When outer array experiments are performed, the analysis includes the transformation of the results into a *Signal to Noise Ratio (S/N)*. This process identifies the optimum condition with the least variability of the controllable as well as the uncontrollable factors.

The actual steps involved in designing the experiments using inner and outer arrays will be discussed in Chapter 5.

EXERCISES

3-1. How does Taguchi's view of quality differ from the conventional practice?

3-2. How does variation affect cost and quality?

3-3. What are the main causes of variation?

3-4. How is a product design optimized?

3-5. How does Taguchi make the design less sensitive to the noise factors?

3-6. What are orthogonal arrays?

3-7. What is implied by the term parameter design and what is its significance in achieving higher product quality?

4

Procedures of the Taguchi Method and Its Benefits

4-1 THE NEW DISCIPLINE

The Taguchi method offers two new powerful elements. First, it is a disciplined way of developing a product or investigating complex problems. Second, it provides a means to cost effectively investigate the available alternatives. Although Taguchi's method was built upon well developed concepts of optimization through the design of experiments, his philosophy regarding the value of quality and the procedure for carrying out experiments were new. The power and popularity of the method lies in the discipline rather than the technique itself. The power and the resultant potential for cost savings will be reviewed in this chapter.

The technique is applied in four steps.

1. Brainstorm the quality characteristics and design parameters important to the product/process.
2. Design and conduct the experiments.
3. Analyze the results to determine the optimum conditions.
4. Run a confirmatory test(s) using the optimum conditions.

These steps are contrasted with typical current practice in Figure 4-1.

Brainstorming is a necessary and important step in the application process. The nature and content of the brainstorming is dependent on the type of project under study and thus no specific guidelines exist. Taguchi recommends the participation of all relevant functional organizations, including marketing. A suggested procedure for brainstorming for a Taguchi experiment design, along with some general guidelines are described in Chapter 8.

Taguchi experiments are designed according to some strict rules. A

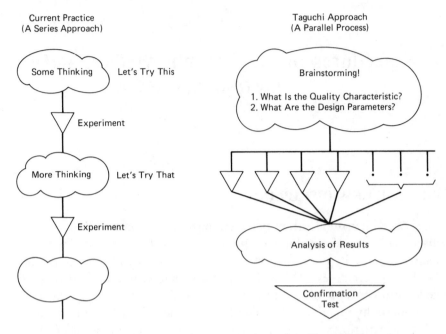

Figure 4-1. Comparison of current practice and the Taguchi approach.

set of OAs are used to design the experiments. A single OA may accomodate several experimental situations. Commonly used OAs are available for 2, 3, and 4 level factors. Some standard arrays accomodate factors of mixed levels. In many situations, a standard OA is modified to suit a particular experiment requiring factors of mixed levels. The process of experiment design includes selecting the suitable OA, assigning the factors to the appropriate columns and determining the conditions for the individual experiments. When noise factors are included in the experiment, the condition of the noise factors for each individual experiment is also determined.

The results of the Taguchi experiments are analyzed in a standard series of phases. First, the factorial effects (main effects) are evaluated and the influence of the factors are determined in qualitative terms. The optimum condition and the performance at the optimum condition are also determined from the factorial effects. In the next phase, analysis of variance (ANOVA) is performed on the result. ANOVA study identifies the relative influence of the factors in discrete terms. When the experiments include multiple runs and the results are measured in quantitative terms, Taguchi recommends signal to noise ratio (*S/N*) analysis. In *S/N* analysis, the multiple results of a trial condition are first transformed into *S/N* ratios and then analyzed.

The optimum design identified in the analysis should be tested to confirm that performance indeed is the best and that it closely matches the performance predicted by analysis.

4-2   UP-FRONT THINKING

The value of brainstorming in product development, or in solving complex problems is well known, yet it was rarely used in solving engineering problems. Brainstorming prior to an experiment is a necessary requirement in the Taguchi approach. However, Taguchi does not give any guidelines to conduct brainstorming for an experiment. The content and outcome of a brainstorming session is largely dependent on the nature of a project, and as such, is a technique learned primarily by experience. Most application specialists consider brainstorming to be the most important element in deriving benefits from the Taguchi method.

Taguchi brings a new breadth to planning experimental studies. He thinks through the whole process before starting the tests. This helps to decide which factors are likely to be most important, how many experiments are needed, and how the results would be measured and analyzed, before actually conducting any experiment. Figure 4-1 shows the typical steps of current practice—some initial thinking, followed by some testing, which, in turn, is followed by some more thinking and so on. In the Taguchi approach, the complete plan of how to test, what to test, and when to analyze the results, will all be decided beforehand. Ideally, a brainstorming session will rely on the collective experience of the group to determine the factors to be selected for testing in an appropriate design. Practice of the Taguchi method fosters a team approach to design optimization since participation of people from engineering, manufacturing, testing, and other activities may be necessary for complete variable identification.

4-3   EXPERIMENTAL EFFICIENCY

In most cases, the Taguchi experiment design requires the least number of test runs. A full factorial experiment with 15 factors at 2 levels each requires a test matrix with $32768(2^{15})$ test runs. A fractional factorial experiment with an orthogonal array suitable for fifteen 2 level factors consists of 16 test runs.

The experimental efficiency Taguchi offers can be described using the following analogy. Assume that you are asked to catch a big fish from a lake with a circular net. You are also told that the fish usually stays around its hideout. But you have no knowledge of where this place is. How do you go about catching this fish? Thinking analytically you may first calculate the area of the net and the lake, then lay out an elaborate scheme to cover the entire lake. You may find, after all this planning, that you need the whole day to locate the spot where the fish is. Wouldn't it be nice to have a fish finder that could tell you the approximate locations where to throw your net. The Taguchi approach in experimental studies, to a great extent, works like a fish finder. It tells you which areas to try first and then from the results of the trials, you determine, with a high degree of certainty, the most probable location of the fish.

4-4   EFFECTIVE USE OF STATISTICAL PROCESS CONTROL

After design and development comes production. When we complete the Taguchi experimental studies, it is time for statistical process control (SPC). But where do we apply controls? Should we control all factors across the board? If we knew which factors were most significant, it would be wise to pay more attention to them. The information about the relative merits of individual factors is obtained by analysis of variance of the experimental results. This knowledge about the factor influence is used to objectively determine the amount of manufacturing process control necessary.

4-5   LONG TERM BENEFITS

Most of the benefits of improved design quality, come after the product is put in use. The reduced variation, a characteristic that is designed in through the optimum combination of the factors, will yield consistent performance of the product. This means that more of the products will perform as designed. There will be happier customers, and therefore, less warranty costs, and increased sales.

4-6   QUANTIFYING COST BENEFITS—TAGUCHI LOSS FUNCTION

As indicated earlier, the major attraction of the Taguchi approach is the discipline it introduces in the engineering practices rather than in the direct benefits in time and cost savings. The value of the discipline is extremely hard to quantify. The direct cost savings in terms of a better product or process, on the other hand, can be experienced in due course of time after the product is sold. Can this potential cost saving be estimated before production begins? Taguchi suggests a way of quantifying such cost savings. He uses his loss function concept to estimate the potential savings based on the improvement achievable, if the product were designed to the optimum condition prescribed by his approach.

Suppose a manufacturer, XYZ Co., of a 9.00 volt transistor battery applied the Taguchi method to improve the quality of its product. Before the experiment, a measured sample of 10 batteries had the following voltages:

BEFORE EXPERIMENT

VOLTAGES				
8.10	8.25	8.90	8.68	8.35
9.25	9.05	8.85	8.45	8.90

With the target value of 9.00 volts, the above measured values produce characteristics as shown below (also see Tables 4-1 and 4-2).

$$\text{Average value } = 8.67$$

$$\text{Standard deviation } = 0.37$$

$$\text{Mean square deviation (MSD)} = [(8.1 - 9.0)^2 + (9.25 - 9.0)^2$$

$$+ \cdots + (8.90 - 9.0)^2]/10$$

$$= 0.23$$

$$S/N \text{ ratio } = -10 \text{ Log}_{10} \text{ (MSD)}$$

$$= 6.36$$

Table 4-1. Standard Statistical Data Before Experiment

Observation No. 1 = 8.100
Observation No. 2 = 8.900
Observation No. 3 = 8.450
Observation No. 4 = 9.250
Observation No. 5 = 8.860
Observation No. 6 = 8.350
Observation No. 7 = 8.250
Observation No. 8 = 8.680
Observation No. 9 = 8.900
Observation No. 10 = 9.050

Target/Nominal value of result (Y_0)	= 9.00
Number of test results (NR)	= 10

AVERAGE AND STANDARD DEVIATION:

Total of all test results	= 86.79001
Average of test results	= 8.679001
Standard deviation (SD)	= 0.376252
Variance	= 0.141565

LOSS FUNCTION PARAMETERS:

Mean square deviation (MSD)	= 0.230449
Signal to noise ratio (S/N)	= 6.374235
Variance (modified form)	= 0.127409
Square of mean value	= 0.103041

VARIANCE DATA (ANOVA):

Target value of data/test result	= 9.00
Mean of data/deviation from target	= -0.321
Total variance (ST)	
(ST = Variance * NR)	= 1.274089
Correction factor (CF)	
(CF = (average of data)^2 * number of data)	= 1.030404
Sums of squares/N	= 2.304499

DEFINITIONS:

$$\text{Standard deviation (SD)} = \sqrt{\sum_{i=1}^{n} (Y_i - \overline{Y})^2/(n - 1)}$$

$$\text{Variance} \ldots\ldots\ldots\ldots = (SD)^2$$

$$\text{Mean square deviation (MSD)} = \sum_{i=1}^{n} (Y_i - Y_o)^2/n$$

$$\text{Signal/noise ratio } (S/N) \ldots = -10 \, \text{Log}_{10} \, (MSD)$$

Table 4-2. Standard Statistical Data After Experiment

Observation No. 1 = 9.100
Observation No. 2 = 9.080
Observation No. 3 = 8.910
Observation No. 4 = 8.940
Observation No. 5 = 8.880
Observation No. 6 = 9.150
Observation No. 7 = 8.690
Observation No. 8 = 9.020
Observation No. 9 = 9.250
Observation No. 10 = 8.920

Target/Nominal value of result	=	9.00
Number of test results (NR)	=	10

AVERAGE AND STANDARD DEVIATION:

Total of all test results	=	89.93999
Average of test results	=	8.993999
Standard deviation (SD)	=	0.159875
Variance	=	0.025560

LOSS FUNCTION PARAMETERS:

Mean square deviation (MSD)	=	0.023040
Signal to noise ratio (S/N)	=	16.37517
Variance (modified form)	=	0.023040
Square of mean value	=	3.6006E-05

VARIANCE DATA (ANOVA):

Target value of data/test result	=	9.00
Mean of data/deviation from target	=	$-6.00004E{-}03$
Total variance (ST)		
(ST = Variance * NR)	=	0.230040
Correction factor (CF)		
(CF = (average of data)^2 * number of data)	=	3.6006E-04
Sums of squares/N	=	0.230040

After the experiment a batch of 10 batteries showed the following characteristics:

AFTER EXPERIMENT

VOLTAGES

9.10	8.93	8.69	8.92	9.08
8.08	9.02	8.91	9.15	9.25

Average value	= 8.99
Standard deviation	= 0.1598
Mean square deviation	= 0.023
S/N ratio	= 16.37

The signal to noise ratio (S/N) expresses the scatter around a target value. The larger the ratio, the smaller the scatter. Taguchi's loss function can be expressed in terms of MSD, and thus S/N ratios. Knowing the S/N ratios of the samples before and after the experiment, Taguchi's loss function may be used to estimate the potential cost savings from the improved product.

Before estimates of savings can be made, some other pertinent information needs to be gathered. Assuming the usual statistical distribution of results, the two samples will exhibit the curve shown in Figure 4-2. The producer, XYZ, Co., makes 100,000 units of the batteries per month which sell for $1.25 each. For most customer applications, the battery voltage should be within ± 1.00 volt, i.e., between 8.00 and 10.00 volts. If the voltage is beyond this range, customers request a refund ($1.25).

Taguchi's approach to the computation of cost savings is based on determining the refund cost associated with variation of batteries, as measured by the mean square deviation (MSD) from the target voltage. Obviously the greater the variation the more likely that some batteries will exceed the limits of customer acceptance. With the above information, the loss is computed as $.288 per battery for the sample before the experiment, and that for the sample after the experiment is $.028 per unit. Since 100,000 units are manufactured per month, the total savings per month is calculated to be $25,950.90 (Fig. 4-3).

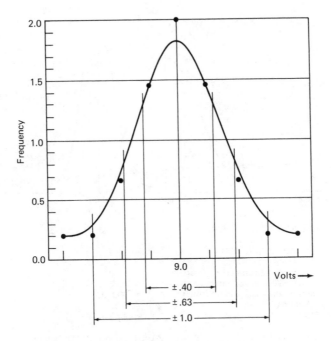

COMPUTATION OF MANUFACTURER & SUPPLIER TOLERANCE
Nominal value of the quality characteristic Y = 9 Volts
Tolerance of Y (range of deviation)   = ± 1 Volt
Cost to repair a nonfunctioning unit by customer   = $ 1.25
Cost to repair a nonfunctioning unit by manufacturer = $ 0.5
Cost to repair a nonfunctioning unit by supplier   = $ 0.25

REQUIRED TOLERANCES
Manufacturer tolerance = 9 ± 0.63
Supplier tolerance   = 9 ± 0.40

NOTE: If these Tolerances were held, there will be no nonfunctional part in the customers hands. For the same cost the Manufacturer will maintain satisfied customers and quality products in the field.

Figure 4-2. Manufacturer and supplier tolerance.

4-7 SPECIFYING TOLERANCE LEVELS

Another application of Taguchi's loss function formulation is in determining the levels of tolerances for various inspection points of the production process. Suppose that the manufacturer XYZ is well aware of the losses in his current production samples (before experiment). He wishes to reduce the warranty costs and wishes to keep his customers satisfied. But he does not want to disturb the current design and production

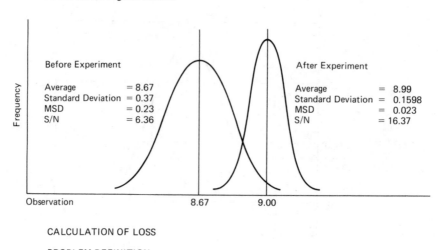

CALCULATION OF LOSS

PROBLEM DEFINITION
Target value of quality characteristic (m) = 9.00
Tolerance of quality characteristic = 1.00
Cost of rejection at production (per unit) = $1.25
Units produced per month (total) = 100000
S/N ratio of current design/part = 6.37
S/N ratio of new design/part = 16.37

COMPUTATION OF LOSS USING TAGUCHI LOSS FUNCTION
Loss function: $L(y) = 1.25 \times (MSD)$ Also $L(y) = K \times (y-m)^2$

BEFORE EXPERIMENT:
Loss/unit due to deviation from target in current design   = $0.288

AFTER EXPERIMENT:
Loss/unit due to deviation from target will be reduced from $0.288 to = $0.028

MONTHLY SAVINGS:
If production were maintained at the improved
condition, then based on 100000 units/month   = $25,950.90

Figure 4-3. Calculation of cost savings.

line. He is, however, willing to explore ways to screen out the bad products. The loss function offers some help here.

Let's say XYZ as the manufacturer of batteries, has a producer who supplies the chemicals needed. Upon investigation, XYZ determines that the chemical which is supplied by the company ABC, is substandard and is the cause of voltage variation. The manufacturer has two options available. He can inspect his production with the hope to screen out all the bad products. Or, he can ask the supplier to prescreen the material so inspection of the product becomes unnecessary. In either case he needs to establish the limits to which the batteries have to conform. We have the customer tolerance, i.e., ± 1.00 volt. A manufacturer tolerance which is what the company XYZ will use in the plant must be established, and the supplier tolerance which the company ABC will be asked to use for inspection must also be set. Taguchi determines these tolerances based on the cost of rejection at the two places. Because the cost of rejecting a finished part is probably greater than the cost of rejection of an ingredient, the tolerances for the manufacturer and the supplier will differ from that of the customers.

In addition to what is already known about the product (battery), two more pieces of information are needed for this calculation:

cost of rejection/replacement at the manufacturer, and
cost of rejection/replacement at the supplier.

Suppose that a part costing 20 cents from a supplier can produce a loss of 50 cents to the manufacturer if the part fails. The loss equations will produce tolerances of ± 0.63 volts and ± 0.4 volts for the manufacturer and the supplier, respectively, as shown in Figure 4-2. Either the supplier or the manufacturer can screen the products. To assure defect free products, the supplier may screen them before they are shipped to the manufacturer, who in turn passes them to the customers. When a supplier doesn't screen, the manufacturer must. (The calculations shown in Figures 4-2 and 4-3 are obtained by using the computer software in Reference 11.)

EXERCISES

4-1. The Taguchi method is considered a technique that helps build quality into a product or process. Explain what aspect of quality it influences and how.

4-2. Compare the roles of the Taguchi method with that of statistical process control (SPC) in a manufacturing process. Explain how the Taguchi method can influence decisions in the SPC activities.

5

Working Mechanics of the Taguchi Design of Experiments

5-1 FORMULAS FOR EXPERIMENT LAYOUT

It should be quite clear by now that the Taguchi method is designed to improve the quality of products and processes where the performance depends on many factors. In laying out a test and development strategy, simple logic will usually be sufficient to establish all possible combinations of factors along with allowable ranges of each of the factors involved. But for engineering projects involving many factors, the number of possible combinations is prohibitively large. In addition higher order interactions among the influencing factors may be needed for specific projects. A customary method of reducing the number of test combinations is to use what are known as partial factorial experiments. Taguchi constructed a special set of general designs for factorial experiments that cover may applications. The special set of designs consist of orthogonal arrays. The use of these arrays helps determine the least number of experiments needed for a given set of factors. The details of using standard (not modified) OAs in designing experiments for a given set of factors is the subject of this chapter.

The OAs provide a recipe for fractional factorial experiments which satisfy a number of situations. When a fixed number of levels for all factors is involved and the interactions are unimportant, standard OAs will satisfy most experimental design needs. A modification of the OAs becomes necessary when mixed levels and interactions are present. Simple designs with smaller number of factors, at fixed levels, will be discussed first.

5-2 BASIC METHODOLOGY

The technique of laying out the conditions (designs) of experiments involving multiple factors was first proposed by the Englishman, Sir R. A. Fisher, in the 1920s. The method is popularly known as the factorial design of experiments. A full factorial design will identify all possible combinations for a given set of factors. Since most industrial experiments usually involve a significant number of factors, a full factorial design results in a large number of experiments. For example, in an experiment involving seven factors, each at two levels, the total number of combinations will be 128 (2^7). To reduce the number of experiments to a practical level, only a small set from all the possibilities, is selected. The method of selecting a limited number of experiments which produces the most information, is known as a partial factorial experiment. Although, this shortcut method is well known, there are no general guidelines for its application or the analysis of the results obtained by performing the experiments. Taguchi's approach complements these two important areas. First, he clearly defines a set of OAs, each of which can be used for many experimental situations. Second, he devised a standard method for analysis of the results. The combination of standard experimental design techniques and analysis methods in the Taguchi approach, produces consistency and reproducibility rarely found in any other statistical method.

Before discussing how Taguchi reduces the number of experiments, an understanding will be helpful of how all possible combinations result from a set of factors.

Suppose that we are concerned about one factor A (say temperature). If we were to study its effect on a product at two levels (say 400 and 500°F) i.e.,

Factor A: Level 1 = A_1 (400°F)   Level 2 = A_2 (500°F)

then two experiments become necessary, one at temperature A_1, the other at A_2.

Consider now 2 factors A and B, each at 2 levels (A_1, A_2 and B_1, B_2). This produces 4 combinations since, when A is held at A_1, B can assume values B_1 and B_2 and when A is held at A_2, B can again be set at values B_1 and B_2.

Symbolically these combinations are expressed as follows:

$A_1(B_1\ B_2)$, $A_2(B_1,\ B_2)$ or as A_1B_1, A_1B_2, A_2B_1 and A_2B_2

With 3 factors, each at 2 levels, there are 2^3 (8) possible experiments as described in the previous section. If A, B and C represent these factors, the 8 experiments can be expressed as:

$A_1B_1C_1, A_1B_1C_2, A_1B_2C_1, A_1B_2C_2,$

$A_2B_1C_1, A_2B_1C_2, A_2B_2C_1, A_2B_2C_2,$

Using the above general rule, the total number of experiments possible for different numbers of factors at 2 or 3 levels and the corresponding suggested Taguchi number of experiments is shown in Table 5-1.

A factorial experiment of 7 factors, at 2 levels each, with 128 possible combinations is represented by Figure 5-1(a). The factors are represented by the letters A, B, C, D, E, F, and G. The subscripts 1 and 2 (Fig. 5-1(b)) represent the value of a factor at level 1 and 2 respectively. Each of the 128 cells corresponds to a unique combination of the factors. Cells T-1 through T-8 indicated the 8 trial numbers defined by Taguchi's partial factorial OA (Fig. 5-1(b)) for this experiment.

Taguchi has established OAs to describe a large number of experimental situations. The symbolic designation for these arrays carries the key information on the size of the experiment. The array of Figure 5-1(b) is designated as L-8 or L_8. The number 8 indicates 8 trials are required. The next lower size of the OA is L_4. An L_4 experiment requires 4 trial runs. The array handles up to 3 factors at 2 levels each. To fit a situation with factors between 4 to 7, all at 2 levels, an L_8 will be used. For situations demanding a larger number of factors, higher levels as well as mixed levels, a number of other OAs are available. (Ref. 4)

Experiment designs by OAs are attractive because of experimental efficiency, but there are some potential tradeoffs. Generally speaking, OA experiments work well when there is minimal interaction among factors, i.e., the factor influences on the measured quality objectives

**Table 5-1. Comparison of Factorial Design and
Taguchi Design**

FACTORS	LEVEL	FACTORIAL DESIGN TOTAL NUMBER OF EXPERIMENTS	TAGUCHI
2	2	$4 \ (2^2)$	4
3	2	$8 \ (2^3)$	4
4	2	$16 \ (2^4)$	8
7	2	$128 \ (2^7)$	8
15	2	$32,768 \ (2^{15})$	16
4	3	$81 \ (3^4)$	9

Full Factorial Experiments				A$_1$				A$_2$			
				B$_1$		B$_2$		B$_1$		B$_2$	
				C$_1$	C$_2$	C$_1$	C$_2$	C$_1$	C$_2$	C$_1$	C$_2$
D$_1$	E$_1$	F$_1$	G$_1$	T−1							
			G$_2$								
		F$_2$	G$_1$								
			G$_2$				T−3				
	E$_2$	F$_1$	G$_1$								
			G$_2$						T−5		
		F$_2$	G$_1$							T−7	
			G$_2$								
D$_2$	E$_1$	F$_1$	G$_1$								
			G$_2$							T−8	
		F$_2$	G$_1$						T−6		
			G$_2$								
	E$_2$	F$_1$	G$_1$				T−4				
			G$_2$								
		F$_2$	G$_1$								
			G$_2$	T−2							

(a) Experiment Structure

Trial Number \ Column	1	2	3	4	5	6	7
	A	B	C	D	E	F	G
T-1	1	1	1	1	1	1	1
T-2	1	1	1	2	2	2	2
T-3	1	2	2	1	1	2	2
T-4	1	2	2	2	2	1	1
T-5	2	1	2	1	2	1	2
T-6	2	1	2	2	1	2	1
T-7	2	2	1	1	2	2	1
T-8	2	2	1	2	1	1	2

(b) Trial Runs and Conditions

Figure 5-1. Experiments using an L_8 array.

are independent of each other and are linear. In other words when the outcome is directly proportional to the linear combination of individual factor main effects, OA design identifies the optimum condition and estimates performance at this condition accurately. If however, the factors interact with each other and influence the outcome in a nonlinear manner, there is still a good chance that the optimum condition will be identified accurately, but the estimate of performance at the optimum can be significantly off. The degree of inaccuracy in performance estimates will depend on the degree of complexity of interactions among all the factors.

5-3   DESIGNING THE EXPERIMENT

The word "design" in the expression design of experiments, is used in a general sense to convey "a mental project or a scheme in which means to an end are laid down." To design the experiment is to develop a scheme or layout of the different conditions to be studied. In engineering, the word takes on a special meaning when used as "a design," "product design," or a "process design." In these expressions, it refers to some form of an engineering communication, such as a set of specifications, drawings, or physical models that describe a concept. Consider a statement like "The Taguchi design of experiments can be used to optimize many designs." The final "design" in this sentence, obviously refers to some engineering design process.

An experiment design must satisfy two objectives. First, the number of trials must be determined. Second, the conditions for each trial must be specified. Taguchi's arrays are versatile recipes that apply to several experimental conditions. For example, the design for experiments involving 4, 5, 6, or 7 factors, may all be accomplished by using the same orthogonal array (L_8). The OAs contain information on both the number as well as the configurations of the experiments.

Before designing an experiment, knowledge of the product/process under investigation is of prime importance for identifying the factors likely to influence the outcome. In order to compile a comprehensive list of the factors, the input to the experiment is generally obtained from all the people involved in the project. Taguchi found brainstorming to be a necessary step for determining the full range of factors to be investigated.

Consider an example.

Table 5-2. Molding Process Factor and Level— Example 5-1

VARIABLES OR FACTORS	LEVEL 1	LEVEL 2
A. Injection Pressure	$A_1 = 250$ psi	$A_2 = 350$ psi
B. Mold Temperature	$B_1 = 150$ °F	$B_2 = 200$ °F
C. Set Time	$C_1 = 6$ sec.	$C_2 = 9$ sec.

Example 5-1

An experimenter has identified three controllable factors for a plastic molding process. Each factor can be applied at two levels (Table 5-2). The experimenter wants to determine the optimum combination of the levels of these factors and to know the contribution of each to product quality.

The Design

There are 3 factors, each at 2 levels, thus an L_4 will be suitable. An L_4 OA with spaces for the factors and their levels is shown in Figure 5-2. This configuration is a convenient way to lay out a design. Since an L_4

	Variable Description	Injection Pressure	Mold Temperature	Set Time	Repetitions			
Level 2		350 Psi	200° F	9 Sec.				
Level 1		250 Psi	150° F	6 Sec.				
Experiment Number	Column	1	2	3	1	2	3	...
1		1	1	1	30			
2		1	2	2	25			
3		2	1	2	34			
4		2	2	1	27			

Figure 5-2. An experiment layout using L_4 array.

has 3 columns, the 3 factors can be assigned to these columns in any order. Having assigned the factors, their levels can also be indicated in the corresponding column.

There are four independent experimental conditions in an L_4. These conditions are described by the numbers in the rows. For an experienced user of the technique, an array with factors assigned as shown in Table 5-2 contains all the necessary information. But for others, a descriptive arrangement of the factors constituting different conditions of the experiment may be helpful. In this case the four conditions can be spelled out as follows:

Experiment No. 1	Injection Pressure	at	250 psi, i.e., A_1
	Mold Temperature	at	150 °F, i.e., B_1
	Set Time	at	6 sec., i.e., C_1
Experiment No. 2	Injection Pressure	at	250 psi, i.e., A_1
	Mold Temperature	at	200 °F, i.e., B_2
	Set Time	at	9 sec., i.e., C_2
Experiment No. 3	Injection Pressure	at	350 psi, i.e., A_2
	Mold Temperature	at	150 °F, i.e., B_1
	Set Time	at	9 sec., i.e., C_2
Experiment No. 4	Injection Pressure	at	350 psi, i.e., A_2
	Mold Temperature	at	200 °F, i.e., B_2
	Set Time	at	6 sec., i.e., C_1

5-3-1 Order of Running the Experiments

Whenever possible, the trial conditions (the individual combinations in a designed experiment) should be run in a random order to avoid the influence of experiment setup. If only one run for each of the above conditions is planned, they could be run as experiment number 2, 4, 3, and 1, or in any other random order. If on the other hand, multiple repetitions are planned, say 3 runs for each of the 4 conditions, then there are two ways to proceed.

Replication

In this approach all the trial conditions will be run in a random order. One way to decide the order is to randomly pull one trial number at a time from a set of trial numbers including repetitions. Often a new setup will be required for each run. This increases the cost of the experiment.

Repetition

Each trial is repeated as planned before proceeding to the next trial run. The trial run sequence is selected in a random order. For example, given the trial sequence 2, 4, 3, and 1, three successive runs of trial number 2 are made followed by 3 runs of trial 4 and so on. This procedure reduces setup costs for the experiment. However a setup error is unlikely to be detected. Furthermore, the effect of external factors such as humidity, tool wear, etc., may not be captured during the successive runs if the runs are short in duration.

5-3-2   Analysis of the Results

Although, a detailed analysis of the results will be discussed in Chapter 6, a brief description of and objectives of such an analysis is introduced here.

Following the specifications as prescribed above, the experimenter conducted the four trials. The molded products were then evaluated and the results, in terms of a quality characteristic, Y, were measured as shown below:

$$Y_1 = 30, \quad Y_2 = 25, \quad Y_3 = 34 \text{ and } Y_4 = 27$$

These results are recorded in the right most column of the OA (Table 5-3). Since, there was only one test for each condition, the results are recorded in one column. For each repetition of the experiment, there will be another column of results.

To speed up analysis, Taguchi has provided some key procedures. When these steps are strictly followed by different individuals performing the analysis, they are likely to arrive at the same conclusions. The ob-

Table 5-3. L_4 with Test Data of Molding Process Experiment

TRIALS	A	B	C	RESULTS (Y)
1	1	1	1	30
2	1	2	2	25
3	2	1	2	34
4	2	2	1	27

jective of the analysis of the Taguchi experimental results is primarily to seek answers to the following three questions:

1. What is the optimum condition?
2. Which factors contribute to the results and by how much?
3. What will be the expected result at the optimum condition?

The predicted result should be verified by running an experiment.

Computation of Average Performance

To compute the average performance of the factor A at level 1, i.e., for A_1, add results (Table 5-3) for trials including factor A_1, and then divide by the number of such trials.

For A_1, we look in the column for A and find that level 1 occurs in experiment numbers 1 and 2. The average effect of A_1, is therefore calculated by adding the results, Y, of these two trials as follows:

$$\overline{A}_1 = (Y_1 + Y_2)/2 = (30 + 25)/2 = 27.5$$

The average effects of other factors are computed in a similar manner.

$$\overline{A}_2 = (Y_3 + Y_4)/2 = (34 + 27)/2 = 30.5$$

$$\overline{B}_1 = (Y_1 + Y_3)/2 = (30 + 34)/2 = 32.0$$

$$\overline{B}_2 = (Y_2 + Y_4)/2 = (25 + 27)/2 = 26.0$$

$$\overline{C}_1 = (Y_1 + Y_4)/2 = (30 + 27)/2 = 28.5$$

$$\overline{C}_2 = (Y_2 + Y_3)/2 = (25 + 34)/2 = 29.5$$

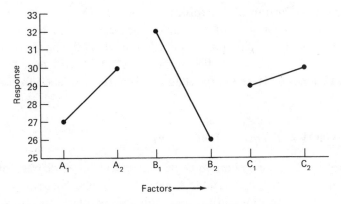

Figure 5-3. Main effects.

The average effects can also be plotted for a visual inspection as appears in Figure 5-3. Frequently the term "factorial effect" or "main effect" is loosely substituted for "average effect." Strictly speaking, the factorial effect is the difference between the two average effects of the factor at the two levels. For instance, the factorial effect of factor C is the difference between average effect of C_1 and C_2.

5-3-3   Quality Characteristics

In the previous chapter the quality characteristics were described as:

- the bigger the better
- the smaller the better
- the nominal the best

For the molding process example, higher strength of the molded plastic part is desired, and thus, "the bigger the better." From Figure 5-3, the $A_2 B_1 C_2$ will likely produce the best result and therefore represents the optimum condition except for the possible effect of interactions between the factors.

In terms of the actual design factors, the probable optimum condition becomes:

A_2 i.e., Injection pressure   at   350 psi

B_1 i.e., Mold temperature   at   150 °F

C_2 i.e., Set time   at   9 sec.

Relative Contribution of Variables

The relative contributions of the factors are determined by comparing their variances. The technique, popularly known as the analysis of variance (ANOVA) is used for this purpose. ANOVA will be covered in detail in Chapter 6. Here the procedure is briefly introduced to complete the analysis.

5-3-4   ANOVA Terms and Notations

The analysis of variance computes quantities known as degrees of freedom, sums of squares, mean squares, etc. and organizes them in a standard tabular format. These quantities and their interrelationships are defined as shown below using the following notation:

V	= Mean squares (variance)	P	= Percent contribution
		T	= Total (of results)
S	= Sum of squares	N	= Number of experiments
S'	= Pure sum of squares	$C.F.$	= Correction factor
f	= Degrees of freedom	n	= Total degrees of freedom
e	= Error (experimental)		
F	= Variance ratio		

Variance

The variance of each factor is determined by the sum of the square of each trial sum result involving the factor, divided by the degrees of freedom of the factor. Thus:

$$V_A = S_A/f_A \quad \text{(for factor } A\text{)}$$

$$V_B = S_B/f_B \quad \text{(for factor } B\text{)}$$

$$V_C = S_C/f_C \quad \text{(for factor } C\text{)}$$

$$V_e = S_e/f_e \quad \text{(for error terms)}$$

Variance Ratio

The variance ratio is the variance of the factor divided by the error variance.

$$F_A = V_A/V_e$$

$$F_B = V_B/V_e$$

$$F_C = V_C/V_e$$

$$F_e = V_e/V_e = 1$$

Pure Sum of Squares

The pure sum of squares is the sum minus the degrees of freedom times the error variance.

$$S'_A = S_A - f_A \times V_e$$

$$S'_B = S_B - f_B \times V_e$$

$$S'_C = S_C - f_C \times V_e$$

$$S'_e = S_e + (f_A + f_B + f_C) \times V_e$$

Percent Contribution

The percent contribution of each factor is the ratio of the factor sum to the total, expressed in percent.

$$P_A = S_A \times 100/S_T$$

$$P_B = S_B \times 100/S_T$$

$$P_C = S_C \times 100/S_T$$

$$P_e = S_e \times 100/S_T$$

5-3-5   Variation Computation—Examples:

Total variation: S_T = Sum of square of all trial run results $- C.F.$

where: $C.F. = T^2/N$ and $T = (Y_1 + Y_2 + Y_3 + Y_4)$

or $S_T = (Y_1^2 + \cdots + Y_4^2) - (Y_1 + Y_2 + Y_3 + Y_4)^2$

$= 30^2 + 25^2 + 34^2 + 27^2 - (30 + 25 + 34 + 27)^2/4$

$= 3410 - 3364$

$= 46$

For the molding process experiment, the totals of the factors are

$A_1 = 30 + 25 = 55$ $A_2 = 34 + 27 = 61$

$B_1 = 30 + 34 = 64$ $B_2 = 25 + 27 = 52$

$C_1 = 30 + 27 = 57$ $C_2 = 25 + 34 = 59$

therefore, the total variance of each factor is:

$$S_A = A_1^2/N_{A1} + A_2^2/N_{A2} - C.F.$$

$$= 55^2/2 + 61^2/2 - 3364$$

$$= 1512.5 + 1860.5 - 3364 = 9.0$$

$$S_B = B_1^2/N_{B1} + B_2^2/N_{B2} - C.F. = 36.0$$

and

$$S_C = C_1^2/N_{C1} + C_2^2/N_{C2} - C.F. = 1.0$$

The error variance

$$S_e = S_T - (S_A + S_B + S_C)$$

$$= 46 - 9 - 36 - 1 = 0 \text{ (in this case)}$$

5-3-6   Degrees of Freedom (DOF)

The number of the degrees of freedom for a factor or a column equals one less than the number of levels. Thus for a 2 level factor assigned to a 2 level column, the DOF is 1. An L_4 OA with three 2 level columns will have a total of 3 DOF or one for each column. The total degrees of freedom of the result T, however is computed as follows:

f_T = total number of result $-$ 1

= (total number of trials $\times$ number of repetition) $-$ 1

= $4 \times 1 - 1 = 3$

For factors

f_A = Number of levels of A − 1 = 1

f_B = Number of levels of B − 1 = 1

f_C = Number of levels of C − 1 = 1

and the DOF for error variance is

$f_e = f_T - f_A - f_B - f_C$

$= 3 - 1 - 1 - 1$

$= 0$

Variance

$V_A = S_A/f_A = 9/1 = 9$

$V_B = S_B/f_B = 36/1 = 36$

$V_C = S_C/f_C = 1/1 = 1$

$V_e = S_e/f_e = 0/0$ indeterminate

Note that if the experiment included repetitions, say 2, then:

$f_T = 4 \times 2 - 1 = 7$

$f_e = 7 - 1 - 1 - 1 = 4$

where S_e need not equal zero, depending on test results, and V_e need not be zero.

Variance Ratio

$F_A = V_A/V_e$ is indeterminate since $V_e = 0$. Similarly F_b and F_C are indeterminate (Table 5-4). However, V_e can be combined (pooled) with another small variance (V_C) to calculate a new error V_e which can then be used to produce meaningful results. The process of disregarding an individual factor's contribution and then subsequently adjusting the contributions of the other factors, is known as *Pooling*. The detailed pro-

Table 5-4. ANOVA Table for Molding Process Experiment

FACTORS	f	S	V	F	s	P
A	1	9	9	—	—	19.62
B	1	36	36			78.28
C	1	1	1			2.10
Error	0	0	0			
Totals	3	46				100.00%

cedure for pooling and the criteria used to determine its use will be discussed in Chapter 6 along with ANOVA.

Consider pooling effects of the factor C. Then the new error variance is computed as:

$$V_e = (S_C + S_e)/(f_C + f_e)$$
$$= (1.0 + 0)/(1.0 + 0) = 1$$

With this new V_e, all sums of squares, S, can be modified as

$$S'_A = S_A - (V_e \times f_A)$$

etc.

The result then can be shown in the ANOVA table with the effect of the factor C pooled. The pooled effects are shown as the error term in the ANOVA table (last row of Table 5-5).

The last column of the ANOVA table indicates the percent contribution of the individual factor. In the example, factor B contributes the most, 76.08%. The contribution of A is 17.39% and that of C is not significant.

Table 5-5. Pooled ANOVA for Molding Process Experiment

SOURCE	f	S	V	F	s	P
A	1	9	9	9	8	17.39
B	1	36	36	36	35	76.08
C	---------	----pooled	-----------	-----------	-----------	-----------
Error	1	1	1			6.74
Totals	3	46				100.00%

Note that the difference in the percentage influences of factors before (Table 5-4) and after pooling (Table 5-5) is not large. To increase the statistical significance of important factors, those factors with small variances should be pooled.

5-3-7   Projection of the Optimum Performance

Recall that for a "bigger is better" quality characteristic, the study of the main effect shows that the optimum condition is $A_2 B_1 C_2$. It happens to be the third trial run. This is just a coincidence. Most of the time, the optimum condition will not be one of the trial runs because the Taguchi experiment represent only a small set of the full factorial experiment. The optimum is one of the trials defined by the full factorial experiment. As a general rule, the optimum performance will be calculated using the following expression.

T = Grand total of all results

N = Total number of results

Y_{opt} = Performance at optimum condition

For optimum combination $A_2 B_1 C_2$ (which happens to be experiment number 3)

$$Y_{opt} = T/N + (\overline{A}_2 - T/N) + (\overline{B}_1 - T/N) + (\overline{C}_2 - T/N)$$

$$= \text{average performance} + \text{contribution of } A_2, B_1, \text{ and } C_2$$
$$\text{above average performance}$$

In this example:

$$T = 116, N = 4, \overline{A}_2 = 30.5, \overline{B}_1 = 32, \overline{C}_2 = 29.5$$

therefore,

$$Y_{opt} = 29 + (30.5 - 29) + (32 - 29) + (29.5 - 29)$$

$$= 34.0$$

which is the result obtained in the trial run 3.

When the optimum is not one of the trial runs already completed, this projection should be verified by running a confirmation test(s). Confirmation testing is a necessary and important step in the Taguchi method as it is direct proof of the methodology. Generally speaking, the average result from the confirmation tests should agree with the optimum performance (Y_{opt}) estimated by the analysis. The correlation can also be established in statistical terms reflecting the level of confidence, influence of number of confirmation tests, etc. The procedure for calculation of confidence interval of the optimum performance is discussed in Section 6-4.

5-4 DESIGNING WITH MORE THAN THREE VARIABLES

In the preceding section, the layout of a simple experiment involving only 3 factors, was discussed. In this section, designs for a larger number of factors will be treated. The designs will use the higher order OAs.

5-4-1 DESIGNS WITH 2-LEVEL VARIABLES

Example 5-2

Design an experiment to investigate

	4 Factors	all at 2 levels,
	5 Factors	all at 2 levels,
	6 Factors	all at 2 levels,
or	7 Factors	all at 2 levels,

Let these factors be A, B, C, D, E, F, and G and their levels A_1, A_2, etc.

Experiment Design
As seen in the last example, the smallest OA i.e., L_4, can handle up to 3 factors. What do we do when there are more than 3 factors?

A list of commonly used OAs is shown in Table A-1. Notice that L_8 can be used for 4 to 7 factors. Therefore, L_8 is suitable for any of the above situations.

An L_8 has 8 trial conditions and 7 columns. To design the experiment, factors must be assigned to appropriate columns and 8 trial conditions must be specified.

Table 5-6. L_8 with Seven 2 Level Factors

FACTORS	A	B	C	D	E	F	G	
EXPERIMENT NUMBER COLUMNS →	1	2	3	4	5	6	7	RESULTS
1	1	1	1	1	1	1	1	
2	1	1	1	2	2	2	2	
3	1	2	2	1	1	2	2	
4	1	2	2	2	2	1	1	
5	2	1	2	1	2	1	2	
6	2	1	2	2	1	2	1	
7	2	2	1	1	2	2	1	
8	2	2	1	2	1	1	2	

Since all factors have the same number of levels, the factor can be assigned to any one column. Thus factor A can be assigned to any of the columns 1 through 7. Then B can be assigned to any one of the remaining columns. You can also assign them in the natural ascending order, like A in column 1, B in column 2 and so on. If there are only 4 factors, ignore the 3 unused columns.

The experimental conditions are defined by reading across the row of the OA. An L_8 OA, as shown in Table A-2, has 8 rows. Thus it represents 8 unique combinations of factors and their levels. An L_8 with the factors assigned to its columns is shown in Table 5-6.

From L_8 trial number 3, is defined as

Trial number 3   1   2   2   1   1   2   2

Example 5-3

Number of factors   = 8 through 11

Number of levels for each = 2

Use array L_{12}

Design

Use L_{12} shown in Table A-3 for this example. Assign factors 1 thru 11 in the 11 columns available, in any order. Express the 12 experimental conditions by using the 12 rows of the OA. Note that L_{12} is a special array prepared for study of the main effects only. In this array the inter-action effects of factors assigned to any two columns is mixed with all other columns which renders the array unsuitable for interaction studies. (Use L_{16}, L_{32} and L_{64} shown in Appendix A to design experiments with higher numbers of 2 level factors.)

5-4-2   Designs with 3 Level Variables

Example 5-4

Number of factors   = 5 through 13

Number of levels for each = 3

Use L_{27} (Table A-8)

5-4-3   Designs with Mixed Levels Using standard Arrays

Example 5-5

Consider the experiments where there are 8 factors to be investigated. To study the nonlinear effect, 7 factors were set at 3 levels. The remaining one (1) factor was examined at only 2 levels.

Design
This is an example of the mixed levels. The L_{18} array shown in Table A-7(b) is used. L_{18} has 8 columns, of which column 1 has 2 levels, and the rest have 3 levels. Obviously, the factor with 2 levels will be assigned to column 1. The remaining 7 factors can be assigned to columns 2 through 8 in any desired manner.

5-5   DESIGNS WITH INTERACTION

The term *Interaction*, expressed by inserting " × " mark between the two interacting factors, is used to describe a condition in which the influence of one factor upon the result, is dependent on the condition of the other. Two factors A and B are said to interact (written as $A \times B$) when the effect of changes in the level of A, determines the influence of B and vice versa. For example, temperature and humidity appear to have strong interaction with respect to human comfort. An increase in temperature alone may cause slight discomfort but the discomfort increases as hu-

Table 5-7. Layout for Experiment with Two 2 Level Factors

(a) The Case with Interaction

	T_1	T_2	TOTAL
H_1	62	80	142
H_2	75	73	148
Total	137	153	290

(b) The Case without Interaction

	T_1	T_2	TOTAL
H_1	67	75	142
H_2	70	78	148
Total	137	153	290

midity increases. Assume the comfort level is dependent only upon two factors T and H, and is measured in terms of numbers ranging from 0 to 100. If T and H are each allowed to assume levels as T_1, T_2, H_1, and H_2, assume that two sets of experimental data (with the same grand total of all observations) were obtained and are represented by Tables 5-7a and 5-7b. The data are plotted in Figures 5-4a and 5-4b. Figure 5-4a shows an interaction between the two factors since the lines cross. Figure 5-4b shows no interaction because the lines are parallel. If the lines are not parallel the factors may interact, albeit weakly.

The graphical method reveals if interaction exists. It is calculated from the experimental data. But how can we know whether the factors will interact before we design the experiment? The Taguchi methods do not specify any general guidelines for predicting interactions. One has to determine that by some other means, perhaps from experience or a previous Taguchi experiment.

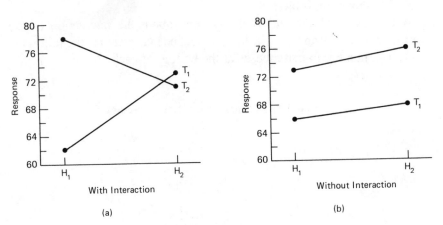

Figure 5-4. Main effects of factors T and H.

Experimental design using Taguchi OA's is simple and straightforward when there is no need to include interactions. It requires a little more care to design an experiment where interactions are to be included. In Taguchi OAs the effect of interactions are mixed with the main effect of a factor assigned to some other column. In the L_4 shown in Table 5-8 with factors A and B assigned to columns 1 and 2, interaction effects of $A \times B$ will be contained in column 3. If the interactions of $A \times B$ were of no interest, a third factor C can be assigned to column 3 (Table 5-8). The effect of interaction $A \times B$ will then be mixed with the main effect of factor C.

The interacting pair of columns along with the column where interaction is shown, constitute an interacting triple. In case of an L_8 OA, the interaction of columns 1 and 2 goes to column 3. Which also means that the interaction between 2 and 3 is reflected in column 1 and that between 3 and 1 shows up in 2. What about interactions between other columns of an L_8 or any other 2 level orthogonal arrays? What about interaction between two columns of 3 level orthogonal arrays? These will be difficult tasks for practicing engineers to keep track of. Taguchi spent much of his research determining relationships for interacting columns. His findings regarding which columns interact with which other columns, are presented in a table called the *Triangular Table of Interaction*. There are tables to suit different levels of OAs. A large triangular table as shown in Table A-6 made for 2 level columns will usually satisfy most commonly used 2 level orthogonal arrays.

Note that the first 7 columns of Table A-6, become the triangular table for L_8 as shown in Table 5-9.

A triangular table contains information about the interaction of the various columns of an OA. The table should be interpreted in the following way. The number in parentheses at the bottom of each column identifies

Table 5-8. L_4 with Two 2 Level Factors

EXPERIMENTS/ COLUMNS	A	B	$A \times B$ C
1	1	1	1
2	1	2	2
3	2	1	2
4	2	2	1

Table 5-9. Interaction Between Two Columns in an L_8 Array

COLUMN:	1	2	3	4	5	6	7
	(1)	3	2	5	4	7	6
		(2)	1	6	7	4	5
			(3)	7	6	5	4
				(4)	1	2	3
					(5)	3	2
						(6)	1
							(7)

the column. To find in which column the interaction between columns 4 and 6 will appear, move horizontally across (4) and vertically from (6), the intersection is "2" in the tables. Thus the interaction effects between columns 4 and 6 will appear at column 2. In a similar manner, other interacting columns can be identified.

The triangular table facilitates laying out experiments with interactions. The table greatly reduces the time and increases the accuracy of assigning proper columns for interaction effects. To further enhance efficiency of the experimental layout, Taguchi created line diagrams based on the triangular tables. These diagrams represent standard experiment designs. He calls such diagrams *Linear Graphs*. Linear graphs for L_4, L_8 and other 2 level orthogonal arrays are shown in Figures A-2 and A-3.

Linear Graphs

Linear graphs are made up of numbers, dots and lines as shown in Figure 5-4-1 where a dot and its assigned number identifies a factor, a connecting line between two dots indicates interaction and the number assigned to the line indicates the column number in which interaction effects will be compounded.

In designing experiments with interactions, the triangular tables are essential; the linear graphs are complementary to the tables. For most industrial experiments, interactions between factors are minor and the

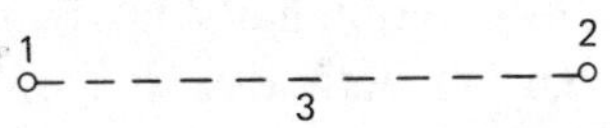

Figure 5-4-1. Linear graphs for L_4.

Table 5-10. Factors for the Cake Baking Experiment

FACTORS/VARIABLES	LEVEL 1	LEVEL 2
A. Egg	2 Eggs (A_1)	3 Eggs (A_2)
B. Butter	1 Stick (B_1)	1.5 Stick (B_2)
C. Milk	2 Cups (C_1)	3 Cups (C_2)
D. Flour	1 Extra scoop (D_1)	2 Extra scoops (D_2)
E. Sugar	1 Extra scoop (E_1)	2 Extra scoops (E_2)

triangular tables suffice. The following example shows how these two tools are used for experimental design.

Example 5-6

In a baking experiment designed to determine the best recipe for a pound cake, five factors and their respective levels were identified as presented in Table 5-10.

Among these factors, milk (factor C) was considered to interact with eggs (A) and butter (B). An experiment was designed to study the interactions $A \times C$ and $B \times C$ in addition to the main effects of factors A, B, C, D, and E.

5-5-1 Steps in the Design and Analysis

Degrees of Freedom (DOF)
Each of the five factors (A, B, C, D, and E) are to be studied at two levels, therefore, each factor has a DOF of 1 (DOF = Number of levels − 1). The DOF for the interaction is computed by multiplying the DOF of each of the interacting factors. Thus, the DOF for $A \times C$ is 1. Likewise the DOF of $B \times C = 1$. The total DOF for the 5 factors and 2 interactions in this case is 7. The appropriate Taguchi array cannot have a DOF less than the total DOF of the experiment.

Selecting the Right OA
The experiment under consideration has 7 DOF and therefore requires an OA with 7 DOF, hence an OA with at least 7 columns. Since an L_4 has 3 columns its DOF is 3. An L_8 has 7 columns and 7 DOF. It possibly

can work. An L_{12} has eleven 2 level columns of which only 7 are needed. L_{12} certainly will work, but would require 12 trial runs in contrast to 8 for L_8. The smallest OA that will do the job should be selected in order to minimize experiment cost and time. How about an L_{16}? That is too large for a 7 DOF experiment. In this case an L_8 is a good match. Would an L_8 always work for an experiment with 7 DOF? Not necessarily. It will depend mainly on how many interactions are expected to be investigated. It will work for Example 5-6.

Column Assignment

In designing experiments with interactions, the columns for interactions must be identified first. We have two interactions, $A \times C$ and $B \times C$. The trick is to select positions for $A \times C$ and $B \times C$, such that there are free columns for each of the factors A, B, and C as well. This can be done by using the triangular table for a 2 level OA or the corresponding linear graphs. Let us examine the linear graph(a) of Figure A-2. C is common to $A \times C$ and $B \times C$. Assign C to column 2, a vertex with two connecting lines. Notice column 2 is a vertex of the triangle with sides 2-3-1 and 2-6-4. With C at 2, assign A to either column 1 or column 4 and B to any remaining column. If A is assigned to 1, and B to 4, then $A \times C$ becomes column 3 and $B \times C$ becomes column 6.

Five columns have been used by factors A, B, C, and interactions $A \times C$ and $B \times C$. The remaining two factors, D and E can be assigned to columns 5 and 7 in any order. Let us assign D to column 5 and E to column 7. With factors and interactions successfully assigned to the available columns, an L_8 is obviously suitable for the design.

Having total DOF less than or equal to that for the OA, is not always a guarantee that a design can be accomplished. Suppose instead of interactions $A \times C$ and $B \times C$, interactions $A \times C$ and $B \times D$ were to be investigated. The total DOF will still be 7, the same as L_8. By examining Figure A-2, notice that both linear graphs (a) and (b) have a common factor such as 1, 2 or 4. Since the interactions $A \times C$ and $B \times D$ do not have a common factor, an L_8 cannot be used. The next higher order array should be tried.

The experiment designed for Example 5-6 uses the L_8 OA with column assignments as shown in Table 5-11.

Table 5-11. L_8 for the Cake Baking Experiment

COLUMNS: TRIAL/NUMBER	A 1	C 2	A × C 3	B 4	D 5	B × C 6	E 7	RESULTS
1	1	1	1	1	1	1	1	66
2	1	1	1	2	2	2	2	75
3	1	2	2	1	1	2	2	54
4	1	2	2	2	2	1	1	62
5	2	1	2	1	2	1	2	52
6	2	1	2	2	1	2	1	82
7	2	2	1	1	2	2	1	52
8	2	2	1	2	1	1	2	78

Total = 521

Description of Combinations

The 8 trial conditions, contained in Table 5-11 can be described for each individual trial as shown in Tables 5-12 and 5-13, for trial runs 1 and 2, respectively. The other trial runs can be similarly described. Note that the numbers in the columns, where interactions are assigned (columns 3 and 6), are not used in the description of trial run 2. Normally the interaction column need not appear in the description and thus is deleted from the description of the trial runs (trial run 2 Table 5-13). The complete design information and analysis for this experiment are shown in Table 5-14.

Table 5-12. Description of Trial NUMBER 1 (Cake Baking)

COLUMN	VARIABLE (FACTOR)	LEVEL	
1	Egg	2 Eggs	(A_1)
2	Milk	2 Cups	(C_1)
3	A × C (Egg × Milk)		
4	Butter	1 Stick	(B_1)
5	Flour	1 Extra scoop	(D_1)
6	B × C (Butter × Milk)		
7	Sugar	1 Extra scoop	(E_1)

Table 5-13. Description of Trial NUMBER 2 (Cake Baking)

COLUMN	VARIABLE (FACTOR)	LEVEL	
1	Egg	2 Eggs	(A_1)
2	Milk	2 Cups	(C_1)
4	Butter	1.5 Stick	(B_2)
5	Flour	2 Extra scoop	(D_2)
7	Sugar	2 Extra scoop	(E_2)

Running the Experiment

The order in which a specific combination of experiments is run is un-affected by the consideration of the interactions. Conditions 1 through 8 should be done in a random order. A minimum of one trial run per condition must be performed. Repetition of trial runs and the order of repetitions are constrained by time and cost.

Quality Characteristic (Results)

Eight cakes were baked, one for each of the trial runs of Table 5-11. The cakes were then examined by several experienced bakers. Before the cakes were baked, evaluation criteria were established. It was agreed that the cakes were to be evaluated not only for taste, but also for appearance and moistness. It was decided that the cakes were to be rated on a scale of 0 to 100, using a scheme to reflect the weighting of each individual attribute of the characteristic. For each condition, the average of the evaluations by the bakers were recorded as shown in the column marked results (Table 5-11). Based on the definition, a higher value of the results was considered favorable. For the purpose of analysis, this constituted "the higher the better" type of quality characteristics.

Analysis of Results

The analysis of data including interactions follows the same steps as are taken when there is no interaction. The objectives are the same: (1) determine the optimum condition, (2) identify the individual influence of each factor, and (3) estimate the performance at the optimum condition. The methods for objectives 2 and 3 are the same as before. For the optimum condition, interactions introduce a minor change in the manner in which the levels of factors are identified. To develop a

Table 5-14. Analysis of the Cake Baking Experiment

(a) Main Effects

COLUMN/FACTOR		FACTOR	LEVEL 1 AVERAGE	LEVEL 2 AVERAGE	DIFFERENCE (2–1)
1	A	Egg	64.25	66.00	1.75
2	C	Milk	68.75	61.50	−7.25
3	A × C	1 × 2	67.75	62.50	−5.25
4	B	Butter	56.00	74.25	18.25
5	D	Flour	70.00	60.25	−9.75
6	B × C	2 × 4	64.50	65.75	1.25
7	E	Sugar	65.50	64.75	−0.75

(b) ANOVA Table

COLUMNS/ FACTOR		FACTORS	DF	SUM OF SQUARES	VARIANCE	F	PERCENT
1	A	Eggs	1	6.125	6.125	5.44	0.49
2	C	Milk	1	105.125	105.125	93.44	10.13
3	A × C	Interaction 1 × 2	1	55.125	55.125	49.00	5.26
4	B	Butter	1	666.125	666.125	592.11	64.76
5	D	Flour	1	190.125	190.125	169.00	18.41
6	B × C	Interaction 2 × 4	1	3.125	3.125	2.77	0.19
7	E	Sugar	(1)	(1.13)	Pooled		
All others/error			0	1.13	1.13		0.78
Total:			7	1026.880			100.00

(c) Estimate of Performance at the Optimum Condition of Design/Process:
   Characteristic: Higher the Better

FACTOR	DESCRIPTION	LEVEL DESCRIPTION	LEVEL NUMBER	CONTRIBUTION
Egg		3 Eggs	2	0.875
Milk		2 Cups	1	3.625
Butter		1.5 Sticks	2	9.125
Flour		1 Extra scoop	1	4.875
Sugar		1 Extra scoop	1	0.375

Contribution from all factors (total) 18.875
Current grand average of performance 65.125
Expected result at optimum condition 84.000

clear understanding of how the optimum condition is selected, the main effects are discussed here in detail. (The details of ANOVA will be covered in Chapter 6, only the results of a computer analysis will be presented.)

The average effect of level 1 of the factor in column 1 (the effect of 2 eggs) is computed by adding the first 4 trial results of Table 5-11 and dividing the sum by 4. Note that for trials 1 to 4, factor A (eggs) is assigned level 1 (2 cups). Thus each of these trial runs contains the effect of factor A at level 1 (A_1). The average effect of A_1, therefore, is found by averaging the results of the first four experiments. The notation $\overline{A}_1$ with a bar is used for this value. Thus,

$$\overline{A}_1 = (66 + 75 + 54 + 62)/4 = 64.25$$

Similarly the average effect of level 2, of A, is obtained by the last four trial runs, since these were runs with factor A at level 2. Hence:

$$\overline{A}_2 = (52 + 82 + 52 + 78)/4 = 66.00$$

Similarly

$$\overline{C}_1 = 68.75$$
$$\overline{C}_2 = 61.50$$

and,

$$\overline{(A \times C)}_1 = 67.75$$
$$\overline{(A \times C)}_2 = 62.50$$

The calculations for each factor and level are presented in Table 5-14(a).

The difference between the average value of each factor at levels 2 and 1 indicates the relative influence of the effect. The larger the difference, the stronger the influence. The sign of the difference, obviously indicates whether the change from level 1 to 2 increases or decreases the result. The main effects are shown visually in Figure 5-5. Figure 5-6 shows the interaction effects of $A \times C$ and $B \times C$.

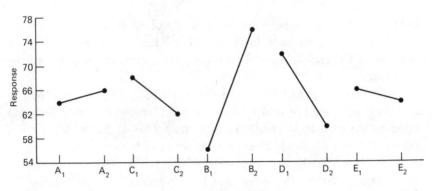

Figure 5-5. Main effects.

Ignoring interaction effects for the moment, notice that Table 5-14(a) and Fig. 5-5 show an improvement at level 2 only for factors A and B while level 2 effects for C, D and E cause a decrease in quality. Hence the optimum levels for the factors based on the data are $A_2 B_2 C_1 E_1$ and E_1. Coincidentally, trial run number 6 tested these conditions and produced the highest result (Table 5-11). Since interaction is ignored, the average effects of $(A \times B)_{1,2}$ and $(A \times C)_{1,2}$ shown in Table 5-14(a) are not used in determining the optimum.

5-5-2 Interaction Effects

To determine whether the interaction is present, a proper interpretation of the results is necessary. The general approach is to separate the influence of an interacting member from the influences of the others. In this

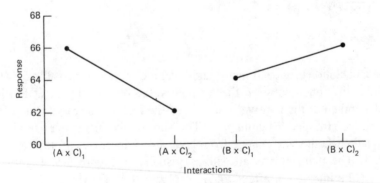

Figure 5-6. Interaction effects.

example $A \times C$ and $B \times C$ are the interactions with C common to both. The information about C can be extracted from the columns assigned to factors A, B, and C, at the two levels of C. The steps involved are described below.

The $(A_1 C_1)$ is first found from the results that contains both A_1 and C_1. Note that $(A_1 C_1)$ is not the same as the average value in level 1 of Table 5-14(a) for interaction $(A \times C)$ assigned to column 3 of Table 5-11. This value is $(A \times C)_1$. In this analysis interaction columns, i.e., columns 3 and 6, are not used. Instead columns of Table 5-11 which represent the individual factors are used. Examination of column 1 shows A_1 is contained in rows (trial runs) 1, 2, 3, and 4, but C_1 is in trial runs 1, 2, 5, and 6. Comparing the two, the rows that contain both A_1 and C_1 are 1 and 2. Therefore, $A_1 C_1$ comes from the results of trial runs 1 and 2.

The average effect of $\overline{(A_1 C_1)} = (66 + 75)/2 = 70.50$. The two common trial runs for $A_1 C_2$ are 3 and 4, and the average effect of $\overline{(A_1 C_2)}$ $= (54 + 62)/2 = 58.00$

In the calculations for $\overline{A_1 C_1}$ and $\overline{A_1 C_2}$, factor level A_1 is common. The difference between result 70.50 for $A_1 C_1$ and 58.00 for $A_1 C_2$ is due only to factor C.

Similarly $\overline{A_2 C_1}$, $\overline{A_2 C_2}$, $\overline{B_1 C_1}$, $\overline{B_1 C_2}$, $\overline{B_2 C_1}$, and $\overline{B_2 C_2}$ are calculated as shown below.

$\overline{(A_1 C_1)} = 70.50$	$\overline{(A_2 C_1)} = 68.50$
$\overline{(A_1 C_2)} = 58.00$	$\overline{(A_2 C_2)} = 65.00$
$\overline{(B_1 C_1)} = 59.00$	$\overline{(B_2 C_1)} = 78.50$
$\overline{(B_1 C_2)} = 53.00$	$\overline{(B_2 C_2)} = 70.00$

These results can be easily visualized by inspection of Figure 5-7.

The intersecting lines on the left represents the interaction between A and C. The parallel lines on the right show that B and C probably do not interact. Recall that in Table 5-14(a), the average influence of interaction $(A \times C)_{1,2}$ assigned to column 3 was -5.25. Further analysis for the significance of this influence is made possible by the ANOVA table in Table 5-14(b) which shows that the interaction $A \times C$ (column 3) is 5.26%, compared to the individual main effects of butter (B) 64.76% and flour (D) 18.4%, etc.

To summarize, the suspected interaction between factors B and C was

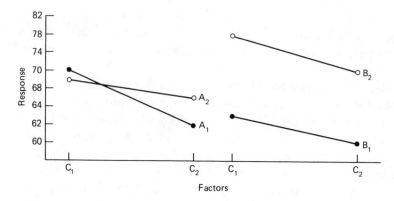

Figure 5-7. Test of interactions.

found not to exist. The suspected interaction between A and C does exist; its value is 5.26%, based on ANOVA.

Now to reexamine the optimum condition determined only from the factors A_2, C_1, B_2, D_1, and E_1, we see from Figure 5-7 that $\overline{A_1 C_1}$ has a higher value than $\overline{A_2 C_1}$. Thus the optimum condition includes levels A_2 and C_1. The new optimum conditions become $A_1 B_2 C_1 D_1 E_1$. However, the performance at the new optimum should be compared with the original optimum before the final determination of the interaction effects.

Consider the initial optimum which excluded the effects of interaction (condition $A_2 C_1 B_2 D_1 E_1$). Using $\overline{T}$ = average result of 8 runs (Table 5-11) = 521/8 = 65.125. Compute the optimum performance using data from Table 5-14(a):

$$
\begin{aligned}
Y_{opt} = {} & \overline{T} + (\overline{A}_2 - \overline{T}) + (\overline{C}_1 - \overline{T}) + (\overline{B}_2 - \overline{T}) \\
& + (\overline{D}_1 - \overline{T}) + (\overline{E}_1 - \overline{T}) \\
= {} & \overline{T} + (66.00 - \overline{T}) + (68.75 - \overline{T}) + (74.25 - \overline{T}) \\
& + (70.00 - \overline{T}) + (65.50 - \overline{T}) \\
= {} & 65.125 + 0.875 + 3.625 + 9.125 + 4.875 + 0.375 \\
= {} & 65.125 + 18.875 \\
= {} & 84.000
\end{aligned}
$$

Similarly for the revised optimum, considering interactic E_1 we compute:

$$Y_{opt} = \overline{T} + (\overline{A_1C_1} - \overline{T}) + (\overline{B_2} - \overline{T}) + (\overline{D_1} - \overline{T})$$
$$= \overline{T} + (70.5 - \overline{T}) + (74.25 - \overline{T})$$
$$+ (70 - \overline{T}) + (65.5 - \overline{T})$$
$$= 65.128 + 5.375 + 9.125 + 4.875 + 0.375$$
$$= 84.875$$

Note that when the estimate of performance at the optimum condition includes the interactions between A and C, the net result is obtained from the combined effect of $\overline{A_1C_1}$.

The second calculation yields a higher value, confirming that the revised optimum is better.

As a final check examine the interaction between B and C. The second pair of lines in Figure 5-7 represents the effect of C at fixed levels of B. The lines are almost parallel thus indicating little interaction. The ANOVA calculations presented in Table 5-14(b) show a small interaction (0.19%). Observe that the highest value for the pair of lines corresponds to C_1B_2. Comparing C_1B_2 to the revised optimum condition, we find that C_1B_2 are included. Thus, the interaction $B \times C$ has no influence on the optimum. The optimum condition remains as revised for interaction $A \times C$ and no further modification is needed.

Optimum condition $= A_1\, C_1\, B_2\, D_1\, E_1.$

Expected performance at optimum condition $= 84.875$

5-5-3 Key Observations

- In designing experiments with interactions, Triangular Tables or Linear Graphs should be used for column assignments. To select the appropriate OA, the types of interactions and their degrees of freedom will have to be considered.
- For the purpose of analysis, interactions are treated as are any other factors, however their presence is ignored for the preliminary deter-

mination of the optimum condition. The relative significance of interactions is obtained from an ANOVA study.

- The determination of the effect of interactions requires a separate study. Such study may suggest a change in the optimum condition.
- When several interactions are included in an experiment, the level selection may become extremely complex.

How should interactions be handled? Should an extra variable be included to study the interaction? If constraints necessitate a choice between including an extra variable or studying an interaction, Taguchi recommends, "dig wide, not down." When there is an extra column, study a new variable, not an interaction. On the second pass, if there are strong feelings about the interactions, then they should be included.

5-5-4   More Designs with Interactions

Example 5-7

Design an experiment with 5 factors at 2 levels each and two interactions.

Variables: A, B, C, D, E

Interactions: $A \times B$ and $C \times D$

Design
The 5 factors and the 2 interactions each have one DOF. Thus the total DOF is 7. In this case an L_8 will not work, because the triangular table (Tables 5-9 and A-6) shows that there is only one independent triplet in the first 7 columns. In other words, if A and B are assigned to columns 1 and 2, column 3 will be reserved for $A \times B$. This means that columns 4, 5, 6, and 7 remain for factors C, D, E, and interaction $C \times D$. However any combination of these columns 4, 5, 6, and 7 contains only the values 1, 2 or 3, hence their interaction would involve columns previously assigned to A, B and $A \times B$. The next higher order OA is an L_{12}. But it is a special array where interaction effects are distributed and thus can't be used to study interactions. An L_{16} OA is the next higher order array. Examination of the triangular table (Table A-6) will show that it can be used.

Using Table A-6, arbitrarily assigns:

A to column 1 C to column 2

B to column 4 D to column 8

Then $A \times B$ is column 5,   and $C \times D$ is column 10

and E is column 3

There were many ways to achieve this column assignment. In this case using Table A-6, A and B were arbitrarily assigned to columns 1 and 4, with column 5 reserved for interaction $A \times B$. C and D were then assigned to two unused columns such that $C \times D$ becomes a column which is 15 or less and not previously assigned. Columns 2, 8, and 10 were the interacting group of columns selected for factors C, D, and $C \times D$, respectively. The factor E was then assigned to one of the remaining 9 columns, column 3. The final design is shown in Table 5-15. Note that columns 6, 7, 9, 11 to 15 are unassigned and not used in the experiment.

Table 5-15. L_{16} Design with Five Factors and Two Interactions

L_{16}	A	C	E	$A \times B$ (B)	$A \times B$			D		$C \times D$	D				
EXPERIMENTS/ COLUMN	1	2	3	4	5	6	7	8	9	10	11	12	13	14	15
1	1	1	1	1	1	0	0	1	0	1	0	0	0	0	0
2	1	1	1	1	1	0	0	2	0	2	0	0	0	0	0
3	1	1	1	2	2	0	0	1	0	1	0	0	0	0	0
4	1	1	1	2	2	0	0	2	0	2	0	0	0	0	0
5	1	2	2	1	1	0	0	1	0	2	0	0	0	0	0
6	1	2	2	1	1	0	0	2	0	1	0	0	0	0	0
7	1	2	2	2	2	0	0	1	0	2	0	0	0	0	0
8	1	2	2	2	2	0	0	2	0	1	0	0	0	0	0
9	2	1	2	1	2	0	0	1	0	1	0	0	0	0	0
10	2	1	2	1	2	0	0	2	0	2	0	0	0	0	0
11	2	1	2	2	1	0	0	1	0	1	0	0	0	0	0
12	2	1	2	2	1	0	0	2	0	2	0	0	0	0	0
13	2	2	1	1	2	0	0	1	0	2	0	0	0	0	0
14	2	2	1	1	2	0	0	2	0	1	0	0	0	0	0
15	2	2	1	2	1	0	0	1	0	2	0	0	0	0	0
16	2	2	1	2	1	0	0	2	0	1	0	0	0	0	0

Example 5-8

Design an experiment with 9 factors at 2 levels each and 5 interactions as described below:

Variables: $A, B, C, D, E, F, G, H, I$

Interactions: $A \times B, A \times C, A \times E, A \times F,$ and $B \times D$

Design

The 9 factors and 5 interactions together have 14 DOF. An L_{16} OA has 15 DOF and is a good candidate. Because of the number of interactions, a linear graph of L_{16} is helpful. Since the factor A is common to 4 of the 5 interactions, a linear graph with a hub will be used. In Figure A-3, the lower left diagram can be adapted for the design by selecting columns of interest as shown in Figure 5-8. Start by assigning A to column 1. Then select ends of four spokes for B, C, E, and F as shown in Table 5-16. If B is assigned to column 15, then D will be column 8 and $B \times D$ column 7. Therefore when all the 5 interactions are assigned to the appropriate columns, the remaining factors can be assigned to the available columns at random.

More examples of experiment designs are described in the later chapters and specifically in Chapter 9.

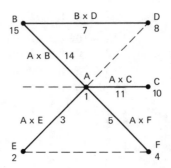

Figure 5-8. A linear graph for Example 5-8.

Table 5-16. L_{16} Design with Nine 2 Level Factors and Five Interactions

L_{16}	A	A×E		A×F				B×D		A×C				A×B	
	A	E	E	F	F	G	D	D	H	C	C	I		B	B
EXPERIMENTS/ COLUMN	1	2	3	4	5	6	7	8	9	10	11	12	13	14	15
1	1	1	1	1	1	1	1	1	1	1	1	1	1	1	1
2	1	1	1	1	1	1	1	2	2	2	2	2	2	2	2
3	1	1	1	2	2	2	2	1	1	1	1	2	2	2	2
4	1	1	1	2	2	2	2	2	2	2	2	1	1	1	1
5	1	2	2	1	1	2	2	1	1	2	2	1	1	2	2
6	1	2	2	1	1	2	2	2	2	1	1	2	2	1	1
7	1	2	2	2	2	1	1	1	1	2	2	2	2	1	1
8	1	2	2	2	2	1	1	2	2	1	1	1	1	2	2
9	2	1	2	1	2	1	2	1	2	1	2	1	2	1	2
10	2	1	2	1	2	1	2	2	1	2	1	2	1	2	1
11	2	1	2	2	1	2	1	1	2	1	2	2	1	2	1
12	2	1	2	2	1	2	1	2	1	2	1	1	2	1	2
13	2	2	1	1	2	2	1	1	2	2	1	1	2	2	1
14	2	2	1	1	2	2	1	2	1	1	2	2	1	1	2
15	2	2	1	2	1	1	2	1	2	2	1	2	1	1	2
16	2	2	1	2	1	1	2	2	1	1	2	1	2	2	1

5-6 DESIGNS WITH MIXED FACTOR LEVELS

Designs without interactions and with all factors at 2 levels are of the simpler kind. They are the least cumbersome and most often can be designed by means of the standard OAs. But there are many occasions when more than two levels will have to be included. In the baking process experiment, a third level of butter (say 1.25 stick, a step between 1 and 1.5) could be specified. The experiment would consist of 4 factors at 2 levels and one at 3 levels. Now we have 4 factors that are of 2 levels and one that has 3 levels. What experiment design is appropriate?

Why are more than 2 levels necessary? First, 3 levels may be important to some factors. Consider an experiment design of a molding process which uses plastic pellet feed stocks from 4 different vendors; or 4 different specifications may include a study of materials at 4 vendor supplied specifications. The factor (material), in such cases, will have 4 levels. Another likely reason for more than 2 levels is that the influence of a factor on the result is suspected to vary nonlinearly. Considering only 2 levels will give a linear output. Nonlinear behavior can only be determined by a third level as shown in Figure 5-9.

There are some standard OAs which treat mixed level factors. But, they may not be the most economical or may not even suit your needs. For most applications involving mixed levels, Taguchi modifies the standard arrays to fit the circumstances. By following his prescription, a 2 level column can be upgraded to a 4 or an 8 level column; a 4 level column can be upgraded into an 8 level column. On the other hand, a column can also be downgraded by lowering the number of levels, say, from 4 to 3. The method of reducing the levels is done by what is known as *Dummy Treatment*.

Before considering column modifications, some additional words about DOF are appropriate. Recall that the DOF for a column is its number of levels less 1. Thus a 2 level column has 1 DOF, a 3 level column has 2 DOF and a 4 level column has 3 DOF.

Thus to create a 4 level column, three 2 level columns are needed to provide the same DOF. To change one column of an L_8 to a 4 level column, 3 columns are combined. Similarly, to change a column of an L_{16} into an 8 level column, seven of the fifteen 2 level columns are combined.

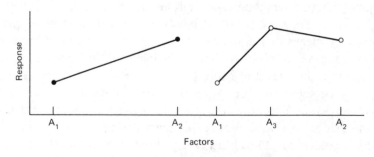

Figure 5-9. Main effects of a factor with two and three levels.

5-6-1   Preparation of a 4 Level Column

A 4 level column is easily prepared from three 2 level columns. To demonstrate, consider an L_8. The procedure will also apply for all 2 level OAs.

Steps

1. From the linear graph for L_8, select a set of three interacting columns (Fig. 5-10). Example: columns 1, 2, and 3.
2. Select any two columns. Suppose 1 and 2 are selected.
3. Combine the two columns row by row, by following the rules of Table 5-17, to get a combined column such as is shown in Table 5-17. Replace the original columns 1, 2, and 3 by the new column which has just been prepared.

Example 5-9

Design an experiment to accommodate one factor at 4 levels and four others at 2 levels each.

Variables: A, B, C, D

Interactions: None

Levels: $A = 4; B, C, D = 2$

The Design

Factor A has 4 levels and 3 DOF. The other four 2 level factors each have 1 DOF. The total DOF is 7. An L_8 OA, shown in Table 5-18, which has 7 DOF appears suitable.

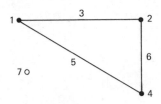

Figure 5-10. Groups of interacting columns for level upgrading.

Table 5-17. Rules for Preparation of a
4 Level Column

LEVEL OF FIRST COLUMN	LEVEL OF SECOND COLUMN	COMBINE TO FORM	LEVEL OF NEW COLUMN
1	1	→	1
1	2	→	2
2	1	→	3
2	2	→	4

Building Columns

The first three columns of an L_8 can be combined to produce a 4 level column following the procedure previously described.

Step 1. Start with an original L_8 and select a set of three interacting columns, say 1, 2, and 3.

Step 2. Ignore column 3 (Table 5-19).

Step 3. Combine column 1 and 2 into a new column. Follow the procedure as shown by Tables 5-20 and 5-21.

Step 4. Assign the 4 level factor to this new column and the others to the remaining original columns as shown in Tables 5-22 and 5-23.

The experimental conditions and the subsequent analysis are handled in a manner similarly to the techniques described before.

Table 5-18. L_8 Array

TRIAL NUMBER	1	2	3	4	5	6	7
1	1	1	1	1	1	1	1
2	1	1	1	2	2	2	2
3	1	2	2	1	1	2	2
4	1	2	2	2	2	1	1
5	2	1	2	1	2	1	2
6	2	1	2	2	1	2	1
7	2	2	1	1	2	2	1
8	2	2	1	2	1	1	2

Table 5-19. L_8 Undergoing Column Upgrade

EXPERIMENTS COLUMN	1	2	3	4	5	6	7
1	1	1		1	1	1	1
2	1	1		2	2	2	2
3	1	2		1	1	2	2
4	1	2		2	2	1	1
5	2	1		1	2	1	2
6	2	1		2	1	2	1
7	2	2		1	2	2	1
8	2	2		2	1	1	2

5-6-2   Preparation of an 8 Level Column

An 8 level column can be prepared by combining a set of seven 2 level columns of an L_{16} OA. The procedure is similar to the one used in creating a 4 level column. First we need to identify the seven columns involved. Then combine the columns using some established guidelines.

Step 1. Select the set of seven columns.

One such set of seven columns consists of columns 1, 2, 3, 4, 5, 6, and 7. The seven columns are an interacting set among three factors, A, B, and C. If A, B, and C are assigned to columns 1, 2, and 4, respectively, the triangular table or the linear graph corresponding to an L_{16}, will show that, the interaction columns are 3 for $A \times B$, 5 for $A \times C$, 6 for $B \times C$ and 7 for $A \times B \times C$. Here $A \times B \times C$ represents the interaction between factor A (column 1) and interaction $B \times C$ (column 6). The six columns may be represented as a closed triangle in the linear graph and

Table 5-20. Rules for 4 Level Column Preparation

OLD COLUMNS			NEW COLUMN
1	1	→	1
1	2	→	2
2	1	→	3
2	2	→	4

Table 5-21. Preparing a 4 Level Column of an L_8 Array

COLUMN→ EXPERIMENT/ NUMBER	1 2	3	4	5	6	7
1	--1-----1 > 1	1	1	1	1	1
2	--1-----1 > 1	2	2	2	2	2
3	--1-----2 > 2	2	1	1	2	2
4	--1-----2 > 2	2	2	2	1	1
5	--2-----1 > 3	2	1	2	1	2
6	--2-----1 > 3	2	2	1	2	1
7	--2-----2 > 4	1	1	2	2	1
8	--2-----2 > 4	1	2	1	1	2

Table 5-22. Modified L_8 Array with One 4 Level Column

EXPERIMENTS/ COLUMN	NEW COLUMN	4	5	6	7
1	1	1	1	1	1
2	1	2	2	2	2
3	2	1	1	2	2
4	2	2	2	1	1
5	3	1	2	1	2
6	3	2	1	2	1
7	4	1	2	2	1
8	4	2	1	1	2

Table 5-23. Modified L_8 with Factors Assigned (One 4 Level Column)

FACTORS → EXPERIMENTS/COLUMN	A NEW COLUMN	B 4	C 5	D 6	E 7
1	1	1	1	1	1
2	1	2	2	2	2
3	2	1	1	2	2
4	2	2	2	1	1
5	3	1	2	1	2
6	3	2	1	2	1
7	4	1	2	2	1
8	4	2	1	1	2

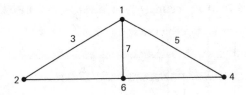

Figure 5-11. Preparation of an 8 level column.

can be selected on this basis. A fourth line connecting the apex and the base represents the interaction $(A \times B \times C)$ as shown in Figure 5-11.

Step 2. Select the three columns to be used to form an 8 level column.

Select the three columns where the three factors, A, B, and C are assigned. In general, select each apex of the triangle of the linear graph for the set to represent the columns. These are columns 1, 2, and 4 for the set. The remaining four columns are eliminated, since the three columns include the four interactive $(A \times B, A \times C, B \times C$ and $A \times B \times C)$.

Step 3. Combine three 2 level columns into an 8 level column.

Compare numbers in each row of the three columns and combine them using the rules shown in Table 5-24. Note the rule is not the previous one for the 4 level array though it follows the same pattern.

Table 5-24. Rules for Preparation of an
8 Level Column for an L_{16} Array

COLUMNS			
FIRST	SECOND	THIRD	NEW COLUMN
1	1	1	1
1	1	2	2
1	2	1	3
1	2	2	4
2	1	1	5
2	1	2	6
2	2	1	7
2	2	2	8

Table 5-25. Converting L_{16} to Include an 8 Level Column

Columns Combined to Form New Columns

L_{16} EXPERIMENTS/COLUMN	1	2		4	8	9	10	11	12	13	14	15
1	1	2	1	1	1	1	1	1	1	1	1	1
2	1	1	1	1	2	2	2	2	2	2	2	2
3	1	1	2	2	1	1	1	1	2	2	2	2
4	1	1	2	2	2	2	2	2	1	1	1	1
5	1	2	3	1	1	1	2	2	1	1	2	2
6	1	2	3	1	2	2	1	1	2	2	1	1
7	1	2	4	2	1	1	2	2	2	2	1	1
8	1	2	4	2	2	2	1	1	1	1	2	2
9	2	1	5	1	1	2	1	2	1	2	1	2
10	2	1	5	1	2	1	2	1	2	1	2	1
11	2	1	6	2	1	2	1	2	2	1	2	1
12	2	1	6	2	2	1	2	1	1	2	1	2
13	2	2	7	1	1	2	2	1	1	2	2	1
14	2	2	7	1	2	1	1	2	2	1	1	2
15	2	2	8	2	1	2	2	1	2	1	1	2
16	2	2	8	2	2	1	1	2	1	2	2	1

(NEW COLUMN)

For the set of columns under consideration, the first, second, and third are columns 1, 2, and 3, respectively (Fig. 5-11). The modified L_{16} array with its upgraded column is shown in Table 5-25. Note that the linear graph (Fig. 5-11) represents seven columns consisting of three main effects and four interactions. Thus combining the column representing the three main effects includes the four interactions.

5-7 DUMMY TREATMENT (COLUMN DEGRADING)

Just as 2 level columns of OA can be combined to higher levels, so a higher level column be decomposed into lower level columns. The method used is known as *Dummy Treatment*.

Consider an experiment involving four factors A, B, C, and D, of which A has only 2 levels, and all the others have 3 levels each. DOF

Table 5-26. Design with Degraded Column of L_9

FACTORS →	B	C	A	D
EXPERIMENTS/ COLUMN	1	2	3	4
1	1	1	1	1
2	1	2	2	1
3	1	3	1'	3
4	2	1	2	3
5	2	2	1'	1
6	2	3	1	2
7	3	1	1'	2
8	3	2	1	3
9	3	3	2	1

(') indicates new modified level
1' = (level 3)

is 7. An L_9 array has four 3 level columns with 8 DOF. It could be used if one column can be reduced to the 2 level for factor A and the three remaining columns occupied by factors B, C, and D. In dummy treatment, the third level of $A = A_3$ is formally treated as A_3, as if A_3 exists. But in reality A_3 is set to be either A_1 or A_2.

The design with the modified column (3) of L_9 is shown in Table 5-26. Factor A can be assigned to any column. Note that column 3 was selected such that the modified level 3 $= 1'$ occurs once in each group of three trial runs. This distribution enhances the experiment.

Example 5-10

In a casting process used to manufacture engine blocks for a passenger car, nine factors and their levels were identified (Table 5-27). The optimum process parameters for the casting operation are to be determined by experiment. Of the nine factors, two are of 3 levels each and another of 4 levels. The remaining six factors are all of 2 levels each. The DOF is at least 13 if no interactions are considered.

The Design

Since most factors are 2 level, a 2 level OA may be suitable. Each 3 level factor can be accommodated by 3 columns (modified) and the 4 level factor can also be described by 3 columns for a subtotal of 9 columns.

Table 5-27. Factors of the Casting Process Experiment—Example 5-10

VARIABLES	LEVEL 1	LEVEL 2	LEVEL 3	LEVEL 4
A: Sand compaction	Plant X	Plant Y	Plant Z	
B: Gating type	Plant X	Plant Y	Plant Z	
C: Metal head	Low	High		
D: Sand supplier	Supplier 1	Supplier 2		
E: Coating type	Type 1	Type 2	Type 3	Type 4
F: Sand permeability	300 perm	400 perm		
G: Metal temperature	1430 F	1460 F		
H: Quench type	450 F	725 F		
I: Gas level	Absent	High amount		

The remaining six 2 level factors require one column each. Thus a minimum of 15 columns is needed. L_{16} satisfies this requirement. Nine columns are to be converted to three 4 level columns, then 2 columns will be reduced by dummy treatment to 3 level columns for this experiment.

Normally a 3 level column will have 2 DOF. But when it is prepared by reducing a 4 level column, it must be counted as 3 DOF since it includes a dummy level. Thus, the total DOF for the experiment is:

6 Variables at 2 levels each	. . .	6 DOF
1 Variable at 4 levels each	. . .	3 DOF
2 Variables at 3 levels each	. . .	6 DOF (Dummy Treated)
Total DOF =		15

L_{16} has 15 DOF and therefore is suitable for the design. The three sets of interacting columns used for column upgrading are 1 2 3, 4 8 12, and 7 9 14. The column preparation and assignment follows these steps.

1. Discard column 3 and use columns 1 and 2 to prepare a 4 level column, then dummy treat it to a 3 level column. Place it as column 1. Assign factor A (sand compaction) to this column.
2. Discard column 12 and use columns 4 and 8 to create a 4 level column first, then dummy treat it to a 3 level column. Call the new column, column 4. Assign factor B (gating type) to this column.
3. Discard column 14 and use columns 7 and 9 to create a 4 level column for factor E (coating type). Call it column 7.

Table 5-28-1. Casting Process Optimization Design—Example 5-10

Design Variables and Their Levels

COLUMN NUMBER	FACTOR NAME	LEVEL 1	LEVEL 2	LEVEL 3	LEVEL 4
1	Sand compaction	Plant X	Plant Y	Plant Z	
2	(Used with Col 1)	M/U			
3	(Used with Col 1)	M/U			
4	Gating type	Plant X	Plant Y	Plant Z	
5	Metal head	Low	High		
6	Sand supplier	Supplier 1	Supplier 2		
7	Coating type	Type 1	Type 2	Type 3	Type 4
8	(Used with Col 4)	M/U			
9	(Used with Col 7)	M/U			
10	Sand perm	200 Perm	300 Perm		
11	Metal temperature	1430 F	1460 F		
12	(Used with Col 4)	M/U			
13	Quench type	450 F	725 F		
14	(Used with Col 7)	M/U			
15	Gas level	None	High		

Note: Modified Cols. 1 2 3   4 8 12 and 7 9 14. No interaction objective: Determine process parameter for best casting characteristic: The higher the better (Siq or other)

4. Assign the remaining seven 2 level factors to the rest of the 2 level columns as shown in Table 5-28-1.

The detail array modified to produce two 3 level and one 4 level column is shown in Table 5-28-2. Table 5-28-3 shows the modifications to create three 4 level columns and the dummy treatment two columns to 3 level. Note that in new column 1, the four dummy levels 1' occur together. In this case, to avoid any undesirable bias due to level 1, the experiment should be carried out by selecting trial conditions in a random order.

Description of Experimental Conditions

Once the factors are assigned, the 16 trial runs are described by the rows of the OA (modified). With experience, the run conditions are easily read from the array. But for the inexperienced, and for large arrays, translating the array notations into actual descriptions of the factor levels may be subject to error. Computer software exists to reduce/eliminate chances

Table 5-28-2. Casting Process Optimization Design—Example 5-10

EXPERIMENT/ COLUMN	1	2	3	4	5	6	7	8	9	10	11	12	13	14	15
Expt 1	1	0	0	1	1	1	1	0	0	1	1	0	1	0	1
Expt 2	1	0	0	2	1	1	2	0	0	2	2	0	2	0	2
Expt 3	1	0	0	3	2	2	3	0	0	1	1	0	2	0	2
Expt 4	1	0	0	1	2	2	4	0	0	2	2	0	1	0	1
Expt 5	2	0	0	1	1	2	3	0	0	2	2	0	1	0	2
Expt 6	2	0	0	2	1	2	4	0	0	1	1	0	2	0	1
Expt 7	2	0	0	3	2	1	1	0	0	2	2	0	2	0	1
Expt 8	2	0	0	1	2	1	2	0	0	1	1	0	1	0	2
Expt 9	3	0	0	1	2	1	4	0	0	1	2	0	2	0	2
Expt 10	3	0	0	2	2	1	3	0	0	2	1	0	1	0	1
Expt 11	3	0	0	3	1	2	2	0	0	1	2	0	1	0	1
Expt 12	3	0	0	1	1	2	1	0	0	2	1	0	2	0	2
Expt 13	1	0	0	1	2	2	2	0	0	2	1	0	2	0	1
Expt 14	1	0	0	2	2	2	1	0	0	1	2	0	1	0	2
Expt 15	1	0	0	3	1	1	4	0	0	2	1	0	1	0	2
Expt 16	1	0	0	1	1	1	3	0	0	1	2	0	2	0	1

of such errors. A printout of the trial conditions for sample trial runs is shown in Table 5-28-4.

Main Effect Plots for 3 Level and 4 Level Factors

The analysis of experimental data follows the same steps as before. The results of a single test run at each of the 16 conditions are shown in Table 5-28-5. The main effects of the factors are presented in Table 5-28-6; the effects for the 3 and 4 level factors are displayed in Figure 5-12. The optimum combination is easily determined by plotting main effects of all factors or from the data of Table 5-28-6 of the main effects, by selecting the higher values (since the quality characteristic is "the bigger the better"). Note that for sand compaction the middle level produces the highest value. Such nonlinear behavior of the factor was suspected from previous experience, hence three levels were selected for the experiment.

Table 5-28-3. Casting Process Optimization Design
(Column Upgrading Procedure)

1 2 and 3 to form a 3 level col. "New 1"				4 8 and 12 to form a 3 level col. "New 4"				7 9 and 14 to form a 4 level col. "New 7"			
1	2	3	NEW 1	4	8	12	NEW 4	7	9	14	NEW 7
1----1----1			1	1----1----1			1	1----1----1			1
1----1----1			1	2----2----1			2	1----2----2			2
1----1----1			1	2----1----2			3	2----1----2			3
1----1----1			1	2----2----1			4 = 1'	2----2----1			4
1----2----2			2	1----1----1			1	2----1----2			3
1----2----2			2	1----2----2			2	2----2----1			4
1----2----2			2	2----1----2			3	1----1----1			1
1----2----2			2	2----2----1			4 = 1'	1----2----2			2
2----1----2			3	1----1----1			1	2----2----1			4
2----1----2			3	1----2----2			2	2----1----2			3
2----1----2			3	2----1----2			3	1----2----2			2
2----1----2			3	2----2----1			4 = 1'	1----1----1			1
2----2----1			4 = 1'	1----1----1			1	1----2----2			2
2----2----1			4 = 1'	1----1----1			2	1----1----1			1
2----2----1			4 = 1'	2----1----2			3	2----2----1			4
2----2----1			4 = 1'	2----2----1			4 = 1'	2----1----2			3

Note: ' indicates dummy treated levels.

5-8 COMBINATION DESIGN

Consider an experiment involving three 3 level factors and two 2 level factors. An experiment design could consider L_{16} OA with 3 columns for each of the 3 level factors and 2 additional columns for the 2 level factors. Such a design will utilize 11 of the available 15 columns and require 16 trial runs for the experiment. Alternatively consider the L_9 OA. Three columns satisfy the 3 level factors. If the fourth column can be used to accommodate two 2 level factors, then L_9 with only 9 trial runs, could be used.

Indeed, it is possible to combine two 2 level factors into a single 3 level factor, with some loss of confidence in the results and loss of opportunity to study interactions. The procedure is given below.

Define a new factor (XY) to be formed out of the combination of X and Y and assign it to column 4. From the four possible combinations X

Table 5-28-4. Description of Individual Trial Conditions

TRIAL NUMBER 1

Sand compaction M/C	= Plant X	. . . Level 1
Gating type	= Plant X	. . . Level 1
Metal head	= Low	. . . Level 1
Sand supplier	= Supplier 1	. . . Level 1
Coating type	= Type 1	. . . Level 1
Sand perm	= 300 perm	. . . Level 1
Metal temperature	= 1430 F	. . . Level 1
Quench type	= 450 F	. . . Level 1
Gas level	= Absent/none	. . . Level 1

TRIAL NUMBER 2

Sand compaction M/C	= Plant X	. . . Level 1
Gating type	= Plant Y	. . . Level 2
Metal head	= Low	. . . Level 1
Sand supplier	= Supplier 1	. . . Level 1
Coating type	= Type 2	. . . Level 2
Sand perm	= 400 perm	. . . Level 2
Metal temperature	= 1460 F	. . . Level 2
Quench type	= 725 F	. . . Level 2
Gas level	= High	. . . Level 2

Table 5-28-5. Casting Process Optimization Data

TRIAL	R_1	R_2	R_3	R_4	R_5	R_6	AVG.
1	67.00						67.00
2	66.00						66.00
3	56.00						56.00
4	67.00						67.00
5	78.00						78.00
6	90.00						90.00
7	68.00						68.00
8	78.00						78.00
9	89.00						89.00
10	78.00						78.00
11	69.00						69.00
12	76.00						76.00
13	78.00						78.00
14	66.00						66.00
15	77.00						77.00
16	87.00						87.00

Table 5-28-6. Casting Process Optimization Design Main Effects

COL. NUMBER	FACTOR NAME	LEVEL 1	LEVEL 2	$(L_2 - L_1)$	LEVEL 3	LEVEL 4
1	Sand compaction	70.50	78.50	8.00	78.00	00.00
4	Gating type	77.50	75.00	−2.50	67.50	00.00
5	Metal head	76.25	72.50	−3.75	00.00	00.00
6	Sand supplier	76.25	72.50	−3.75	00.00	00.00
7	Coating type	69.25	72.75	3.50	74.75	80.75
10	Sand perm	75.25	73.50	−1.75	00.00	00.00
11	Metal temperature	75.00	73.75	−1.25	00.00	00.00
13	Quench type	72.50	76.25	3.75	00.00	00.00
15	Gas level	75.50	73.25	−2.25	00.00	00.00

and Y (X_1Y_1, X_2Y_1, X_1Y_2, and X_2Y_2), select any three and label them as stated below.

call X_1Y_1 as (XY_1) i.e., level 1 of new factor (XY)

X_2Y_1 as $(XY)_2$ i.e., level 2 of new factor (XY)

X_1Y_2 as $(XY)_3$ i.e., level 3 of new factor (XY).

Note that one combination, X_2Y_2, is not included. With factor XY assigned, L_9 OA is shown in Table 5-29. From the array, the trial run conditions defined for trial number 1 (row 1) are A_1 B_1 C_1 $(XY)_1$ where $(XY)_1$ is X_1Y_1, which was defined above.

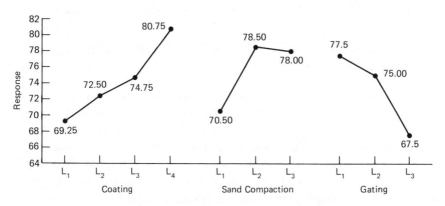

Figure 5-12. Plots of main effects—Example 5-10.

Table 5-29. L_9 with Five Factors

FACTORS	A	B	C	(XY)
NUMBER/COLUMN	1	2	3	4
1	1	1	1	1
2	1	2	2	2
3	1	3	3	3
4	2	1	2	3
5	2	2	3	1
6	2	3	1	2
7	3	1	3	3
8	3	2	1	3
9	3	3	2	1

The total data are analyzed with the two factors X and Y treated as one (XY). The analysis yields the main effect of (XY). The individual effect of the constituents, X and Y is then obtained as follows:

Main effect of $X = \overline{(XY)}_1 - \overline{(XY)}_2$ and

Main effect of $Y = \overline{(XY)}_1 - \overline{(XY)}_3$

Note that the first equation has Y constant as Y_1 and the second equation has X constant as X_1.

After determining the main effects, the optimum condition, including the levels of the two factors used in combination design, can be identified. However, the interaction effects between factors X and Y cannot be obtained from the data by this method. Should interaction be important, the experiment design must be based on a larger array such as L_{16}.

5-9 DESIGNING EXPERIMENTS TO INVESTIGATE NOISE FACTORS

Throughout this text the terms *factors, variables* and *parameters* are synonymously used to refer to factors which influence the outcome of the product or process under investigation. Taguchi further categorized the factors as controllable factors and noise factors. The factors identified for the baking process experiment, namely sugar, butter, eggs, milk, and flour, were easily controlled factors. Other factors which are less controllable, such as oven temperature distribution, humidity, oven temperature cycle band width, etc., may also influence the optimum product. Since the goal is a robust optimum which is influenced minimally by these less controllable variables, the study of the impact of noise factors on the optimum parameters is desirable.

Taguchi fully recognizes the potential influence of uncontrollable factors. No attempt is made to remove them from the experiment. Before describing how the uncontrollable factors are treated, additional definitions are needed.

Controllable Factors—Factors whose levels can be specified and controlled during the experiment and in the final design of the product or process.

Noise Factors—These are factors which have influence on the product or process results, but generally are not maintained at specific levels during the production process or application period.

Inner Array—The OA of the controllable factors. All experiment designs discussed to this point fall in this category.

Outer Array—The OA of recognized noise factors. The term outer or inner refers to the usage rather than the array itself, as will be clear soon.

Experiment—The experiment refers to the whole experimental process.

Trial Condition—The combination of factors/levels at which a trial run is conducted.

Conditions of Experiment—Unique combinations of factor levels described by the *inner array* (orthogonal array).

Repetitions or Runs—These define the number of observations under the same conditions of an experiment.

The experiment requires a minimum of one run per condition of the experiment. But one run does not represent the range of possible variability in the results. Repetition of runs enhances the available information in the data. Taguchi suggests guidelines for repetitions.

5-10 BENEFITING FROM REPETITIONS

For some experiments, trial runs are easily and inexpensively repeated. For others, repetitions of tests are expensive as well as time consuming. Whenever possible trials should be repeated, particularly if strong noise factors are present. Repetition offers several advantages. First, the additional trial data confirms the original data points. Second, if noise factors vary during the day, then, repeating trials through the day may reveal their influence. Third, additional data can be analyzed for variance around a target value.

When the cost of repetitive trials is low, repetition is highly desirable. When the cost is high, or interference with the operation is high, then the number of repetitions should be determined by means of an expected payoff for the added cost. The payoff can be the development of a more robust production procedure or process, or by the introduction of a production process that greatly reduces product variance.

Repetition permits determination of a variance index called the *Signal to Noise Ratio* (*S/N*). The greater this value, the smaller the product variance around the target value. The signal to noise ratio concept has been used in the fields of acoustics, electrical and mechanical vibrations, and other engineering disciplines for many years. Its broader definition and application will be covered in Chapter 6. The basic definition of the *S/N* ratio is introduced here.

5-11   DEFINITION OF *S/N* RATIO

$$S/N = -10 \, \text{Log}_{10} \, (\text{MSD})$$

Where MSD = Mean squared deviation from the target value of the quality characteristic.

Consistent with its application in engineering and science, the value of *S/N* is intended to be large, hence the value of MSD should be small. Thus the mean squared deviation (MSD) is defined differently for each of the three quality characteristics considered, smaller, nominal or larger.

For smaller is better:

$$\text{MSD} = (y_1^2 + y_2^2 + y_3^2 + \ldots)/n$$

For nominal is the best

$$\text{MSD} = ((y_1 - m)^2 + (y_2 - m)^2 + \ldots)/n$$

For bigger is better

$$\text{MSD} = (1/y_1^2 + 1/y_2^2 + 1/y_3^2 + \ldots)/n$$

Where y_1, y_2, etc. = Results of experiments, observations or quality characteristics such as length, weight, surface finish, etc.

m = Target value of results (above)

n = Number of repetitions (y_i)

Consider an experiment with three repetitions, using an L_4 orthogonal array as shown in Table 5-30.

In the table, trial number 1 is repeated three times with results 5, 6, and 7. The average of these three is 6. The average is used for the study of the main effects in a manner similar to that described for nonrepeated trials. Slight differences in the analysis of variance for the repetitive case is covered in Chapter 6. For experiments with repetitions, analysis should always use the S/N ratios computed as follows.

Assume that bigger is better is the quality characteristic sought by the experimental data of Table 5-30. Then,

$$MSD = (1/y_1^2 + 1/y_2^2 + 1/y_3^2 + \ldots)/n$$

Now, for row 1, $y_1^2 = 5 \times 5 = 25$ $y_2^2 = 6 \times 6 = 36$

$$y_3^2 = 7 \times 7 = 49 \qquad n = 3$$

Therefore, MSD = (1/25 + 1/36 + 1/49)/3

$= (.04 + .02777 + .020408)/3$

$= .088185/3$

or   MSD = .029395, a small value.

Table 5-30. L_4 with Results and Averages

TRIAL NUMBER COLUMN	1	2	3	R_1	R_2	R_3	AVERAGE
1	1	1	1	5	6	7	6
2	1	2	2	3	4	5	4
3	2	1	2	7	8	9	8
4	2	2	2	4	5	6	5

Table 5-31. L_4 with Results and S/N Ratios

TRIAL NUMBER COLUMN	1	2	3	R_1	R_2	R_3	S/N RATIO
1	1	1	1	5	6	7	15.316
2	1	2	2	3	4	5	11.47
3	2	1	2	7	8	9	17.92
4	2	2	2	4	5	6	13.62

The S/N ratio is calculated as:

$$S/N = -10 \, \text{Log}_{10} \, (\text{MSD})$$

$$= -10 \, \text{Log}_{10} \, (.029395)$$

$$= 15.31$$

S/N values for all rows are shown in Table 5-31.

In analysis, the S/N ratio is treated as a single data point at each of the test run conditions. Normal procedure for studies of the main effects will follow. The only difference will be in the selection of the optimum levels. In S/N analysis, the value of MSD or greatest value of S/N represents a more desirable condition.

5-12 REPETITIONS UNDER CONTROLLED NOISE CONDITIONS

Repetitions show the variation of the product or process. The variation occurs principally as a result of the uncontrollable factors (noise factors). By expanding the design of the experiment to include noise factors in a controlled manner, optimum conditions insensitive to the influence of the noise factors can be found. These are Taguchi's robust conditions that control production close to the target value despite noise in the production process. To incorporate noise factors into the design of the experiment the factors and their levels are identified in a manner similar to those used for other product and process factors (control factors). For example, if humidity is considered noise, the low and high levels may be considered a factor for the design. After determining the noise factors and their levels for the test, OAs are used to design the conditions of the noise factors which dictate the number of repetitions for the trial runs. The OA used for designing the noise experiment is called an *outer array*.

Assume that three noise factors are identified for the cake baking experiment (Tables 5-10 and 5-14) which utilized an L_8 OA. The noise factors are to be investigated at 2 levels each. There are four possible combinations of these factors. To obtain complete data, each trial run of L_8 must be repeated for each of the four noise combinations. The noise array selected is an L_4 OA. This outer array, with four combinations of noise of the three noise factors, tests each of the 8 trial conditions four times. The experiment design with *inner* and *outer array* is shown by Figure 5-13. Note that for the *outer array*, column 3 represents both the third noise factor and the interaction of the first and second noise factor. Note also the arrangement of each array, with the noise (*outer*) array perpendicular to the *inner array*. The complete design is shown by Figure 5-14.

For most simple applications, the *outer array* describes the noise conditions for the repetitions. This formal arrangement of the noise factors and the subsequent analysis influences the combination of the controllable

Outer Array — Noise Factors

Columns	1	2	3	4
Noise Factor 1	1	1	2	2
Noise Factor 2	1	2	1	2
Noise Factor 3	1	2	2	1

Inner Array

Experiment Number	\ Column Number	Control Factors							Results			
		1	2	3	4	5	6	7	1	2	3	4
1		1	1	1	1	1	1	1				
2		1	1	1	2	2	2	2				
3		1	2	2	1	1	2	2				
4		1	2	2	2	2	1	1				
5		2	1	2	1	2	1	2				
6		2	1	2	2	1	2	1				
7		2	2	1	1	2	2	1				
8		2	2	1	2	1	1	2				

Figure 5-13. Inner and outer orthogonal arrays.

Experiment Number → Column Number ↓	1	2	3	4	5	6	7	8
1	1	1	1	1	2	2	2	2
2	1	1	2	2	1	1	2	2
3	1	1	2	2	2	2	1	1
4	1	2	1	2	1	2	1	2
5	1	2	1	2	2	1	2	1
6	1	2	2	1	1	2	2	1
7	1	2	2	1	2	1	1	2

Column Number	Factor Description	Level 1	Level 2
1	Egg	2 Eggs	3 Eggs
2	Milk	2 Cups	3 Cups
3			
4	Butter	1 Stick	1.5 Sticks
5	Flour	1 Extra Scoop	2 Extra Scoops
6			
7	Sugar	1 Spoon	2 Spoons

		Type of Oven 1. Gas 2. Electric	Baking Time 1. + 5 min. 2. – 5 min.	Humidity 1. 80% 2. 60%
	Columns	1	2	3
R_1	1	1	1	1
R_2	2	1	2	2
R_3	3	2	1	2
R_4	4	2	2	1

Figure 5-14. Cake baking experiment with noise factors.

factors for the optimum condition. The use of S/N ratio in analysis, is strongly recommended.

5-13 DESIGN AND ANALYSIS SUMMARY

Application of the Taguchi technique is accomplished in two phases: (1) design of the experiment, which includes determining controllable and noise factors and the levels to be investigated, which determines the number of repetitions, and (2) analysis of the results to determine the best possible factor combination from individual factor influences and interactions. The two activities, experiment design and analysis of

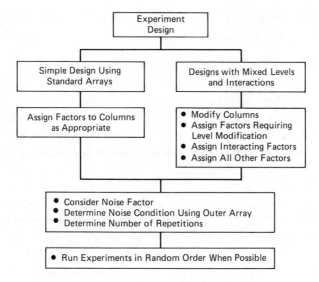

Figure 5-15. Experiment design flow diagram.

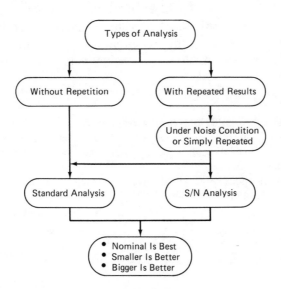

Figure 5-16. Analysis flow diagram.

test data are presented (flow charts) in Figures 5-15 and 5-16. The steps involved are briefly described here.

Design

Depending on the factors and levels identified, follow one of the two paths (Fig. 5-16). If all the factors are of the same level, say 2, one of the standard OAs can probably be used. In this case, the factors can be assigned to the columns without much consideration about where they should be placed. On the other hand, if the factors require many levels, or one or more interactions are to be investigated, then carefully select certain specific columns for factor assignments or level changes. No matter how simple the design, the applicable noise conditions should be identified, and a second array (*outer array*) selected to include noise effects. The number of repetitions will be dictated by the number of noise factors. In the absence of a formal layout such as Figure 5-13 the number of repetitions will be influenced by time and cost considerations.

Analysis

Analysis of results follows either paths (Fig. 5-16) of repetitions or no repetition. Generally, for a single observation for each trial condition, the standard analysis approach is followed. When there are repetitions of the trial runs, whether by outer array designed noise condition, or under random noise condition, S/N analysis should be performed. The final analysis for the optimum condition is based on one of the three characteristics greatest, smallest, or nominal value of quality.

EXERCISES

5-1. Identify each element (8, 2, 7, etc.) of the notation for an orthogonal array $L_8(2^7)$.

5-2. Design an experiment to study four factors A, B, C, and D and three interactions $A \times C$, $C \times D$ and $A \times D$. Select the orthogonal array and identify the columns for the three interactions.

5-3. An experiment with three 2 level factors yielded the following results. Determine the average effect of factor C at levels C_1 and C_2.

TRIALS/ COLUMNS	A	B	C	RESULTS
1	1	1	1	30
2	1	2	2	25
3	2	1	2	34
4	2	2	1	27

Table 5-32. Design Variables and Their Levels

COLUMN NUMBER	VARIABLE NAMES	LEVEL-1	LEVEL-2
1	Speed	2100 RPM	250 RPM
2	Oil viscosity	At low TP	At high t
3	Interaction 1 × 2	N/A	N/A
4	Clearance	Low	High
5	Pin straightness	Perfect	Bend
6	(Unused)	M/U	
7	(Unused)	M/U	

5-4. Describe the procedure you will follow to design an experiment to study one 3 level factor and four 2 level factors.

5-5. In an experiment involving piston bearings, an L_8 OA was used in a manner shown in Table 5-32. Determine the description of the trial number 7.

5-6. The average effects of the factors involved in Problem 5 are as shown in Table 5-33. If the quality characteristic is "the bigger the better," determine (a) the optimum condition of the design, (b) the grand average of performance, and (c) the performance at the optimum condition. (Ans. (b) 35.01 (c) 37.03)

Table 5-33. Average Factor Effects

COLUMN NUMBER	VARIABLE NAMES	LEVEL-1	LEVEL-2
1	Speed	34.39	35.63
2	Oil viscosity	35.50	34.52
3	Interaction 1 × 2	33.60	36.42
4	Clearance	35.62	34.40
5	Pin straightness	35.31	34.70

6

Analysis of Variance (ANOVA)

6-1 THE ROLE OF ANOVA

Taguchi replaces the full factorial experiment with a lean, less expensive, faster, partial factorial experiment. Taguchi's design for the partial factorial is based on specially developed OAs. Since the partial experiment is only a sample of the full experiment, the analysis of the partial experiment must include an analysis of the confidence that can be placed in the results. Fortunately, there is a standard statistical technique called Analysis of Variance (ANOVA) which is routinely used to provide a measure of confidence. The technique does not directly analyze the data, but rather determines the variability (variance) of the data. Confidence is measured from the variance.

Analysis provides the variance of controllable and noise factors. By understanding the source and magnitude of variance, robust operating conditions can be predicted. This is a second benefit of the methodology.

6-2 ANOVA TERMS, NOTATIONS AND DEVELOPMENT

In the analysis of variance many quantities such as degrees of freedom, sums of squares, mean squares, etc., are computed and organized in a standard tabular format. These quantities and their interrelationships are defined below and their mathematical development is presented.

DEFINITIONS:

$C.F.$ =	Correction factor	n =	Number of trials
e =	Error (experimental)	r =	Number of repetitions
F =	Variance ratio	P =	Percent contribution
f =	Degrees of freedom	T =	Total (of results)
f_e =	Degrees of freedom of error	S =	Sum of squares
f_T =	Total degrees of freedom	S' =	Pure sum of squares
		V =	Mean squares (variance)

Total Number of Trials
In an experiment designed to determine the effect of factor A on response Y, factor A is to be tested at L levels. Assume n_1 repetitions of each trial that includes A_1. Similarly at level A_2 the trial is to be repeated n_2 times. The total number of trials is the sum of the number of trials at each level, i.e.,

$$n = n_1 + n_2 + \cdots + n_L$$

Degrees of Freedom (DOF)
DOF is an important and useful concept that is difficult to define. It is a measure of the amount of information that can be uniquely determined from a given set of data. DOF for data concerning a factor equals one less than the number of levels. For a factor A with four levels, A_1 data can be compared with A_2, A_3 and A_4 data and not with itself. Thus a 4 level factor has 3 DOF. Similarly an L_4 OA with three columns representing 2 level factors, has 3 DOF.

The concept of DOF can be extended to the experiment. An experiment with n trial and r repetitions of each trial has $n \times r$ trial runs. The total DOF becomes:

$$f_T = n \times r - 1$$

Similarly, the DOF for a sum of squares term is equal to the number of terms used to compute the sum of squares and the DOF of the error term f_e is given by:

$$f_e = f_T - f_A - f_B - f_C$$

Sum of Squares
The sum of squares is a measure of the deviation of the experimental data from the mean value of the data. Summing each squared deviation emphasizes the total deviation. Thus

$$S_T = \sum_{i=1}^{n} (Y_i - \overline{Y})^2$$

Where $\overline{Y}$ is the average value of Y_i.

Similarly the sum of squares of deviations S_T, from a target value Y_0, is given by;

$$S_T = \sum_{i=1}^{n} (Y_i - \bar{Y})^2 + n(\bar{Y} - Y_0)^2 \qquad (6\text{-}1\text{-}1)^*$$

Variance measures the distribution of the data about the mean of the data. Since the data is representative of only a part of all possible data, DOF rather than the number of observations is used in the calculation.

$$\text{Variance} = \frac{\text{Sum of Squares}}{\text{Degrees of Freedom}}$$

or $V = S_T/f$

When the average sum of squares is calculated about the mean, it is called the general variance. The general variance σ^2 is defined as.

$$\sigma^2 = \frac{1}{n} \sum_{i=1}^{n} (Y_i - \bar{Y})^2 \qquad (6\text{-}1\text{-}2)$$

$$* \quad S_T = \sum_{i=1}^{n} (Y_i - Y_0)^2$$

$$= \sum_{i=1}^{n} (Y_i - \bar{Y} + \bar{Y} - Y_0)^2$$

$$= \sum_{i=1}^{n} [(Y_i - \bar{Y})^2 + 2(Y_i - \bar{Y})(\bar{Y} - Y_0) + (\bar{Y} - Y_0)^2]$$

$$= \sum_{i=1}^{n} (Y_i - \bar{Y})^2 + \sum_{i=1}^{n} 2(Y_i - \bar{Y})(\bar{Y} - Y_0) + \sum_{i=1}^{n} (\bar{Y} - Y_0)^2$$

since $\sum_{i=1}^{n} (Y_i - Y) = \sum_{i=1}^{n} Y_i - \sum_{i=1}^{n} \bar{Y} = n\bar{Y} - n\bar{Y} = 0$

and $\sum_{i=1}^{n} (\bar{Y} - Y_0)^2 = n(\bar{Y} - Y_0)^2$

The above equation becomes,

$$S_T = \sum_{i=1}^{n} (Y_i - \bar{Y})^2 + n(\bar{Y} - Y_0)^2$$

Let m represent the deviation of the mean $\overline{Y}$ from the target value Y_0, i.e.,

$$m = (\overline{Y} - Y_0) \tag{6-1-3}$$

Substituting Eqs. (6-1-2) and (6-1-3) into Eq. (6-1-1),

$$S_T = n\sigma^2 + nm^{2\cdot} = n(\sigma^2 + m^2) \tag{6-1-4}$$

Thus the total sum of squares of deviations (S_T) from the target value Y_0 is the sum of the variance about the mean, and the square of the deviation of the mean from the target value multiplied by the total number of observations made in the experiment.

S_T of Eq. (6-1-4) also represents the expected statistical value of S_T. In this book, rigorous proofs are omitted unless necessary to clarify an idea or concept. Further, the symbol S_T is used for both the expected value and the computed value for a given sample.

The total sum of squares S_T (Eq. 6-1-4) gives an estimate of the sum of the variations of the individual observations about the mean $\overline{Y}$ of the experimental data and the variation of the mean about the target value Y_0. This information is valuable for controlling manufacturing processes, as the corrective actions to reduce the variations around the mean $\overline{Y}$, i.e., to reduce σ^2, are usually not identical to those actions which move the mean toward the target value. When the total sum of squares S_T, is separated into its constituents, the variation can be understood and an appropriate strategy to bring the process under control can be easily developed. Furthermore, the information thus acquired can be effectively utilized in Statistical Process Control (SPC).

Mean Sum (of Deviations) Squared

Let $T = \sum\limits_{i=1}^{n} (Y_i - Y_0)$ the sum of all deviations from the target value.

Then, the mean sum of squares of the deviation is:

$$S = T^2/n = \left[\sum_{i=1}^{n} (Y_i - Y_0)\right]^2 \Big/ n \tag{6-2}$$

Eq. (6-2) can thus be written as:

$$S_m = nm^{2}*$$

It is important to note that even though from an over-simplistic derivation of the value of $S_m = nm^2$, its statistical estimate or the expected value, includes one part of the general variance. Therefore, representing the statistically expected value by $E(S_m)$:

$$E(S_m) = S_m = \sigma^2 + nm^2 \tag{6-3}$$

The term $(S_T - S_m)$ is usually referred to as the error sum of squares and can be obtained from Eqs. (6-1-4) and (6-3).

Therefore,

$$S_e = S_T - S_m = (n - 1)\sigma^2$$

Rewriting the equation, $S_T = S_e + S_m$. Thus the total effect of variance S_T can be decomposed into the mean deviation S_m and the deviation S_e about the mean. Thus individual effects can be analyzed. Let

$$Y_1 - Y_0 = 3 \qquad Y_4 - Y_0 = 4$$
$$Y_2 - Y_0 = 5 \qquad Y_5 - Y_0 = 6$$
$$Y_3 - Y_0 = 7 \qquad Y_6 - Y_0 = 8$$

$*S_m = \dfrac{1}{n} [(Y_1 - Y_0) + \cdots + (Y_n - Y_0)]^2$

Which can also be expressed as:

$S_m = \dfrac{1}{n} [(Y_1 + Y_2 + \cdots + Y_n - nY_0)]^2$

or

$S_m = \dfrac{1}{n} [(n\bar{Y} - nY_0)]^2$

or

$S_m = \dfrac{n^2}{n} [(\bar{Y} - Y_0)]^2$

$S_m = nm^2$

where Y_0 is a target value, then

$$S_T = 3^2 + 5^2 + 7^2 + 4^2 + 6^2 + 8^2$$

$$= 199$$

$$S_m = (3 + 5 + 7 + 4 + 6 + 8)^2/6$$

$$= 33^2/6$$

$$= 181.5$$

$$\bar{Y} = (3 + 5 + 7 + 4 + 6 + 8)/6$$

$$= 5.5$$

and

$$S_e = [(3 - \bar{Y})^2 + (5 - \bar{Y})^2 + \ldots]$$

$$= [(3 - 5.5)^2 + (5 - 5.5)^2 + \ldots (8 - 5.5)^2]$$

$$= 17.5$$

Note that

$$S_e = S_T - S_m = 199 - 181.5 = 17.5$$

Also, since the standard deviation of the data 3, 5, 7, 4, 6, and 8, is equal to 1.8708.

$$S_e = (n - 1)^2$$

$$= (6 - 1) \times (1.8708)^2$$

$$= 17.5$$

Degrees of Freedom Sums
The DOF f_e, f_T, and f_m of the sum of squares S_e, S_T, and S_m are as follows:

$$f_T = n = \text{number of data points.}$$

$$f_m = 1 \text{ (always for the mean)}$$

$$f_e = f_T - f_m = (n - 1)$$

As pointed out earlier, the DOF f_T is equal to n because there are n independent values of $(Y_i - Y_0)^2$. For investigating the effect of factors at different levels, the DOF are usually one less than the number of observations.

To summarize:

$$S_T = n\sigma^2 + nm^2 \qquad (6\text{-}4)$$

$$S_m = \sigma^2 + nm^2 \qquad (6\text{-}5)$$

$$S_e = S_T - S_m = (n - 1)\sigma^2 \qquad (6\text{-}6)$$

Also as stated earlier, variance V, is

$$V = S/f$$

Therefore:

$$V_T = S_T/f_T = \sigma^2 + m^2 \qquad \text{(total variance)}$$

$$V_m = S_m/f_m = \sigma^2 + nm^2 \qquad \text{(mean variance)}$$

$$V_e = (S_T - S_m)/f_e = \sigma^2 \qquad \text{(error variance)}$$

The example that follows should clarify the application of the concepts developed above. The data for this example are fictitious but suffice for the purpose of illustrating the principles.

6-3   ONE WAY ANOVA

One Factor One Level Experiment
When one dimensional experimental data are analyzed using ANOVA, the procedure is termed a one way analysis of variance. The following problem is an example of one way ANOVA. Later ANOVA will be extended to multi-dimensional problems.

Example 6.1

To obtain the most desirable iron castings for an engine block, a design engineer wants to maintain the material hardness at 200 BHN. To measure the quality of the castings being supplied by the foundry the hardness of

Table 6-1. Hardness of Cylinder Block Castings—Example 6-1

SAMPLE	HARDNESS	SAMPLE	HARDNESS
1	240	6	180
2	190	7	195
3	210	8	205
4	230	9	215
5	220	10	215

10 castings chosen at random from a lot is measured, and displayed in Table 6-1.

The analysis:

$$f_T = \text{Total number of results} - 1$$

$$= 10 - 1 = 9$$

$$Y_0 = \text{Desired value} = 200$$

the mean value is:

$$\overline{Y} = (240 + 190 + 210 + 230 + 220 + 180 + 195 + 205$$

$$+ 215 + 215)/10$$

$$= 210$$

then

$$S_T = (240 - 200)^2 + (190 - 200)^2 + (210 - 200)^2$$

$$+ (230 - 200)^2 + (220 - 200)^2 + (180 - 200)^2$$

$$+ (195 - 200)^2 + (205 - 200)^2 + (215 - 200)^2$$

$$+ (215 - 200)^2$$

$$= 4000$$

and $S_m = n(\overline{Y} - Y_0)^2 = 10(210 - 200)^2 = 1000$

$$S_e = S_T - S_m = 4000 - 1000 = 3000$$

Table 6-2. Analysis of Variance (ANOVA) Table—Example 6-1

SOURCE OF VARIATION	f	SUM OF SQUARES	VARIANCE (MEAN SQUARE) V	VARIANCE RATIO F	PURE SUM OF SQUARES S'	PERCENT CONTRIBUTION P
Mean (m)	1	1000	1000.00			
Error (e)	9	3000	333.33			
Total	10	4000				

And the variance is calculated as follows:

$$V_T = S_T/f_T = 4000/9 = 444.44$$

$$V_m = 1000/1 = 1000$$

$$V_e = (S_T - S_m)/f_e = (4000 - 1000)/9 = 333.33$$

These results are summarized in Table 6-2. Table 6-3 represent a generalized format of the ANOVA table.

The data cannot be analyzed further, but analysis of the variance of the data can provide additional information about the data.

Let F be the ratio of total variance to the error variance. F coupled with the degrees of freedom for V_T and V_e provides a measure for the confidence in the results.

To complete the analysis, the error variance V_e is removed from S_m and added to S_e. The new values are renamed as

S_m' = pure sum of squares

S_e' = pure error.

Table 6-3. ANOVA Table for Randomized One Factor Designs— Example 6-1

SOURCE OF VARIATION	f	SUM OF SQUARES	VARIANCE (MEAN SQUARES) V	VARIANCE RATIO F	PURE SUM OF SQUARES S'	PERCENT CONTRIBUTION P
Mean (m)	f_m	S_m	S_m/f_m			
Error (e)	f_e	S_e	S_e/f_e			
Total	f_T	S_T				

This reformulation allows calculation of the percent contribution, P, for the mean, P_m, or for any individual factor (P_A, P_B, etc.)

Table 6-3 presents the complete format for analysis F, S and P. These parameters are described below in greater detail.

Variance Ratio

The variance ratio, commonly called the F statistic, is the ratio of variance due to the effect of a factor and variance due to the error term. (The F statistic is named after Sir Ronald A. Fisher.) This ratio is used to measure the significance of the factor under investigation with respect to the variance of all the factors included in the error term. The F value obtained in the analysis is compared with a value from standard F-tables for a given statistical level of significance. The tables for various significance levels and different degrees of freedom are available in most handbooks of statistics. Table C-1 through C-5 in Appendix A provides a brief list of F factors for several levels of significance.

To use the tables enter the DOF of the numerator to determine the column and the DOF of the denominator for the row. The intersection is the F value. For example, the value of $F_{.1}$ (5,30) from the table is 2.0492, where 5 and 30 are the DOF of the numerator and the denominator, respectively. When the computed F value is less than the value determined from the F tables at the selected level of significance, the factor does not contribute to the sum of the squares within the confidence level. Computer software, such as Reference 11, simplifies and speeds the determination of the level of significance of the computed F values.

The F values are calculated by:

$$F_m = V_m/V_e$$

$$F_e = V_e/V_e = 1 \tag{6-7}$$

and for a factor A it is given by:

$$F_A = V_A/V_e \tag{6-8}$$

Pure Sum of Squares

In Equations (6-4), (6-5), and (6-6) for each of the sum of squares, there is a general variance σ^2 term expressed as (DOF) $\times$ σ^2.

When this term is subtracted from the sum of squares expression, the remainder is called the pure sum of squares. Since S_m has only one degree of freedom, it therefore contains only one σ^2 i.e., V_e. Thus the pure sum of square for S_m is:

$$S'_m = S_m - V_e = \sigma^2 + nm^2 - \sigma^2 = nm^2$$

The portion of error variance subtracted from the sum of squares for S_m is added to the error term. Therefore,

$$S'_e = S_e + V_e \tag{6-9}$$

If factors A, B, and C, having DOF f_A, f_B, and f_C are included in an experiment, their pure sum of squares are determined by:

$$S'_A = S_A - f_A \times V_e \tag{6-10}$$
$$S'_B = S_B - f_B \times V_e$$
$$S'_C = S_C - f_C \times V_e$$
$$S'_e = S_e + (f_A + f_B + f_C) \times V_e \tag{6-11}$$

Percent Contribution

The percent contribution for any factor is obtained by dividing the pure sum of squares for that factor by S_T and multiplying the result by 100. The percent contribution is denoted by P and can be calculated using the following equations.

$$P_m = S'_m \times 100/S_T$$
$$P_A = S'_A \times 100/S_T$$
$$P_B = S'_B \times 100/S_T$$
$$P_C = S'_C \times 100/S_T$$
$$P_e = S'_e \times 100/S_T \tag{6-12}$$

The ANOVA Table 6-2 can now be completed as follows: Using Eqs. (6-7) and (6-8) gives:

$$F_m = V_m/V_e = 1000/333.33^{**} = 3.00$$
$$F_e = V_e/V_e = 333.33/333.33 = 1.00$$

Table 6-4. Analysis of Variance (ANOVA) Table—Example 6-1

SOURCE OF VARIATION	f	SUM OF SQUARES	VARIANCE (MEAN SQUARES) V	VARIANCE RATIO F	PURE SUM OF SQUARES S'	PERCENT CONTRIBUTION P
Mean (m)	1	1000	1000.00	3.00	666.67	16.67
Error (e)	9	3000	333.33	1.00	3333.33	83.33
Total	10	4000				100.00

The pure sum of squares obtained using Eqs. (6-9) and (6-10) is shown below:

$$S'_m = S_m - V_e = 1000 - 333.33 = 666.67$$
$$S'_e = S_e + V_e = 3000 + 333.33 = 3333.33$$

And the percent contribution is calculated using Eqs. (6-11) and (6-12):

$$P_m = S'_m \times 100/S_T = 666.67/4000 = 16.67$$
$$P_e = S'_e \times 100/S_T = 3333.33/4000 = 83.33$$

The completed ANOVA tables are shown in Table 6-4.

A generalized ANOVA table for one factor randomized design is shown in Table 6-5.

Returning to Table 6-3, the computed value for F_m, 3.00, is less than the value from Table C-1 for $F_{.1}$ (1,9) i.e., 3.3603. Hence with 90% confidence (10% risk) the castings appear to be similar. The apparent data spread contributes only 16.67% to the sample variability (sum of

Table 6-5. ANOVA Table for Randomized One Factor Design— Example 6-1

SOURCE OF VARIATION	f	SUM OF SQUARES	VARIANCE (MEAN SQUARES) V	VARIANCE RATIO F	PURE SUM OF SQUARES S'	PERCENT CONTRIBUTION $P/100$
Mean (m)	f_m	S_m	$V_m = S_m/f_m$	V_m/V_e	$S_m - V_e$	S'_m/S_T
Error (e)	f_e	S_e	$V_e = S_e/f_e$	—	$S_m + V_e$	S'_e/S_T
Total	f_T	S_T				

squares) whereas the remaining 83.33% variation is caused by other factors.

6-4   ONE FACTOR TWO LEVEL EXPERIMENTS (ONE WAY ANOVA)

Example 6.2

In Example 6-1 an experiment with one factor at one level was considered, the factor being the hardness of the cylinder blocks being supplied by one source. Now consider the case with two different vendors suppling the castings. These two sources are assumed to use similar casting processes. Therefore, a new experiment is described with one factor, hardness of castings, from two sources A_1 and A_2. The question to be resolved is whether the castings being supplied by the two vendors are statistically of the same quality. If not, which one is preferable. The target hardness, 200 BHN, is unchanged.

Ten samples from each of the two castings sources were drawn at random and their hardness was measured. The test yielded the results shown in Table 6-6.

The analysis of this test proceeds as for the experiment of Example 6.1. Note that the error sum of squares term, S_e, as given in Eq. (6.11), contains the variation of the mean and that of the factor A. Therefore to separate the effect of vendors, i.e., factor A, the sum of squares term S_A must be isolated from S_e. The sum of squares for the factor A can be calculated by:

$$S_A = \sum_{k=1}^{L} \frac{1}{n_k} \left[\sum_{i=1}^{n} (A_{ik} - Y_0) \right]^2 - \frac{T^2}{n} \qquad (6\text{-}13)$$

Table 6-6. Measured Hardness—Example 6-2

HARDNESS OF CASTINGS FROM VENDOR A_1			HARDNESS OF CASTINGS FROM VENDOR A_2		
240	180	190	197	202	198
195	210	205	205	203	192
230	215	220	208	199	195
215			201		

Where,

L = number of levels

n_i, n_k = number of test samples at levels A_i and A_k, respectively

T = sum total of all deviations from the target value

n = total number of observations = $n_1 + n_2 + \cdots + n_j$

The T^2/n in Eq. (6-13) is a term similar to S_m and is called the correction factor, C.F.

The expression for the total sum of squares can now be written as

$$S_T = S_e + S_m + S_A \qquad (6\text{-}14)^*$$

The DOF equation will be:

$$f_T = f_e + f_A$$

The Analysis:

Y_0 = 200 (unchanged from Example 6.1)

$$
\begin{aligned}
S_T &= (240 - 200)^2 + (180 - 200)^2 + \cdots + (215 - 200)^2 \\
&\quad + (197 - 200)^2 + \cdots + (195 - 200)^2 \\
&\quad + (201 - 200)^2 - \text{C.F.} \\
&= 4206 - 500 = 3706
\end{aligned}
$$

As
$$
\begin{aligned}
T^2/n = \text{C.F.} &= [(Y_1 - Y_0) + (Y_2 - Y_0) + \ldots]^2/n \\
&= [(40 - 20 + \ldots - 15 + 15) \\
&\quad + (-3 + 2 \ldots - 5 + 1)]^2/20 \\
&= 500
\end{aligned}
$$

---

*Taguchi considers deviation from the target more significant than that about the mean. The cost of quality is measured as a function of the deviations from the target. Therefore, Taguchi eliminates the variation about the mean from Eq. (6-14) by redefining S_T as follows:

$$S_T = \sum_{i=1}^{n} (Y_i - Y_0)^2 - \text{C.F.} = S_e + S_A$$

or $S_e = S_T - S_A$

Using Eq. (6-13), the value of S_A, the square sum for the effect of factor A (vendors) is obtained as:

S_A = Squares of sum for vendor A_1

    + Square of sum for vendor A_2

    − Correction factor

or

$$S_A = [(Y_{iA_1} - Y_0)]^2/n_{A_1} + [(Y_{iA_2} - Y_0)]^2/n_{A_2} + T^2/n$$

$$= \frac{[(240 - 200) + \cdots + (215 - 200)]^2}{10}$$

$$+ \frac{[(197 - 200) + \cdots + (201 - 200)]^2}{10} - 500$$

$$= 1000 + 0 - 500 = 500$$

Also

$$S_e = S_T - S_A$$
$$= 3706 - 500$$
$$= 3206$$

and the DOF will be:

$$f_T = 20 - 1 = 19$$
$$f_A = 2 - 1 = 1$$
$$f_e = 19 - 1 = 18$$

Also,

$$V_A = S_A/f_A = 500/1 = 500$$

and

$$V_e = S_e/f_e = 3206/18 = 178.11$$

The variance ratio F will, therefore, be as shown below:

$$F_A = V_A/V_e = 500/178.11 = 2.81$$

$$F_e = V_e/V_e = 1$$

In order to complete the ANOVA table, the pure sum of squares and the percentage contributions are needed. The pure sum of squares are computed using Eq. (6-10), whereas the percentage contribution is calculated using Eq. (6-12).

The pure sum of squares are:

$$S'_A = S_A - f_A \times V_e = S_A - 1 \times V_e = 500 - 178.11 = 321.87$$

$$S'_e = S_e + f_A \times V_e = S_e - 1 \times V_e = 3206 + 178.11 = 3384.11$$

and the percentage contributions are given by:

$$P_A = S'_A \times 100/S_T = 321.89 \times 100/3706 = 8.68$$

$$P_e = S'_e \times 100/S_T = 3384.11 \times 100/3706 = 91.31$$

The complete ANOVA table is shown in Table 6-7.

Since the degrees of freedom for the numerator is 1 and that for the denominator 18, from the F-Tables at 0.10 level of significance (90% confidence), we obtain $F_{.1} (1,18) = 3.007$. Since the computed values of the F factor is smaller than the limiting values obtained from the table, no significant difference between the two sources of the castings can be concluded. Of the observed variation only 8.68% is due to the vendor and 91.32% is due to the error and other factors not included in the study. The range of the hardness data of Table 6-6 is 180 to 240 from vendor

Table 6-7. ANOVA Table for Cylinder Block Castings From Two Sources—Example 6-2

SOURCE OF VARIATION	f	SUM OF SQUARES	VARIANCE (MEAN SQUARES) V	VARIANCE RATIO F	PURE SUM OF SQUARES S'	PERCENT CONTRIBUTION P
Factor A	1	500.00	500.00	2.81	321.89	8.68
Error (e)	18	3206.00	178.00	1.00	3384.11	91.30
Total	19	3706.00				100.00

A_1 and 192 to 208 from vendor A_2. The difference in range suggests that vendor A_2 may be preferred intuitively.

6-4-1   Confidence Intervals

The calculations shown in the ANOVA table are only estimates of the population parameters. These statistics are dependent upon the size of the sample being investigated. As more castings are sampled the precision of the estimate would be improved. For large samples, the estimates approach the true value of the parameter. In statistics, it is therefore customary to represent the values of a statistical parameter as a range within which it is likely to fall, for a given level of confidence. This range is termed as the confidence interval (C.I.). If the estimate of the mean value of a set of observations is denoted by $E(m)$, then the C.I. for the mean is given by:

$$\text{C.I. } (m) = E(m) \pm \sqrt{\frac{F_\alpha(f_1, f_2) \times V_e}{n_e}} \tag{6-15}$$

Where,

$F_\alpha (f_1, f_2)$ = Variance ratio for DOF f_1 and f_2 at the level of significance α. The confidence level is $(1 - \alpha)$.

f_1 = DOF of mean (which always equals 1)

f_2 = DOF of error term.

V_e = variance of the error term.

n_e = number of equivalent replications and is given by:

$$n_e = \frac{\text{(Number of trials)}}{\text{[DOF of mean (always 1) + DOF of all factors used in the estimate]}}$$

To determine the C.I. for the estimated value of the mean for the above data, we proceed as follows:

$$E(m) = [240 + 190 + \cdots + 215 + 215$$
$$+ 197 + 202 + \cdots + 195 + 201]/20$$
$$= 205$$

The number of experiments is 20 and there are two factors m and A involved in the estimates. Therefore,

$$n_e = \frac{20}{f_A + f_m} = \frac{20}{1 + 1} = 10$$

Since,

$$F_{.1}(1,18) = 3.007$$

and

$$V_e = 178.11$$

$$m = 205 \pm \sqrt{\frac{3.007 \times 178.11}{10}}$$

$$= 205 \pm 7.32$$

$$= (197.68, 212.32)$$

Therefore, it can be stated that there is a 90% probability that the true value of the estimated mean will lie between 197.68 and 212.32.

The confidence interval can similarly be calculated for other statistics.

6-5 TWO WAY ANOVA

The one way ANOVA discussed above included one factor with two levels. This section extends ANOVA to experimental data of two or more factors with two or more levels. The following examples illustrate the procedure.

Example 6-3

The wear characteristics of two brands of tires, Wearwell and Superwear are to be compared. Several factors such as load, speed, and air temperature have significant effect on the useful life of the tires. The problem will be limited to only one factor, i.e., the temperature. Let T_w and T_s represent winter (low) and summer (high) temperatures, respectively. Tire life is measured in hours of operation at constant speed and load. The experiment design for this example is given in Table 6-8. This

Table 6-8. Tire Wear Experiment—Example 6-2

	TIRE TYPE	TEMPERATURE A		SUM
		$A_1 = T_w$	$A_2 = T_s$	
	Wearwell	70	65	135
	B_1	Y_1	Y_3	
B	Superwear	75	60	135
	B_2	Y_2	Y_4	
	Sum	145	125	270 = Grand total

is called a two factor two level experiment. It has 4 possible trial runs and the results of each run can be interpreted as follows:

With A at A_1 and B at B_1 the life is $= 70$ Hrs.
With A at A_1 and B at B_2 the life is $= 75$ Hrs.
With A at A_2 and B at B_1 the life is $= 65$ Hrs.
With A at A_2 and B at B_2 the life is $= 60$ Hrs.

The analysis of the data follows exactly the same procedures presented in the previous example. In this case the total degrees of freedom, $f_T = n - 1 = 3$. The degrees of freedom and the ANOVA quantities in this case become:

$$n = 2^2 = 4$$

$$f_T = n - 1 = 4 - 1 = 3$$

$$f_A = \text{number of levels} - 1 = 2 - 1 = 1$$

$$f_B = \text{types of tires} - 1 = 2 - 1 = 1$$

$$f_{A \times B} = 1 \times 1 = 1$$

$$f_e = f_T - f_A - f_B - f_{A \times B}$$

$$\text{C.F.} = \text{Correction Factor} = T^2/n = (270)^2/4 = 18225.0$$

$$Y_o = \text{Target value} = 0$$

$$S_T = \text{sum of square of all results} - \text{C.F.}$$

$$= (Y_1^2 + \cdots + Y_4^2) - \text{C.F.}$$
$$= 70^2 + 65^2 + 75^2 + 60^2 - 18225.0$$
$$= 18350.0 - 18225.0 = 125.0$$

The total contribution of each factor is calculated as shown below:

$A_1 = 70 + 75 = 145$ $\qquad A_2 = 65 + 60 = 125$

$B_1 = 70 + 65 = 135$ $\qquad B_2 = 75 + 60 = 135$

and,

$$S_A = A_1^2/N_{A_1} + A_2^2/N_{A_2} - \text{C.F.}$$

$$S_B = B_1^2/N_{B_1} + B_2^2/N_{B_2} - \text{C.F.}$$

$$S_{AB} = \sum_{i=1}^{2}\sum_{j=1}^{2} (A_iB_j)^2/r_{ij} - \text{C.F.}$$

$$S_{A \times B} = S_{AB} - S_A - S_B$$

$$S_T = S_e + S_A + S_B + S_{A \times B}$$

where N_{A_1}, N_{A_2} etc., refer to the number of trial runs included in the sums A_1, A_2 etc. A_iB_j is the total experimental response for the factor A at level i and the factor B at level j whereas r_{ij} is the number of replications (observations) for the cell ij. The term $S_{A \times B}$ represents the interaction sum of squares.

For the above example,

$$S_A = 145^2/2 + 125^2/2 - 18225.0 = 18325.0 - 18225.0 = 100.0$$

$$S_B = 135^2/2 + 135^2/2 + 18225.0 = 18225.0 - 18225.0 = 0.0$$

Since $r = 1$ (one observation per cell)

$$S_{AB} = 70^2/1 + 75^2/1 + 65^2/1 + 60^2/1 - 18225.0 = 125.0$$

and

$$S_{A \times B} = 125.0 - 100. - 0 = 25.0$$

Therefore, using Eq. (6-11), the error variation becomes,

$$S_e = S_T - (S_A + S_B + S_{A \times B})$$
$$= 125 - 100 - 0 - 25 = 0$$

Variance Calculations:

$$V_A = S_A/f_A \qquad = 100/1 = 100$$
$$V_B = S_B/f_B \qquad = 0/1 \quad = 0$$
$$V_{A \times B} = S_{A \times B}/f_{A \times B} = 25/1 \quad = 25$$
$$V_e = S_e/f_e \qquad = 0/0 \qquad \text{indeterminate, hence not useful.}$$

Variance Ratio

Once all the variances are computed, the results can be arranged, in a tabular form as appears in Table 6-9.

Observe that the DOF and S_e of the error terms are zero, hence F, the ratio of the variances, cannot be computed. Thus this experimental design is not effective for studying the interaction of factors A and B. Additional degrees of freedom are necessary for a complete analysis of the interactions and main effects. This can be accomplished by repeating the observations for each setup so that there will be an error term which will have non-zero degrees of freedom and variance terms.

Table 6-9. ANOVA Table for Tire Wear Characteristics—Example 6-3

SOURCE OF VARIATION	f	SUM OF SQUARES	VARIANCE (MEAN SQUARES) V	VARIANCE RATIO F	PURE SUM OF SQUARES S'	PERCENT CONTRIBUTION P
A	1	100.00	100.00			
B	1	0.00	0.00			
$A \times B$	1	25.00	25.00			
Error (e)	0	0.00				
Total	3	125.00				

6-6   EXPERIMENTS WITH REPLICATIONS

Example 6-4

Example 6-3 is extended to two observations per cell as shown in Table 6-10. In Table 6-11, the data in each cell are replaced by a single value obtained by adding the two data points. The total of the degrees of freedom f_T is increased:

since, $n = r \times 2^2 = 2 \times 4 = 8$

and $f_T = n - 1 = 8 - 1 = 7$

The degrees of freedom for other factors are as follows:

$$f_A = \text{number of levels} - 1 = 2 - 1 = 1$$

$$f_B = \text{types of tires} - 1 = 2 - 1 = 1$$

$$f_{A \times B} = 1 \times 1 = 1$$

$$f_e = f_T - f_A - f_B - f_{A \times B} = 7 - 1 - 1 - 1 = 4$$

and

$$\text{C.F.} = \text{Correction Factor} = T^2/n = (542)^2/8 = 36720.5$$

Table 6-10. Tire Wear Experiments
with Repetitions—Example 6-4

	TIRE TYPE	TEMPERATURE A	
		$A_1 = T_w$	$A_2 = T_s$
	Wearwell B_1	70, 72 Y_1	65, 62 Y_3
B	Superwear B_2	75, 77 Y_2	60, 61 Y_4

Table 6-11. Tire Wear Experiments with Repetitions—Example 6-4

	TIRE TYPE	TEMPERATURE A		SUM
		$A_1 = T_w$	$A_2 = T_s$	
B	Wearwell B_1	142 Y_1	127 Y_3	269
	Superwear B_2	152 Y_2	121 Y_4	273
	Sum	294	248	542 = Grand total

Assuming

Y_0 = target value = 0

S_T = sum of square of all 8 data points − C.F.

$\quad = (Y_1^2 + \cdots + Y_8^2) -$ C.F.

$\quad = 70^2 + 72^2 + 75^2 + 77^2 + 65^2 + 62^2 + 60^2 + 61^2 - 36720.5$

$\quad = 37028.0 - 36720.5 = 307.5$

The contribution of each factor is shown below:

$A_1 = 142 + 152 = 294 \qquad A_2 = 127 + 121 = 248$

$B_1 = 142 + 127 = 269 \qquad B_2 = 152 + 121 = 273$

and

$S_A = 294^2/4 + 248^2/4 - 36720.5 = 264.5$

$S_B = 269^2/4 + 273^2/4 - 36720.5 = 2.0$

$S_{A \times B} = (A_1B_1)^2/2 + (A_1B_2)^2/2 + (A_2B_1)^2/2 + (A_2B_2)^2/2 -$ C.F.

$\qquad = [(142)^2 + (152)^2 + (127)^2 + (121)^2]/2 - 36720.5$

$\qquad = 37019 - 36720.5 = 298.5$

Also:

$$S_{A \times B} = 298.5 - 264.5 - 2 = 32$$

$$S_e = S_T - (S_A + S_B + S_{A \times B})$$

$$= 307.5 - 264.5 - 2 - 32 = 9.0$$

Variance Calculations:

$$V_A = S_A/f_A = 264.5/1 = 264.5$$

$$V_B = S_B/f_B = 2/1 = 2$$

$$V_{A \times B} = S_{A \times B}/f_{A \times B} = 32/1 = 32$$

$$V_e = S_e/f_e = 9/4 = 2.25$$

Also

$$F_A = V_A/V_e = 264.5/2.25 = 117.6$$

$$F_B = V_B/V_e = 2/2.25 = 0.89$$

$$F_{A \times B} = V_{A \times B}/V_e = 32/2.25 = 14.22$$

Pure Sum of Squares:

$$S'_A = S_A - f_A \times V_e = 264.5 - 1 \times 2.25 = 262.25$$

$$S'_B = S_B - f_B \times V_e = 2 - 1 \times 2.25 = -0.25$$

$$S'_{A \times B} = S_{A \times B} - f_{A \times B} \times V_e = 32 - 1 \times 2.25 = 29.75$$

$$S'_e = S_e + (f_A + f_B + f_{A \times B}) \times V_e = 9 + 3 \times 2.25 = 15.75$$

and the percentage contributions will be:

$$P_A = S'_A \times 100/S_T = 262.25 \times 100/307.5 = 85.28$$

$$P_B = S'_B \times 100/S_T = -0.25 \times 100/307.5 = -0.08$$

$$P_{A \times B} = S'_{A \times B} \times 100/S_T = 29.75 \times 100/307.5 = 9.68$$

$$P_e = S'_e \times 100/S_T = 15.75 \times 100/307.5 = 5.12$$

Table 6-12. ANOVA Table for Tire Wear with Repetitions—Example 6-4

SOURCE OF VARIATION	f	SUM OF SQUARES	VARIANCE (MEAN SQUARES) V	VARIANCE RATIO F	PURE SUM OF SQUARES S'	PERCENT CONTRIBUTION P
A	1	264.50	264.50	117.50	262.50	85.28
B	1	2.00	2.00	0.80	−00.25	−0.08
A × B	1	32.00	32.00	14.20	29.75	9.68
Error (e)	4	9.00	2.25	1.00	1.00	5.12
Total	7	307.50				100.00

Since the number of the degrees of freedom for the numerator is 1 (see Table 6-12) and that for the denominator is 4, from the F Tables at .05 level of significance (95% confidence), we obtain $F_{.05}(1,4) = 7.7086$. The computed values of variance ratios F for factor A and interaction $A \times B$, are greater than the limiting values obtained from the table. Therefore, there is a significant difference in the wear life of the tires under summer and winter conditions. The interaction term, $F_{A \times B}$ indicates that the influence of temperature on the two brands of tires is also significant. However, F_B is less than the table F factor. Thus, there is no difference between tire brands within the confidence level.

6-6-1   Procedures for Pooling

When the contribution of a factor is small, as for B in the above example, the sum of squares for that factor is combined with the error S_e. This process of disregarding the contribution of a selected factor and subsequently adjusting the contributions of the other factor, is known as *Pooling*. Pooling is usually accomplished by starting with the smallest sum of squares and continuing with the ones having successively larger effects. Pooling is recommended when a factor is determined to be insignificant by performing a test of significance against the error term at a desired confidence level. A general guideline for when to pool is obtained by comparing error DOF with the total factor DOF. Taguchi recommends pooling factors until the error DOF is approximately half the total DOF of the experiment (Ref. 10, pp. 293–295). Approaching the matter technically, one could test for significance and pool all factor influences below the 90% confidence level. The procedure for significance testing will be discussed later in this chapter. For now, we will arbitrarily select small factor effects and pool. Consider the pooling effects of the factor B. If the variance for this factor is pooled with the error term, the new error variance is computed as:

$$V_e = (S_B + S_e)/(f_B + f_e)$$

$$= (2.0 + 9.0)/(1 + 4) = 2.2$$

With a pooled V_e, all S' values must be modified to reflect pooling:

$$S'_A = S_A - (V_e \times f_A) = 264.50 - 2.20 = 262.30$$

$$S'_{A \times B} = S_{A \times B} - (V_e \times f_{A \times B}) = 32.0 - 2.2 \times 1 = 29.8$$

$$S'_e = S_e + V_e(f_A + f_{A \times B}) = 11.0 + 2.2 \times 2 = 15.4$$

The results of this procedure are summarized in Table 6-13, which makes it apparent that pooling in this particular case does not appreciably change the results. But in certain cases, the process may significantly affect the results. No matter the effect on the results, insignificant factors should always be pooled.

It is quite evident from these considerations, that the ANOVA procedure is cumbersome and extremely time-consuming. The computations needed increase tremendously as the size of the matrix increases. The design of the experiment and the subsequent analysis of the test results can be simplified using available software specifically made for analysis of Taguchi experimental designs. Most of the computations shown in this book have been carried out using QUALITEK-3 software (Ref. 11). To

Table 6-13. ANOVA Table for Tire Wear with Repetitions and Pooling— Example 6-4

SOURCE OF VARIATION	f	SUM OF SQUARES	VARIANCE (MEAN SQUARES) V	VARIANCE RATIO F	PURE SUM OF SQUARES S'	PERCENT CONTRIBUTION P
A	1	264.50	264.50	120.20	262.50	85.30
B			Pooled			
$A \times B$	1	32.00	32.00	14.50	29.80	9.69
Error (e)	5	11.00	2.20	1.00	15.40	5.01
Total	7	307.50				100.00

further clarify the step by step procedure involved in analysis of variance, the following numerical example is presented.

6-7   STANDARD ANALYSIS WITH SINGLE AND MULTIPLE RUNS

Example 6-5

A Taguchi experiment was designed (Table 6-14) to investigate five 2 level factors (A, B, C, D, and E) and two interactions ($A \times C$ and $B \times C$) of a certain manufacturing operation. The L_8 orthogonal array was used for the design and one sample that was produced under each experimental configuration was examined. The results are shown in Table 6-15.

6-7-1   Analysis Using Single Run

Level Totals and Their Averages
The factor averages at each factor level are obtained by adding the results of all trial conditions at the level considered, and then dividing by the numbers of data points added.

$$\overline{A}_1 = (y_1 + y_2 + y_3 + y_4)/4 = (42 + 50 + 36 + 45)/4$$

$$= 173/4 = 43.25$$

Table 6-14. Factors and Their Levels—Example 6-5

COLUMN	FACTOR NAMES	LEVEL 1	LEVEL 2	LEVEL 3	LEVEL 4
1	Factor A	A_1	A_2		
2	Factor C	C_1	C_2		
3	Interaction $A \times C$	N/A			
4	Factor B	B_1	B_2		
6	Factor D	D_1	D_2		
7	Interaction $B \times C$	N/A			
8	Factor E	E_1	E_2		

Objective: Determine best design parameters.
Characteristic: The smaller the better.

Table 6-15. Layout and Results—Example 6-5

FACTORS: TRIAL/COLUMN	A 1	C 2	A × C 3	B 4	D 5	B × C 6	E 7	RESULTS (y)
Trial 1	1	1	1	1	1	1	1	42.00
Trial 2	1	1	1	2	2	2	2	50.00
Trial 3	1	2	2	1	1	2	2	36.00
Trial 4	1	2	2	2	2	1	1	45.00
Trial 5	2	1	2	1	2	1	2	35.00
Trial 6	2	1	2	2	1	2	1	55.00
Trial 7	2	2	1	1	2	2	1	30.00
Trail 8	2	2	1	2	1	1	2	54.00

Total = 347.00

$$\overline{A}_2 = (y_5 + y_6 + y_7 + y_8)/4 = (35 + 55 + 30 + 54)/4$$

$$= 174/4 = 43.50$$

$$\overline{C}_1 = (y_1 + y_2 + y_5 + y_6)/4 = (42 + 50 + 35 + 55)/4$$

$$= 182/4 = 45.50$$

$$\overline{C}_2 = (y_3 + y_4 + y_7 + y_8)/4 = (36 + 45 + 30 + 54)/4$$

$$= 165/4 = 41.25$$

Similarly

$$B_1 = 143 \qquad \overline{B}_1 = 35.75$$

$$B_2 = 204 \qquad \overline{B}_2 = 51.00$$

$$D_1 = 187 \qquad \overline{D}_1 = 46.75$$

$$D_2 = 160 \qquad \overline{D}_2 = 40.00$$

$$E_1 = 172 \qquad \overline{E}_1 = 43.00$$

$$E_2 = 175 \qquad \overline{E}_2 = 43.75$$

and

$$\overline{(A \times C)}_1 = (y_1 + y_2 + y_7 + y_8)/4 = 176/4 = 44.00$$

$$\overline{(A \times C)_2} = (y_3 + y_4 + y_5 + y_6)/4 = 171/4 = 42.75$$

$$\overline{(B \times C)_1} = (y_1 + y_4 + y_5 + y_8)/4 = 176/4 = 44.00$$

$$\overline{(B \times C)_2} = (y_2 + y_3 + y_6 + y_7)/4 = 171/4 = 42.75$$

The results are shown in Table 6-16 and the main effects are plotted in Figure 6-1.

Ignoring interaction effects and assuming the "smaller is better" characteristic is desired, the optimum condition becomes:

$$A_1 \quad C_2 \quad B_1 \quad D_2 \quad E_1$$

Computation of Interaction

Interaction effects are always mixed with the main effects of the factors assigned to the column designated for interaction. The relative significance of the interaction effects is obtained by ANOVA just as are the relative significance of factor effects. To determine whether two factors A and C interact, the following calculations are performed.

Level Totals and Their Averages for A and C

$$\overline{A_1 C_1} = (y_1 + y_2)/2 = (42 + 50)/2 = 92/2 = 46.0$$

$$\overline{A_1 C_2} = (y_3 + y_4)/2 = (36 + 45)/2 = 81/2 = 40.5$$

$$\overline{A_2 C_1} = (y_5 + y_6)/2 = (35 + 55)/2 = 90/2 = 45.0$$

$$\overline{A_2 C_2} = (y_7 + y_8)/2 = (30 + 54)/2 = 84/2 = 42.0$$

Table 6-16. Average Effects—Example 6-6

COLUMN	FACTORS	LEVEL 1	LEVEL 2	$(L_2 - L_1)$	LEVEL 3	LEVEL 4
1	Factor A	43.25	43.50	−0.25		
2	Factor C	45.50	41.25	−4.25		
3	Interaction $A \times C$	44.00	42.75	−1.25		
4	Factor B	35.75	51.00	15.25		
6	Factor D	46.75	40.00	−6.75		
7	Interaction $B \times C$	44.00	42.75	−1.25		
8	Factor E	43.00	43.75	0.75		

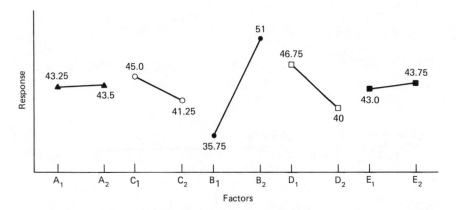

Figure 6-1. Main effects—Example 6-6.

Level Totals and Their Averages for B and C

$$\overline{B_1C_1} = (y_1 + y_5) = (42 + 35)/2 = 77/2 = 38.5$$
$$\overline{B_1C_2} = (y_3 + y_7) = (36 + 30)/2 = 66/2 = 33.0$$
$$\overline{B_2C_1} = (y_2 + y_6) = (50 + 55)/2 = 105/2 = 52.5$$
$$\overline{B_2C_2} = (y_4 + y_8) = (45 + 54)/2 = 99/2 = 49.5$$

These results are plotted in Figure 6-2. Note that lines B_1 and B_2 appear almost parallel. Hence, B and C interact slightly. Note also that A_1 and A_2 intersect, thus, A and C interact.

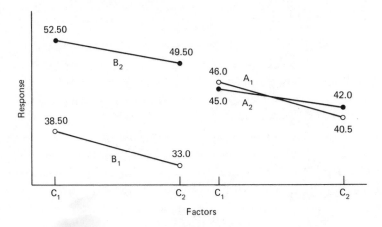

Figure 6-2. Interaction $A \times C$ and $B \times C$—Example 6-6.

The minor interaction of $B \times C$ is ignored but interaction $A \times C$ is included in the optimum condition. For the "smaller is better" situation, A_1C_2 (40.5) produces the lowest average value. Therefore, A_1C_2 is included in the optimum condition. It so happens that A_1C_2 was already included in the optimum condition, based on the main effects alone. (A_1 $C_2 B_1 D_2 E_1$)

Analysis of Variance (ANOVA)

ANOVA establishes the relative significance of the individual factors and the interaction effects. The steps are as follows.

Step 1.   Total of All Results:

$$T = 42 + 50 + 36 + 45 + 35 + 55 + 30 + 54 = 347$$

Step 2.   Correction Factor:

$$\text{C.F.} = T^2/n = 347^2/8 = 15051.125$$

Note: n = Total number of experiments, 8.

Step 3.   Total Sum of Squares:

$$S_T = \sum_{i=1}^{8} y_i^2 - \text{C.F.}$$

$$= (42^2 + 50^2 + 36^2 + \cdots + 54^2) - 15051.125$$

$$= 599.88$$

Step 4.   Factor Sum of Squares:

$$S_A = A_1^2/N_{A1} + A_2^2/N_{A2} - \text{C.F.}$$

$$= 173^2/4 + 174^2/4 - 15051.125 = 0.125$$

$$S_B = B_1^2/N_{B1} + B_2^2/N_{B2} - \text{C.F.}$$

$$= 143^2/4 + 204^2/4 - 15051.125 = 465.125$$

$$S_C = C_1^2/N_{C1} + C_2^2/N_{C2} - \text{C.F.}$$

$$= 182^2/4 + 165^2/4 - 15051.125 = 36.125$$

$$S_D = D_1^2/N_{D1} + D_2^2/N_{D2} - \text{C.F.}$$

$$= 187^2/4 + 160^2/4 - 15051.125 = 91.125$$

$$S_E = E_1^2/N_{E1} + E_2^2/N_{E2} - \text{C.F.}$$

$$= 172^2/4 + 175^2/4 - 15051.125 = 91.125$$

$$S_{A \times C} = (A \times C)_1^2/N_{(A \times C)1} + (A \times C)_2^2/N_{(A \times C)2} - \text{C.F.}$$

$$= 176^2/4 + 171^2/4 - 15051.125 = 3.125$$

$$S_{B \times C} = (B \times C)_1^2/N_{(B \times C)1} + (B \times C)_2^2/N_{(B \times C)2} - \text{C.F.}$$

$$= 176^2/4 + 171^2/4 - 15051.125 = 3.125$$

Alternative Formula for 2 Level Factors

In the case of 2 level factors, the sums of squares can be computed using the following formulas:

$$S_A = \frac{(A_1 - A_2)^2}{(N_{A_1} + N_{A_2})} = \frac{(173 - 174)^2}{(4 + 4)} = 0.125$$

$$S_B = \frac{(B_1 - B_2)^2}{(N_{B_1} + N_{B_2})} = \frac{(143 - 204)^2}{(4 + 4)} = 465.125$$

$$S_C = \frac{(C_1 - C_2)^2}{(N_{C_1} + N_{C_2})} = \frac{(182 - 165)^2}{(4 + 4)} = 36.125$$

$$S_D = \frac{(D_1 - D_2)^2}{(N_{D_1} + N_{D_2})} = \frac{(187 - 160)^2}{(4 + 4)} = 91.125$$

$$S_E = \frac{(E_1 - E_2)^2}{(N_{E_1} + N_{E_2})} = \frac{(172 - 175)^2}{(4 + 4)} = 1.125$$

$$S_{A \times C} = \frac{((A \times C)_1 - (A \times C)_2)^2}{(N_{(A \times C)_1} + N_{(A \times C)_2})} = 3.125$$

$$S_{B \times C} = \frac{((B \times C)_1 - (B \times C)_2)^2}{(N_{(B \times C)_1} + N_{(B \times C)_2})} = 3.125$$

$$S_e = S_T - (S_A + S_B + S_C + S_D + S_E + S_{A \times C} + S_{B \times C})$$

$$= 599.88 - 599.88 = 0$$

where

N_{A_1} = Total number of experiments in which factor A_1 is present

N_{B_1} = Total number of experiments in which factor B_1 is present

A_1 = Sum of results (Y_i) where factor A_1 is present

B_1 = Sum of results (Y_i) where factor B_1 is present

Step 5. Total and Factor Degrees of Freedom (DOF):

DOF total = Number of test runs minus 1

or $f_T = n - 1 \quad = 8 - 1 \quad = 7$

DOF of each factor is 1 less than the number of levels:

f_A = (Number of levels of factor A) $-$ 1

$\quad = 2 - 1 \qquad = 1$

f_B = (Number of levels of factor B) $-$ 1

$\quad = 2 - 1 \qquad = 1$

f_C = (Number of levels of factor C) $-$ 1

$\quad = 2 - 1 \qquad = 1$

f_D = (Number of levels of factor D) $-$ 1

$\quad = 2 - 1 \qquad = 1$

f_E = (Number of levels of factor E) $-$ 1

$\quad = 2 - 1 \qquad = 1$

Also,

$f_{(A \times C)} = f_A \times f_C$

$\quad = 1 \times 1 \qquad = 1$

$f_{(B \times C)} = f_B \times f_C$

$\quad = 1 \times 1 \qquad = 1$

DOF of the error term in this example:

$$f_e = f_T - (f_A + f_B + f_C + f_D + f_E + f_{A \times C} + f_{B \times C})$$

$$= 7 - 7 \qquad = 0$$

With the error degrees of freedom equal to zero, $f_e = 0$, information regarding the error sum of squares cannot be determined. In addition F ratios for factors cannot be calculated since the calculations involve f_e. To complete the calculations, smaller factorial effects are added together (pooled) to form a new nonzero estimate of the error term. This is discussed in the following section.

Step 6.   Mean Square (Variance):

$$V_A = S_A/f_A = \quad 0.125/1 = \quad 0.125$$

$$V_B = S_B/f_B = 456.125/1 = 465.125$$

$$V_C = S_C/f_C = \quad 36.125/1 = \quad 36.125$$

$$V_D = S_D/f_D = \quad 91.125/1 = \quad 91.125$$

$$V_E = S_E/f_E = \quad 1.125/1 = \quad 1.125$$

$$V_e = S_e/f_e = \qquad 0/0 = \text{Indeterminate}$$

As the variance of error term (V_e) is zero, the variance ratio and pure sum of squares (S') cannot be calculated. In this case the percentage contributions are first calculated using sums of squares. Then, if there are insignificant factors, pool them and recalculate percentages using the pure sums of squares.

Step 7.   Percentage Contribution:

$$P_A = S_A/S_T \quad = \quad 0.125/599.88 = \quad 0.02$$

$$P_B = S_B/S_T \quad = 465.125/599.88 = 77.54$$

$$P_C = S_C/S_T \quad = \quad 36.125/599.88 = \quad 6.02$$

$$P_D = S_D/S_T \quad = \quad 91.125/599.88 = 15.20$$

$$P_E = S_E/S_T \quad = \quad 1.125/599.88 = \quad 0.19$$

$$P_{A \times C} = S_{A \times C}/S_T = \quad 3.125/599.88 = \quad 0.52$$

$$P_{B \times C} = S_{B \times C}/S_T = \quad 3.125/599.88 = \quad 0.52$$

and P_e cannot be calculated as $V_e = 0$

The results of the analysis of variance are summarized in Table 6-17.

6-7-2 Pooling

Note that in Step 7, the effects of factors A, E, and interactions $B \times C$ and $A \times C$ are small, totalling slightly more than 1% (1.2%). These factors are pooled to obtain new, nonzero estimates of S_e and f_e.

Sum of Squares of Error:

Let: $S_e = S_A + S_B + S_{A \times C} + S_{B \times C}$

then $S_e = S_T - (S_B + S_C + S_D) = 599.9 - (592.4) = 7.5$

Degree of Freedom of Error Term:

$$f_e = f_T - (f_B + f_C + f_D)$$
$$= 7 - 3 = 4$$

Variance of Error Term:

$$V_e = S_e/f_e = 7.5/4 = 1.875$$

Table 6-17. ANOVA Table—Example 6-6

COLUMN	FACTORS	f	S	V	F	P
1	Factor A	1	0.125	0.125		0.02
2	Factor C	1	36.125	36.125		6.02
3	Interaction $A \times C$	1	3.125	3.125		0.52
4	Factor B	1	465.125	465.125		77.54
5	Factor D	1	91.125	92.125		15.20
6	Interaction $B \times C$	1	3.125	3.125		0.52
7	Factor E	1	1.125	1.125		0.19
All other/error		0	0	0		
Total		7	599.880			100.00%

Factor F Ratios, for Significant Factors:

$$F_C = V_C/V_e = 36.125/1.875 = 19.267$$

$$F_B = V_B/V_e = 465.125/1.875 = 248.067$$

$$F_D = V_D/V_e = 91.125/1.875 = 48.600$$

Pure Sum of Squares S', for Significant Factors:

$$S_C' = S_C - (V_e \times f_C)$$
$$= 36.125 - (1.875 \times 1) = 34.25$$
$$S_B' = S_B - (V_e \times f_B)$$
$$= 465.125 - (1.875 \times 1) = 463.25$$
$$S_D' = S_D - (V_e \times f_D)$$
$$= 91.125 - (1.875 \times 1) = 89.25$$

Note that the ANOVA in Table 6-18, the pure sum of squares, S' is not shown.

Percentage Contribution:

$$P_c = S_C'/S_T = 34.25/599.88 = 5.71\%$$

$$P_B = S_B'/S_T = 463.25/599.88 = 77.22\%$$

Table 6-18. Pooled ANOVA—Example 6-6

COLUMN	FACTORS	f	S	V	F	P
1	Factor A	(1)	(0.13)	Pooled		
2	Factor C	1	36.125	36.125	19.267	5.71
3	Interaction $A \times C$	(1)	(3.125)	Pooled		
4	Factor B	1	465.125	265.125	248.067	77.22
5	Factor D	1	91.125	91.125	48.600	14.88
6	Interaction $B \times C$	(1)	(3.125)	Pooled		
7	Factor E	(1)	(1.125)	Pooled		
All other/error		4	7.500	1.88		2.19
Total:		7	599.880			100.00%

$$P_D = S_D'/S_T = 89.25/599.88 = 14.88\%$$

$$P_e = 100\% - (P_C + P_B + P_D) = 2.19\%$$

The ANOVA terms which are modified after pooling are shown in Table 6-18.

Taguchi's guideline for pooling (Ref. 10, pp. 293–295), requires a start with the smallest main effect and successively includes larger effects, until the total pooled DOF equals approximately half of the total DOF. The larger DOF for the error term, as a result of pooling, increases the confidence level of the significant factors.

Note that as small factor effects are pooled, the percentage contributions and the confidence level of the remaining factors decrease ($P_C = 5.71$ versus $P_C = 6.02$). By pooling, the error term is increased and in comparison the other factors, appear less influential. The greater the number of factors pooled the worse the unpooled factor effects look. Then we must consider why are column effects pooled?

Error variance represents the degree of inter-experiment error when the DOF of the error term is sufficiently large. When the error DOF is small or zero, which is the case when all columns of the OA are occupied and trials are not repeated, small column effects are successively pooled to form a larger error term (this is known as a pooling up strategy). The factors and interactions that are now significant in comparison with the larger magnitude of the error term are now influential. Taguchi prefers this strategy as it tends to avoid the mistake (alpha mistake) of ignoring helpful factors.

A large error DOF naturally results when trial conditions are repeated and standard analysis is performed. When the error DOF is large, pooling may not be necessary. Therefore, one could repeat the experiment and avoid pooling. But, to repeat all trial conditions just for information on the error term may not be practical.

A sure way to determine if a factor or interaction effect should be pooled is to perform a test of significance (1- confidence level). But what level of confidence do you work with? No clear guidelines are established. Generally, a confidence level between 90 and 99% is recommended. However, if the confidence level is below 90%, then it is a common practice to pool the factor for Example 6.5, factor C is tested for significance at a 99% confidence level. Since factor C contributes only 5.71%, test for significance and determine if this factor should be pooled. From the ANOVA table.

$F_C = 19.267$

From the F Table, find the F value at

$n_1 = $ DOF of factor $C = 1$

$n_2 = $ DOF of error term $= 4$

at a confidence level (say the 99% confidence level).

$F = 21.198$ (From Table C-4)

As F_C from experiment (19.267) is smaller than the F Table value (21.198), factor C should be pooled.

SUMMARY RESULT

Description of the factor $\qquad = $ Factor C

Column the factor is assigned to $= 2$

Variance ratio for this factor is $\quad = 19.267$

DOF of the factor $\qquad\qquad = 1$

DOF of error term, f_e $\qquad\quad = 4$

Confidence level % $\qquad\qquad = 99$

Based on the level of confidence desired (99%), the following is recommended.

"Pool this factor"

The revised values are calculated as shown below:

$S_e = S_T - (S_B + S_D) = 599.9 - (556.25) = 43.625$

$f_e = f_T - (f_B + f_D) = 7 - 2 = 5$

$V_e = S_e/f_e = 43.625/5 = 8.725$

$F_B = V_B/V_e = 465.125/8.725 = 53.309$

$F_D = V_D/V_e = 91.125/8.725 = 10.444$

$$S'_B = S_B - (V_e \times f_B) = 465.125 - (8.725 \times 1) = 456.40$$

$$S'_D = S_D - (V_e \times f_D) = 91.125 - (8.725 \times 1) = 82.40$$

$$P_B = S'_B/S_T = (456.40 \times 100)/599.88 = 76.08$$

$$P_D = S'_D/S_T = (82.40 \times 100)/599.88 = 13.74$$

$$P_e = 100\% - (P_B + P_D) = 10.18$$

6-7-3   Confidence Interval of Factor Effect

The confidence interval of estimates of the main effect is calculated using the following expression:

$$\text{C.I.} = \pm \sqrt{(F(1,n_2) \times V_e/N_e)}$$

Where

$F(1,n_2) = F$ value from the F Table at a required confidence level and at DOF 1 and error DOF n_2

V_e = Variance of error term (from ANOVA)

N_e = Effective number of replications

$$= \frac{\text{Total number of results (or number of } S/N \text{) ratios)}}{\text{DOF of mean } (=1, \text{ always}) + \text{ DOF of all factors}}$$
included in the estimate of the mean.

Thus for the factor C at level C_1, the C.I. is calculated by first determining the F factor:

$$n_2 = 4$$

$$N_e = 8/(1 + 1) = 4$$

$$F(1,4) = 7.7086 \text{ at 95\% confidence level}$$

then   C.I. $= \pm 1.9034$ at 95% confidence level.

since $C_1 = 45.50$ (Table 6-16)

expected value of $C_1 = 45.50 \pm 1.9034$

SUMMARY RESULTS

Based on:

F value from the table (at a confidence level) = 7.7086

Error variance, V_e = 1.88

Number of effective replications = 4

The confidence interval C.I. is calculated as follows:

$$\text{C.I.} = \pm \sqrt{(F(1,n_2) \times V_e)/N_e)}$$

C.I. represents the variation of the estimated value of the main effect of a factor of the result at the optimum at a confidence level used for the F values.

Confidence interval (C.I.) = ± 1.9034

6-7-4   Estimated Result at Optimum Condition

The performance at the optimum condition is estimated only from the significant factors. Therefore, the pooled factors are not included in the estimate.

Grand average of performance: $\overline{T} = 347/8 = 43.375$

As the factors B, C, and D are considered significant, the performance at the optimum condition will be estimated using only these three factors.

$$= \overline{T} + (\overline{B}_1 - \overline{T}) + (\overline{D}_2 - \overline{T}) + (\overline{C}_2 - \overline{T})$$
$$= 43.375 + (35.75 - 43.375) + (40 - 43.375)$$
$$+ (33 - 43.375)$$
$$= 22.000$$

Note that the optimum condition for the "smaller is better" quality characteristic is $B_1 \, C_2 \, D_2$. The average values at these conditions were previously calculated as summarized in Table 6-19.

Table 6-19. Estimate of Performance at the Optimum Condition—Example 6-6

FACTOR DESCRIPTION	LEVEL DESCRIPTION	LEVEL	CONTRIBUTION
Factor C	C_1	1	-10.3750
Factor B	B_1	1	-7.6250
Factor D	D_2	2	-3.3750
Contribution from all factors (total)			-21.375
Current grand average of performance			43.375
Expected result at optimum condition			22.000

6-7-5   Confidence Interval of the Result at the Optimum Condition

The expression for computing the confidence interval, for performance at the optimum condition, is calculated in the same way as are the factor effects.

$$\text{C.I.} = \pm \sqrt{(F(1,n_2) \times V_e/N_e)}$$

Where

$F(1,n_2) =$ The F value from the F Table at a required confidence level at DOF 1 and error DOF n_2

$V_e =$ Variance of error term (from ANOVA)

$N_e =$ Effective number of replications

$$= \frac{\text{Total number of results (or number of } S/N \text{ ratios)}}{\text{DOF of mean } (=1, \text{ always}) + \text{DOF of all factors included in the estimate of the mean.}}$$

Three factors, B_1, C_2, and D_2 are included in the making of the performance estimate at the optimum condition. Therefore, the effective number of replication, F value and the confidence intervals are calculated as shown below. A confidence level of 90 to 99% is the normal range of selection for common industrial experiments. A 90% confidence level is arbitrarily selected for the following calculations.

$$n_2 = 4$$

$$N_e = 8/(1 + 3) = 2$$

$$F(1,4) = 4.5448 \text{ at the 90\% confidence level}$$

$$V_e = 1.88$$

$$\text{C.I.} = \pm 2.067 \text{ at the 90\% confidence level.}$$

Therefore the result at the optimum condition is 22.0 ± 2.067 at the 90% confidence level.

SUMMARY RESULTS

Expression: $\text{C.I.} = \pm \sqrt{(F(1,n_2) \times V_e)/N_e}$

where $F(n_1,n_2)$ = Computed value of F with $n_1 = 1$, n_2 = error DOF, at a desired confidence level,

V_e = Error variance

N_e = Number of effective replications

Based on $F = 4.5448$, $n_1 = 1$ and $n_2 = 4$, $V_e = 1.88$ $N_e = 2$

The confidence interval $(\text{C.I.}) = \pm 2.067$

Which is the variation of the estimated result at the optimum i.e., the mean result, (m) lies between $(m + \text{C.I.})$ and $(m - \text{C.I.})$ at 90% confidence level.

The confidence interval formula assumes a sufficiently large number of data points so that the sample approximates the population characteristics. With a "small" sample, its characteristics may deviate from the population. When the sample is small, i.e., only a finite number of confirmation tests are planned, the C.I. of the expected result is expressed as:

$$\text{C.I.} = \pm \sqrt{[F(n_1,n_2) \times V_e \times (N_e + N_r)]/N_e \times N_r}$$

Where

$$F(n_1, n_2) = \text{Computed value of } F \text{ at a desired confidence level with}$$
$$n_1 = 1 \text{ and error DOF } n_2$$

$$V_e = \text{Error variance}$$

and N_e = Effective number of replications.

Based on:

$$n_1 = 1 \qquad n_3 = 4 \qquad V_e = 1.88$$

$$N_e = 2 \qquad N_r = 3$$

$$F_{.1}(1,4) = 4.5448 \text{ at the 90\% confidence level,}$$

then C.I. = $\pm$ 2.668 at the 90% confidence level. This is a wider interval than previously calculated based on a large number of repetitions.

6-7-6 Analysis with Multiple Runs

Assume the trial runs of the experiment were each repeated three times and that the average result of each trial as shown Table 6-20, is the same as that for a single trial in Table 6-15. The analysis takes a slightly different form. Since the averages of these hypothetical results were kept the same, the main effects remain unchanged as shown in Tables 6-21

Table 6-20. Results with Three Repetitions—Example 6-6

TRIAL/ REPETITIONS	R_1	R_2	R_3	R_4	R_5	R_6	AVERAGE
1	38.00	42.00	46.00				42.00
2	45.00	50.00	55.00				50.00
3	38.00	36.00	34.00				36.00
4	55.00	45.00	35.00				45.00
5	30.00	35.00	40.00				35.00
6	65.00	55.00	45.00				55.00
7	40.00	30.00	20.00				30.00
8	58.00	54.00	50.00				54.00

Table 6-21. The Main Effects—Example 6-6

COLUMNS	FACTOR NAMES	LEVEL 1	LEVEL 2	$(L_2 - L_1)$	LEVEL 3	LEVEL 4
1	Factor A	43.25	43.50	-0.25		
2	Factor C	45.50	41.25	-4.25		
3	Interaction $A \times C$	44.00	42.75	-1.25		
4	Factor B	35.75	51.00	15.25		
6	Factor D	46.75	40.00	-6.75		
7	Interaction $B \times C$	44.00	42.75	-1.25		
8	Factor E	43.00	43.75	0.75		

and 6-16. However, the results of ANOVA (Table 6-22) are significantly different from the corresponding result of the single run (Table 6-18).

Computation for ANOVA:

$$DOF = \text{total number of results} - 1$$
$$= \text{number of trial} \times \text{number of repetitions} - 1$$
$$= 8 \times 3 - 1 = 23$$

Sample Calculations Using Factor B:

$$B_1 = (38.0 + 42.0 + 46.0) + (38.0 + 36.0 + 34.0)$$
$$+ (30.0 + 35.0 + 40.0) + (40.0 + 30.0 + 20.0) = 429$$

Table 6-22. Pooled ANOVA

COLUMN	FACTORS	f	S	V	F	P
1	Factor A	(1)	(0.38)	Pooled		
2	Factor C	1	108.375	108.375	2.728	2.67
3	Interaction $A \times C$	(1)	(9.380)	Pooled		
4	Factor B	1	1395.375	1395.375	35.126	52.72
5	Factor D	1	273.375	273.375	6.882	9.09
6	Interaction $B \times C$	(1)	(9.380)	Pooled		
7	Factor E	(1)	(3.380)	Pooled		
All other/error		20	794.500	39.72		35.53
Total:		23	2571.630			100.00%

Note that the trial condition for calculating B_1 is (1,3,5, and 7)

$$B_2 = (45.0 + 50.0 + 55.0) + (55.0 + 45.0 + 35.0)$$
$$+ (65.0 + 55.0 + 45.0) + (58.0 + 54.0 + 50.0) = 612$$

Using the sum of squares formula for 2 level factor,

$$S_B = \frac{(B_1 - B_2)^2}{(N_{B1} + N_{B2})} = \frac{(429 - 612)^2}{24} \qquad = 1395.375$$

$$V_B = S_B/f_B \qquad = 1395.375/1 \qquad = 1395.375$$

$$F_B = V_B/V_e \qquad = 1395.375/39.72 \qquad = 35.126$$

$$S_B' = S_B - V_e \times f_B = 1395.275 - 39.72 \qquad = 1355.650$$

$$P_B = 100 \times S_B'/S_T \qquad = 100 \times 1355.65/2571.63 = 52.70\%$$

The ANOVA and the performance at the optimum condition are as shown in Table 6-22 and Table 6-23, respectively.

When trial runs are repeated, ANOVA produces different results with larger error DOF and thus a higher level of confidence in the estimate optimum performance and the factor influences. ANOVA results from multiple repetitions should always be preferred as this will yield the robust design and reproducible performance estimate. For this reason repetition is highly desirable. But, since repeating trial runs may be expensive, it must be weighed against the need for robustness.

Table 6-23. Estimate of Performance at the Optimum Condition—Example 6-6

FACTOR DESCRIPTION	LEVEL DESCRIPTION	LEVEL	CONTRIBUTION
Factor C	C_2	2	-2.1250
Factor B	B_1	1	-7.6250
Factor D	D_2	2	-3.3750
Contribution from all factors			-13.375
Current grand average of performance			43.375
Expected result at optimum condition			30.250

6-8   APPLICATION OF THE S/N RATIO

The change in the quality characteristics of a product under investigation, in response to a factor introduced in the experimental design is the "signal" of the desired effect. However, when an experiment is conducted, there are numerous external factors not designed into the experiment which influence the outcome. These external factors are called the noise factors and their effect on the outcome of the quality characteristic under test is termed "the noise." The signal to noise ratio (S/N ratio) measures the sensitivity of the quality characteristic being investigated in a controlled manner, to those external influencing factors (noise factors) not under control. The concept of S/N originated in the electrical engineering field. Taguchi effectively applied this concept to establish the optimum condition from the experiments.

The aim of any experiment is always to determine the highest possible S/N ratio for the result. A high value of S/N implies that the signal is much higher than the random effects of the noise factors. Product design or process operation consistent with highest S/N, always yields the optimum quality with minimum variance.

From the quality point of view, there are three possible categories of quality characteristics. They are:

1. Smaller is better, e.g., minimum shrinkage in a cast iron cylinder block casting.
2. Nominal is best, e.g., dimension of a part consistently achieved with modest variance.
3. Bigger is better, e.g., maximum expected life of a component.

The S/N analysis is designed to measure quality characteristics.

6-8-1   Conversion of Results into S/N Ratios

The conversion of a set of observations into a single number, the S/N ratio, is performed in two steps. First, the Mean Squared Deviation (MSD) of the set is calculated. Second, the S/N ratio is computed from the MSD by the equation,

$$S/N = -10 \, \text{Log}_{10} \, (\text{MSD}) \qquad (6\text{-}16)$$

Note that for the S/N to be large, the MSD must have a value that is small.

The smaller is better quality characteristic:

$$\text{MSD} = (Y_1^2 + Y_2^2 + \cdots + Y_N^2)/N \qquad (6\text{-}17)$$

The nominal is the best quality characteristic, $Y_0 = $ nominal or target value:

$$\text{MSD} = ((Y_1 - Y_0)^2 + (Y_2 - Y_0)^2 + \cdots + (Y_N - Y_0)^2)/N \qquad (6\text{-}18)$$

The bigger is better quality characteristic:

$$\text{MSD} = (1/Y_1^2 + 1/Y_2^2 + \cdots + 1/Y_N^2)/N \qquad (6\text{-}19)$$

The Mean Squared Deviation (MSD) is a statistical quantity that reflects the deviation from the target value. The expressions for the MSD are different for different quality characteristics. For the nominal is best characteristic, the standard definition of MSD is used. For the other two characteristics, the definition is slightly modified. For smaller is better, the unstated target value is zero. For larger is better, the inverse of each large value becomes a small value and again, the unstated target is zero. Thus for all three MSD expressions, the smallest magnitude of MSD is being sought. In turn this yields the greatest discrimination between controlled and uncontrolled factors. This is Taguchi's solution to robust product or process design.

Alternate forms of definitions of the S/N ratios exist (Ref. 7, pp. 172–173), particularly for the nominal is the best characteristic. The definition in terms of MSD is preferred as it is consistent with Taguchi's objective of reducing variation around the target. Conversion to S/N ratio can be viewed as a scale transformation for convenience of better data manipulation.

6-8-2   Advantage of S/N Ratio over Average

To analyze the results of experiments involving multiple runs, use of the S/N ratio over standard analysis (use average of results) is preferred. Analysis using the S/N ratio will offer the following two main advantages:

1. It provides a guidance to a selection of the optimum level based on least variation around the target and also on the average value closest to the target.
2. It offers objective comparison of two sets of experimental data with respect to variation around the target and the deviation of the average from the target value.

To examine how the S/N ratio is used in analysis, consider the following two sets of observations which have a target value of 75.

Observation A: 55 58 60 63 65   Mean $= 60.2$

   Deviation of mean from target $= (75 - 60.2) = 14.8$

Observation B: 50 60 76 90 100   Average $= 75.00$

   Deviation of mean from target $= (75 - 75) = 0.0$

These two sets of observations may have come from the two distributions shown in Figure 6-3. Observe that the set B has an average value

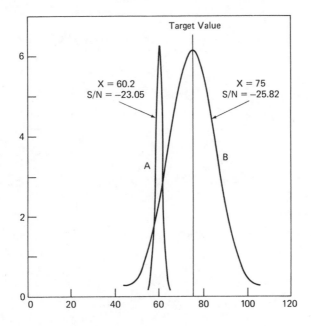

Figure 6-3. Comparison of two distributions.

which equals the target value, but has a wide spread around it. On the other hand for the set A, the spread around its average is smaller, but the average itself is quite far from the target. Which one of the two is better? Based on average value, the product shown by observation B, appears to be better. Based on consistency, product A is better. How can one credit A for less variation? How does one compare the distances of the averages from the target? Surely, comparing the averages is one method. Use of the S/N ratio offers an objective way to look at the two characteristics together.

6-8-3 Computation of the S/N Ratio

Consider the first of the two sets of observations shown above. That is set A: 55 58 60 63 65.

Case 1. The nominal is the best.
Using Eq. 6-18, and with the target value of 75,

$$MSD = ((55 - 75)^2 + (58 - 75)^2 + (60 - 75)^2 + (63 - 75)^2$$
$$+ (65 - 75)^2)/5$$
$$= (400 + 289 + 225 + 144 + 100)/5$$
$$= 1158/5$$
$$= 231.6$$

therefore,

$$S/N = -10 \, Log_{10} \, (MSD)$$
$$S/N = -10 \times Log_{10} \, (231.6)$$
$$= -23.65$$

Case 2. The smaller is the better.
Using Eq. 6-17,

$$MSD = (55^2 + 58^2 + 60^2 + 63^2 + 65^2)/5$$
$$= (3025 + 3364 + 3600 + 3969 + 4425)/5$$
$$= 18183/5$$
$$= 3636.6$$

and

$$S/N = -10 \text{ Log } (3636.6)$$

$$= -35.607$$

Case 3. The bigger the better.
Using Eq. 6-19,

$$MSD = (1/55^2 + 1/58^2 + 1/60^2 + 1/63^2 + 1/65^2)/5$$

$$= (1/3025 + 1/3364 + 1/3600 + 1/3969 + 1/4425)/5$$

$$= (3.305 + 2.972 + 2.777 + 2.519 + 2.366) \times 10^{-4}/5$$

$$= (13.939) \times 10^{-4}/5$$

$$= .0002728$$

therefore,

$$S/N = -10 \text{ Log } (MSD) = -10 \text{ Log } (.0002787) = 35.548$$

The three S/N ratios computed for the data sets A and B under the three different quality characteristics are shown in Table 6-24. The three columns N, S and B, under the heading "S/N ratios" are for nominal, smaller, and the bigger the better characteristics, respectively.

Now select the best data set on the basis of minimum variation. By definition lower deviation is indicated by a higher value of the S/N ratio (regardless of the characteristics of quality). If the nominal the better characteristic applies, then using column N, the S/N ratio for A is -23.65 and is -25.32 for B. Since -23.65 is greater than -25.32, set A has less variation than st B, although set B has an average value equal to the desired target value.

Table 6-24. S/N Ratios for Three Quality Characteristics

				S/N RATIOS		
OBSERVATIONS			AVERAGE	N	S	B
A: 55 58 60 63 65			60.2	-23.65	-35.61	35.54
B: 50 60 75 90 100			75.0	-25.32	-37.76	36.65

Similarly, set A is selected for the smaller is better characteristic and B is selected for the bigger is better characteristic.

6-8-4 Effect of the S/N Ratio on the Analysis

Use of the S/N ratio of the results, instead of the average values, introduces some minor changes in the analysis.

- Degrees of freedom of the entire experiment is reduced.

  DOF with S/N ratio = number of trial conditions − 1
  (i.e., Number of repetitions is reduced to 1)

  Recall that the DOF in the case of the standard analysis is

  DOF = (Number of trial × Number of repetition) − 1

  The S/N ratio calculation is based on data from all observations of a trial condition. The set of S/N ratios can then be considered as trial results without repetitions. Hence the DOF, in case of S/N is the number of trials − 1. The rest of the analysis follows the standard procedure.

- S/N must be converted back to meaningful terms. When the S/N ratio is used, the results of the analysis, such as estimated performance from the main effects or confidence interval are expressed in terms of S/N. To express the analysis in terms of the experimental result, the ratio must be converted back to the original units of measurement.

To see the specific differences in the analysis using the S/N ratio, let us compare the two analyses of the same observations for the Cam-Lifter Noise Study shown in Table 6-25-1 (standard analysis) and in Table 6-25-2 (S/N ratio analysis). In this study the three factors (spring rate, cam profile, and weight of the push rod) each at two levels, were investigated. The L_4 OA defined the four trial conditions. At each of the four trial conditions, three observations (in some noise scale of 0 to 60) were recorded. The results were then analyzed both ways as shown in these two tables.

A subtable "results" of the standard analysis (Table 6-25-1) presents the average of the three repetitions for each trial run at the extreme right hand column. The averages are used in calculating the main effects. The values shown in the subtable titled "Main Effects" have the same units as the original observations. Similarly, the expected value at the optimum

Table 6-25-1. Cam-Lifter Noise Study Standard Analysis

COLUMN	FACTORS	LEVEL 1	LEVEL 2	LEVEL 3	LEVEL 4
1	Spring rate	Current	Proposed		
2	Cam profile	Type 1	Type 2		
3	Wt. of push rod	Lighter	Heavier		

Individual Results and Their Average

TRIAL/ REPETITIONS	R_1	R_2	R_3	R_4	R_5	R_6	AVERAGE
1	23.00	30.00	37.00				30.00
2	35.00	40.00	45.00				40.00
3	50.00	30.00	40.00				40.00
4	45.00	48.00	51.00				48.50

The Main Effects

COLUMN	FACTORS	LEVEL 1	LEVEL 2	$(L_2 - L_1)$	LEVEL 3	LEVEL 4
1	Spring rate	35.00	44.00	9.00	00.00	00.00
2	Cam profile	35.00	44.00	9.00	00.00	00.00
3	Wt. of push rod	39.00	40.00	1.00	00.00	00.00

ANOVA Table

COLUMN	FACTORS	DOF	SUM OF SQUARES	VARIANCE	F	PERCENT
1	Spring rate	1	243.00	243.00	5.93	23.63
2	Cam profile	1	243.00	243.00	5.93	23.63
3	Wt. of push rod	(1)	(3.00)	POOLED		
All others/error		9	369.00	41.00		52.76
Total:		11	855.00			100.00

Estimate of the Optimum Condition of Design/Process:
For Smaller the Better Characteristic

FACTOR DESCRIPTION	LEVEL DESCRIPTION	LEVEL	CONTRIBUTION
Spring rate	Current	1	-4.5000
Cam profile	Type 1	1	-45.000
Contribution from all factors (total)			-9.00
Current grand average of performance			39.50
Expected result at optimum condition			30.50

Table 6-25-2. Cam-Lifter Noise Study—*S/N* Analysis

Design Factors and Their Levels

COLUMN	FACTORS	LEVEL 1	LEVEL 2	LEVEL 3	LEVEL 4
1	Spring rate	Current	Proposed		
2	Cam profile	Type 1	Type 2		
3	Wt. of push rod	Lighter	Heavier		

Results and the *S/N* Ratios

TRIAL/ REPETITIONS	R_1	R_2	R_3	R_4	R_5	R_6	*S/N*
1	23.00	30.00	37.00				-29.70
2	35.00	40.00	45.00				-32.09
3	50.00	30.00	40.00				-32.22
4	45.00	48.00	51.00				-33.64

The Main Effects

COLUMN	FACTORS	LEVEL 1	LEVEL 2	$(L_2 - L_1)$	LEVEL 3	LEVEL
1	Spring rate	-30.9	-32.93	-2.04	00.00	00.00
2	Cam profile	-30.96	-32.86	-1.91	00.00	00.00
3	Wt. of push rod	-31.67	-32.16	-0.49	00.00	00.00

ANOVA Table

COLUMN	FACTORS	DOF	SUM OF SQUARES	VARIANCE	F	PERCENT
1	Spring rate	1	4.141	4.141	17.61	48.79
2	Cam profile	1	3.629	3.629	15.43	42.39
3	Wt. of push rod	(1)	(3.00)	Pooled		
All others/error		1	0.24	0.24		8.82
Total:		3	8.01			100.00

Estimate of the Optimum Condition of Design/Process:
For Smaller the Better Characteristic

FACTOR DESCRIPTION	LEVEL DESCRIPTION	LEVEL	CONTRIBUTION
Spring rate	Current	1	1.0175
Cam profile	Type 1	1	0.9525
Contribution from all factors (total)			1.9699
Current grand average of performance			-31.9125
Expected result at optimum condition			-29.9425

condition, 30.5, has the same units as the original recorded data. The degrees of freedom for the experiment (DOF column in ANOVA table) is 11 ($4 \times 3 - 1$).

Comparing the standard analysis with the analysis using the S/N ratio (Table 6-25-2), note that the average value of the results is replaced by the S/N ratio. The S/N ratios are then used to compute the main effects as well as the estimated performance at the optimum condition. Notice also that the degrees of freedom for the experiment is 3. This difference in DOF produces a big difference in the way the two analyses compute ANOVA, i.e., the percentage contribution of the factors involved (for spring rate the value is 23.6% from standard analysis as compared to 48.79% from S/N analysis). Likewise, the other factors will have different magnitudes of contribution in the two methods.

In estimating the result at the optimum condition, only the factors that will have significant contributions are included. In this case, both methods selected level 1 of factors in columns 1 (spring rate) and 2 (cam profile). This may not always be true.

When the S/N ratio is used, the estimated result can be converted back to the scale of units of the original observations. For example, the expected result in terms of S/N ratio is -29.9425 (Table 6-25-2, bottom line). This is equivalent to an average performance, Y', which is calculated as follows.

Since

$$S/N = -10 \text{ Log (MSD)}$$

and

$$MSD = (Y_1^2 + \ldots Y_N^2)/N \qquad \text{(For "smaller is better")}$$
$$\cong Y_{\text{expected}}^2$$

Therefore,

$$MSD = 10^{(-S/N)/10} = 10^{-(-29.9425)/10} = 986.8474$$

or

$$Y_{\text{expected}} \cong (MSD)^{1/2} = (986.8474)^{1/2} = 31.41$$

which is comparable to 30.5 shown at the bottom of Table 6-25-1.

Table 6-26. Orthogonal Array and Test Data

TRIAL/ COLUMN	A 1	B 2	A × B 3	C 4	D 5	6	7	R_1	R_2	R_3
Trial 1	1	1	1	1	1	0	0	45.00	56.00	64.00
Trial 2	1	1	1	2	2	0	0	34.00	45.00	53.00
Trial 3	1	2	2	1	1	0	0	67.00	65.00	60.00
Trial 4	1	2	2	2	2	0	0	45.00	56.00	64.00
Trial 5	2	1	2	1	2	0	0	87.00	81.00	69.00
Trial 6	2	1	2	2	1	0	0	78.00	73.00	68.00
Trial 7	2	2	1	1	2	0	0	45.00	56.00	52.00
Trial 8	2	2	1	2	1	0	0	42.00	54.00	47.00

6-8-5   When to Use the S/N Ratio for Analysis

Whenever an experiment involves repeated observations at each of the trial conditions, the S/N ratio has been found to provide a practical way to measure and control the combined influence of deviation of the population mean from the target and the variation around the mean. In standard analysis, the mean and the variation around the mean are treated separately by a main effect study and ANOVA respectively. The analysis of the Taguchi experiments using S/N ratios for the observed results, can be conveniently performed by using computer software such as the one in Ref. 11.

Table 6-27. ANOVA

COLUMN	FACTORS	f	S	V	F	P
1	Speed	1	3.036	3.036	4.432	9.56
2	Oil viscosity	(1)	(1.91)	Pooled		
	Interaction	1	15.820	15.820	23.093	61.57
4	Clearance	1	2.987	2.987	4.361	9.36
5	Pin straightness	(1)	(0.75)	Pooled		
All others/error		4	2.740	0.685		19.51
Total:		7	24.584			100.00%

Note: Insignificant factorial effects are pooled as shown ( ).

EXERCISES

6-1. In an experiment involving four factors (A, B, C, and D) and one interaction ($A \times B$), each trial condition as repeated three times and the observations recorded as shown in Table 6-26. Determine the total sum of squares and the sum of squares for factor A.

6-2. Assuming "the bigger the better" quality characteristic, transform the results to the corresponding S/N ratios. (Ans. ± 0.962)

6-3. Table 6-27 shows the product of ANOVA performed on the observed results of an experiment. Determine the following from the ANOVA table.

  a. Percent influence of the clearance factor.
  b. Degrees of freedom of the speed factor.
  c. Error degrees of freedom.
  d. Influence of noise factors and all other factors not included in the experiment.
  e. Confidence interval (90%) of the performance at the optimum condition (use F Table for 90% confidence level).

7

Loss Function

+ p/0

7-1 DERIVATION OF LOSS FUNCTION

In Chapter 2 Taguchi's philosophy regarding the cost of quality was stressed. He believes that a poorly designed product causes society to incur losses from the initial design stage through to product usage. Therefore, he emphasizes good quality at the conceptual stage of a product and onward, by optimizing the product design parameters as well as the production conditions, to create a robust product. A question commonly asked is how much effort should an organization expend on quality. How can the point of diminishing returns be determined. In this section the basic mathematical formulation of Taguchi's loss function is developed and an outline of the steps used to apply the loss function is presented. The loss function has proven to be an excellent tool for determining the magnitude of the process (manufacturer) and supplier tolerances, based upon quality as perceived by the customer. The methodology for realignment of tolerances is beyond the scope of this text.

Taguchi defined the loss function as deviation as a quantity proportional to the deviation from the target quality characteristic. At zero deviation, the performance is on target, the loss is zero. If Y represents the deviation from the target value, then the loss function $L(Y)$ is:

$$L(Y) = k(Y - Y_0)^2 \tag{7-1}$$

Where

$Y =$ The quality characteristics, such as a dimension, performance, etc.

$Y_0 =$ The target value for the quality characteristic.

$k =$ A constant which is dependent upon the cost structure of a manufacturing process or an organization.

It is important to note that:

1. The term $(Y - Y_0)$ represents the deviation of the quality characteristic Y from the target value Y_0.
2. The equation for the loss function is of the second order in terms of deviation of the quality characteristic.

The loss function represented by Eq. 7-1 is graphically shown in Figure 7-1; it possesses the following characteristics:

1. The loss must be zero when the quality characteristic of a product meets its target value.
2. The magnitude of the loss increases rapidly as the quality characteristic deviates from the target value.
3. The loss function must be a continuous (second order) function of the deviation from the target value.

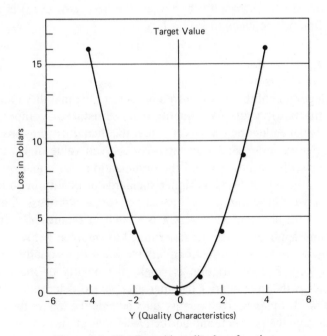

Figure 7-1. The Taguchi quality loss function.

Taguchi determined the loss function from a Taylor Theorem expansion about the target value Y_0. Thus,

$$L(Y) = L(Y_0) + L'(Y_0)(Y - Y_0) + \frac{1}{2!} L''(Y_0)(Y - Y_0)^2 \quad (7\text{-}2)$$

where the terms with powers of $(Y - Y_0)$ higher than 2 are ignored as being too small for consideration.

In Eq. 7-2, $L(Y)$ is the minimum at $Y = Y_0$ hence its first derivative $L'(Y_0)$ is zero. Therefore, Eq. 7-2 can be written as

$$L(Y) = L(Y_0) + \frac{1}{2!} L''(Y_0)(Y - Y_0)^2 \quad (7\text{-}3)$$

The expression $(1/2)L''(Y_0)$ in Eq. 7-3, is a constant and can be replaced by a constant k. Also if Y_0 is the mean value of the product/process, then Eq. 7-3 is interpreted as the loss about the product/process mean plus the loss due to displacement of the process mean from the target. If the process mean coincides with the target, the loss term $L(Y_0)$ is zero and the loss function reduces to Eq. 7-1,

$$L(Y) = k(Y - Y_0)^2$$

The magnitude of the loss incurred because of the inability of a process to meet the target value of a quality characteristic, as computed using Eq. 7-1, is dependent on the target value, the manufacturing process, the cost of rework, scrap, and warranty. For a given value of Y_0, the value of k varies with the process and the organization. An organization seriously committed to achieving higher standards of quality in an optimum manner may develop families of loss curves for each process. One family of curves with different values of k is shown in Figure 7-2. The value of k for any application can be determined as outlined below.

Any mass produced product exhibits variation in its quality characteristic. As long as the variation is small, the quality of the product is acceptable to the customer. Customer acceptance determines the range of variation. If the perceived quality falls outside the range, the customer will not accept the product, and corrective actions at the design or process level are required.

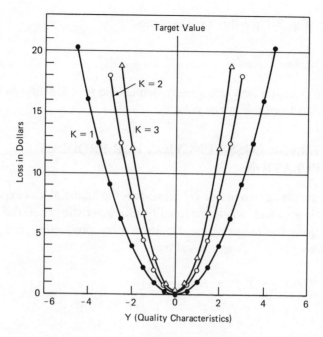

Figure 7-2. Family of loss functions.

Let this tolerance zone be $\pm \Delta$, then the quality characteristic at the extremes can be denoted as:

$$Y_0 + \Delta \quad \text{and} \quad Y_0 - \Delta$$

Poor quality exceeding the extremes, necessitates corrective action such as a warranty cost of L_0.

Let L_0 be the loss at $Y = Y_0 + \Delta$

Then from Eq. 7-1:

$$L_0 = k(Y_0 + \Delta - Y_0)^2$$

or

$$K = \frac{L_0}{\Delta^2}$$

Therefore, Eq. 7-1 for this case becomes:

$$L(Y) = L_0/2 \, (Y - Y_0)^2$$

The above equation now completely defines the loss function in terms of the deviation from the target value.

7-2   AVERAGE LOSS FUNCTION FOR PRODUCT POPULATION

The loss function given in Eq. 7-1 represents the financial loss experienced by a single product when the quality characteristic Y of the product deviates from the target value Y_0. In a mass production process, the average loss per unit is expressed by:

$$L(Y) = [k(Y_1 - Y_0)^2 + k(Y_2 - Y_0)^2$$
$$+ \, k(Y_3 - Y_0)^2 + \cdots + k(Y_n - Y_0)^2]/n$$

where n is the number of units in a given sample.

In the above equation the factor k is common with every term, and therefore, it can also be written as:

$$L(Y) = k[(Y_1 - Y_0)^2 + (Y_2 - Y_0)^2$$
$$+ \, (Y_3 - Y_0)^2 + \cdots + (Y_n - Y_0)^2]/n$$

Note that the expression within the brackets is the mean squared deviation (MSD), the average of the squares of all deviations from the target value Y_0. The average loss per unit can now simply be expressed by:

$$L(Y) = k(\text{MSD}) \qquad (7\text{-}4)$$

7-3   APPLICATION OF LOSS FUNCTION CONCEPTS

The loss function concept has two practical applications. The primary application is for estimating the potential cost savings resulting from the improvements achieved by optimizing a product or a process design. The loss function can serve regardless of the method of the quality improvement. As long as variation is reduced by corrective actions or design improvements, the loss function presents a means for estimating the savings in terms of dollars and cents. The second application is to determine manufacturer and supplier tolerances based on the customer's perception of the quality range. In this case, the loss function provides an objective way to set the limits for the inspection of products at manufacturer or supplier location. The following examples illustrate the use of the loss function.

Example 7-1
Machine Bracket Casting Process (Cost Savings)

Engineers involved in casting a machine bracket designed an experimental study to improve the process and reduce scrap rate. As a result of the study, a number of improvements were incorporated. Data were taken from 10 samples before and after the experiments. The foundry had a production rate of 1500 castings per month. The quality inspection criterion was a length dimension of 12 ± 0.35 inches. The parts which did not fall within the limits were rejected. The average unit cost for scrap or rework of the rejects was $20. The potential cost savings of the optimized process was calculated by the Taguchi loss function.

Test Data before the Experiment:

| 11.80 | 12.30 | 12.20 | 12.4 | 12.1 | 12.2 | 11.9 | 11.8 | 11.85 | 12.15 |

Readings After the Experiment:

| 11.9 | 12.2 | 12.1 | 12.2 | 12.1 | 12.1 | 11.9 | 11.95 | 11.95 | 12.1 |

Other Data:

Target value   = 12.00 in.

Tolerance   = ± 0.35 in.

Cost of rejection = $20.00

Production rate   = 1500 per month.

Solution

For this application the expression of loss in terms of the MSD will be used.

$$L(Y) = k(Y - Y_0)^2 \quad \text{for a single sample}$$

and

$$L(Y) = k(\text{MSD}) \quad \text{for multiple samples.}$$

Using Eq. 7-1, the constant k is determined as follows:

$$L = k(Y - Y_0)^2$$

i.e., $L = k(Y_0 \pm \text{Tolerance} - Y_0)^2$

But the loss L is equal to the cost of rejecting a part ($20.00) and the tolerance is .35

or $20 = k (.35)^2$

or $k = 20/(.35)^2 = 163.265$

Therefore, from Eq. 7-4

$$L = 163.265 \, (\text{MSD}) \tag{7-5}$$

Using the data from samples before the experiment,

$$\text{MSD} = [(11.8 - 12)^2 + (12.3 - 12)^2 + \ldots]/10$$
$$= 0.0475$$

The MSD and other statistical parameters for this example, as shown in Tables 7-1, 7-2 and 7-3, are obtained by using the software in Reference 11. The format of the design descriptions and the results are presented in the manner displayed by the software.

From Eq. 7-5 the average loss per unit is calculated as

$$L = 163.265 \times .0475 = 7.754 \text{ (in dollars)}$$

Table 7-1. Machine Bracket Casting Process
(Before Experiment)

```
Observation   1  =  11.800
Observation   2  =  12.300
Observation   3  =  12.200
Observation   4  =  12.400
Observation   5  =  12.100
Observation   6  =  12.200
Observation   7  =  11.900
Observation   8  =  11.800
Observation   9  =  11.850
Observation  10  =  12.150
```

Target/nominal value of result	=	12.00
Number of test results (NR)	=	10

AVERAGE AND STANDARD DEVIATION:

Total of all test results	=	120.70000
Average of test results	=	12.07000
Standard deviation (SD)	=	00.21756
Variance	=	00.04733

LOSS FUNCTION PARAMETERS:

Mean square deviation (MSD)	=	00.04749
Signal to noise ratio (S/N)	=	13.23307
Variance (modified form)	=	00.04259
Square of mean value	=	00.00489

VARIANCE DATA (ANOVA):

Target value of data/test result	=	12.00
Mean of data/deviation from target	=	00.069999
Total variance (ST)	=	00.04899
(ST = Variance × NR)		
Correction factor (CF)	=	00.04899
(CF = (average of data)^2 × number of data)		
Sums of squares/N	=	00.47499

Table 7-2. Machine Bracket Casting Process
(After Experiment)

Observation   1 = 11.900
Observation   2 = 12.200
Observation   3 = 12.100
Observation   4 = 12.200
Observation   5 = 12.100
Observation   6 = 12.100
Observation   7 = 11.900
Observation   8 = 11.950
Observation   9 = 11.950
Observation 10 = 12.100

Target/nominal value of result	=	12.00
Number of test results (NR)	=	10

AVERAGE AND STANDARD DEVIATION:

Total of all test results	=	120.50000
Average of test results	=	12.05000
Standard deviation (SD)	=	00.11547
Variance	=	00.01333

LOSS FUNCTION PARAMETERS:

Mean square deviation (MSD)	=	00.01450
Signal to noise ratio (S/N)	=	18.38631
Variance (modified form)	=	00.01200
Square of mean value	=	00.00250

VARIANCE DATA (ANOVA):

Target value of data/test result	=	12.00
Mean of data/deviation from target	=	00.05000
Total variance (ST)	=	00.12000

(ST = Variance × NR)

Correction factor (CF)	=	00.02500

(CF = (average of data)^2 × number of data)

Sums of squares/N	=	00.14500

Table 7-3. Calculation of Loss

PROBLEM DEFINITION
Target value of quality characteristic (m)	=	12.00
Tolerance of quality characteristic	=	0.35
Cost of rejection at production (per unit)	=	$20.00
Units produced per month (total)	=	1500
S/N ratio of current design/part	=	13.23307
S/N ratio of new design/part	=	18.38631

COMPUTATION OF LOSS USING TAGUCHI LOSS FUNCTION
Loss function: $L(y) = 163.26 \times (MSD)$ Also $L(y)$ $= K \times (y - m)^2$

BEFORE EXPERIMENT:
Loss/unit due to deviation from target in current design   = $7.754

AFTER EXPERIMENT:
Loss/unit due to deviation from target will be reduced from
$7.754 to   = $2.367

MONTHLY SAVINGS:
If production were maintained at the improved condition, then
based on 1500 units/month   = $8081.34

Using the data from samples after the experiment,

$$MSD = [(11.9 - 12)^2 + (12.2 - 12)^2 + \ldots]/10$$
$$= 0.0145$$

From Eq. 7-6, the average loss per unit is calculated to be

$$L = 163.265 \times .0145 = 2.367 \text{ (in dollars)}$$

The average savings per unit is calculated by subtracting the loss after the experiment ($2.367) from that before the experiment ($7.754). The total savings is then obtained by multiplying the average savings by the production rate as shown here.

$$\text{Total saving per month} = (7.754 - 2.367) \times 1500$$
$$= \$8080.50$$

Example 7-2
Dryer Motor Belt (Manufacturer/supplier tolerance)

Alarmed by a high rate of warranty repairs of drive-belts for one of its products, the distributor sought to reduce such defects. The field reports suggested that the problem was mainly caused by the lack of adjustment of tension in the drive belt. To correct the situation at the customer's location, the field repairmen had to adjust the tension to 100 ± 15 lbs. Field service cost is $40 per unit. Alternately, the adjustment of tension could be made by the manufacturer at a unit cost of $15. The distributor wants to ask the manufacturer to make such adjustments prior to shipment in order to eliminate the field service and maintain satisfied customers. What range of tolerance in belt tension should the distributor specify for the manufacturer?

Solution

For this application, an understanding of the role of the three parties, namely customer, manufacturer, and supplier will be helpful. In the context of tolerance specification, the three terms correspond to three stages of product life. The supplier is the one who supplies a component or part of the finished product to the manufacturer. The manufacturer is the one who assembles the final product. The customer is the one who uses the product and experiences its performance. In this example, the distributor and the customers are considered to be the end users. The customer and the manufacturer may have a supplier (not identified) for the motor and belt assembly. The relationships among the three can be represented in the following way.

Supplier   →   Manufacturer   →   Customer

(Belt + Motor)   (Washer)   (Washer in use)

Tolerance required:

  (unknown)   (unknown) $\pm$ 15 lbs.)

From Eq. 7-1 we have

$$L(Y) = k(Y - Y_0)^2 = k \text{ (Tolerance)}^2$$

where

Tolerance $= Y$(max. or min.) $- Y_0$

Based on a repair cost of $40 at the customer's installation, the loss per unit is $40.

Since

$Y_0 = 100$, $\quad Y = 100 + 15$ (max.), $\quad$ and $\quad L(Y) = 40$

$k = 40/(100 + 15 - 100)^2 = 0.17778$

Therefore,

$$L(Y) = .17778 \text{ (Tolerance)}^2 \tag{7-6}$$

Using the repair cost of $15 at the manufacturers facility as the loss, the tolerance now can be determined by using the above relation.

Tolerance $\quad = (L/.17778)^{1/2} = 9.18$

(Manufacturer)

or

Tolerance Limits $= 100 \pm 9.8$

If the manufacturer determined the problem to be caused by a specific component, then correction at the supplier's facilities would be appropriate. A different set of specification may be required. Assuming the cost to make an adjustment at the supplier is $5 per unit. What tolerance should the manufacturer require of the supplier to assure the required quality?

Using Eq. 7-4 with $L(Y) = 5$

$5 = .178 \text{ (Tolerance)}^2$

and

Tolerance $= (5/.17778)^{1/2} = 5.30$

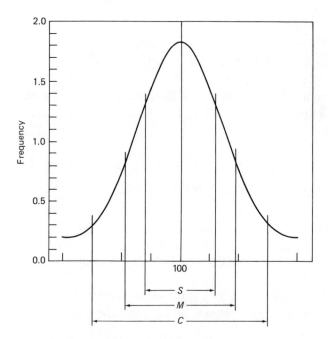

S = Supplier tolerance 100 ±5.8
M = Manufacturer tolerance 100 ±9.18
C = Customer tolerance 100 ±15

COMPUTATION OF MANUFACTURER $ SUPPLIER TOLERANCE
Nominal value of the quality characteristic Y = 100 Lbs.
Tolerance of Y (range of deviation)   = ±15 Lbs.
Cost to repair a nonfunctioning unit by customer   = $40.0
Cost to repair a nonfunctioning unit by manufacturer = $15.0
Cost to repair a nonfunctioning unit by supplier   = $ 5.0

REQUIRED TOLERANCES
Manufacturer tolerance = 100 ±9.18
Supplier tolerance   = 100 ±5.3

NOTE: If these Tolerances were held, there will be no nonfunctional part in the customers hands. For the same cost the Manufacturer will maintain satisfied customers and quality products in the field.

Figure 7-3. Manufacturer and supplier tolerances.

Therefore

Tolerance limits for supplier $= 100 \pm 5.3$

The solutions are presented in Figure 7-3.

Example 7-3
Fuel Pump Noise Study

In an experimental study of an automotive fuel pump noise, three 2 level factors were included as shown in Table 7-4-1. The Taguchi L_4 orthogonal array was used to define the four trial conditions. Six samples at each of the trial conditions were tested and the results were recorded as shown in Table 7-4-2. The levels were selected so that the trial condition 1 represents the current design of the fuel pump. If the decision is made to change the design to the determined optimum configuration, estimate the performance at the optimum design and the cost savings when the new fuel pump is produced.

Table 7-4-1. Fuel Pump Noise Study—Example 7-3

Fuel Pump Noise Study
Design Factors and Their Levels

COLUMNS	FACTORS	LEVEL 1	LEVEL 2	LEVEL 3	LEVEL 4
1	Seal thickness	Present	Thicker		
2	Rotor chuck type	Present	New design		
3	Finger to drive C_1	Present	Increase		

Note: Three 2 level factors studied.
Objective: Design least noisy and best performing pump.
Characteristic: Nominal the best (SIQ = 60 Target).

This experiment will use L_4

TRIAL/COLUMN	1	2	3
Trial 1	1	1	1
Trial 2	1	2	2
Trial 3	2	1	2
Trial 4	2	2	1

Table 7-4-2. Fuel Pump Noise Study (Result: Main Effect and ANOVA)

Original Observations and Their S/N Ratios
Quality Characteristic: Nominal is Best

TRIAL/ REPETITIONS	R_1	R_2	R_3	R_4	R_5	R_6	S/N
1	67.00	85.00	87.00	65.00	59.00	76.00	-20.71
2	65.00	65.00	66.00	54.00	73.00	58.00	-18.99
3	54.00	45.00	56.00	45.00	63.00	46.00	-25.89
4	56.00	67.00	45.00	54.00	56.00	74.00	-23.36

The Main Effects

COLUMN	FACTOR NAME	LEVEL 1	LEVEL 2	$(L_1 - L_1)$	LEVEL 3	LEVEL 4
1	Seal thickness	-19.85	-24.63	-4.78	00.00	00.00
2	Rotor chuck type	-23.30	-21.18	2.12	00.00	00.00
3	Finger to drive	-22.04	-22.44	-0.41	00.00	00.00

ANOVA Table

COLUMN	FACTOR	DOF	SUM OF SQUARES	VARIANCE	F	PERCENT
1	Seal thickness	1	22.801	22.801		82.97
2	Rotor chuck type	1	4.512	4.512		16.43
3	Finger to drive	1	0.164	0.164		00.60
All others/error		0				
Total:		3	27.480			100.00

Assume that the following information is used.

Target value of quality characteristic   = 70

Tolerance value of quality characteristic = ± 20

Cost of replacement/rejection   = \$45.00

Production Rate   = 20,000

Table 7-4-3. Fuel Pump Noise Study (Optimum and Cost Savings)

Estimate of the Optimum Condition of Design/Process:
for Nominal the Best Characteristic

FACTOR DESCRIPTION	LEVEL DESCRIPTION	LEVEL	CONTRIBUTION
Seal thickness	Present design	1	2.3875
Rotor chuck type	New design	2	1.0625
Finger to drive clearance	Present design	1	0.2025
Contribution from all factors (total)			3.6524
Current grand average of performance			− 22.2375
Expected result at optimum condition			− 18.5850

This estimate includes only those variables that have a significant contribution, i.e., pooled variables are excluded from the estimate. Estimates may also be made with variables of choice.

CALCULATION OF LOSS

PROBLEM DEFINITION

Target value of quality characteristics (m)	=	70.00
Tolerance of quality characteristic	=	20.00
Cost of rejection at production (per unit)	=	$45.00
Units produced per month (total)	=	20000
S/N ratio of current design/part	=	− 20.71
S/N ratio of new design/part	=	− 18.585

COMPUTATION OF LOSS USING TAGUCHI LOSS FUNCTION
Loss function: $L(y) = 0.11 \times (MSD)$ Also $L(y)$ $= K \times (y - m)^2$

BEFORE EXPERIMENT:
Loss/unit due to deviation from target in current design   = $12.953

AFTER EXPERIMENT:
Loss/unit due to deviation from target will be reduced from $12.953
to   = $7.941

MONTHLY SAVINGS:
If production were maintained at the improved condition, then based on 20000 units/month   = $100246.90

Solution

The complete solution of this problem is shown in Tables 7-4-2 and 7-4-3. In calculating the cost savings, notice that the S/N ratios at the trial condition 1 and the optimum condition, are taken directly from the analysis of the Taguchi experimental results. (Solutions used software of Ref. 11.)

EXERCISES

7-1. The manufacturer of a 10.5 volt smoke alarm battery employed the Taguchi method to determine the better design parameters. The experimenters estimated the signal to noise (S/N) ratio for the proposed design to be 6.3. Based on a sample inspection of the current production process, the S/N ratio was calculated to be 5.2. The analysis of warranty showed that when the battery voltage was beyond (10.50 ± 0.75) volts, the smoke alarm malfunctioned and customers returned the batteries for $6.50 each. Determine the monthly savings the proposed new design is expected to generate if 20,000 units are manufactured each month.

7-2. Suppose that the manufacturer in Problem 7-1 decides not to adopt the new design, but chooses to screen all defective batteries in his manufacturing plant before they are shipped to the customers. The cost for inspection in the plant is estimated to be $3 per battery. If the same amount of warranty cost is incurred in the inspection process, determine the tolerance limits for the inspection.

8

Brainstorming—An Integral Part of the Taguchi Philosophy

8-1 THE NECESSITY OF BRAINSTORMING

Taguchi regards brainstorming as an essential step in the design of effective experiments. Taguchi uses brainstorming to cross organizational barriers. By including representatives of all departments, from design through marketing, the quality demanded by the customer can be considered and those production factors which may contribute towards quality can be identified and incorporated into the design of the experiments.

The benefits of brainstorming are obvious. The design does not belong to any one group, it belongs to all. Brainstorming identifies characteristic effects and the environment known to the group as a whole. Measurement techniques can draw on many disciplines. The outcome is better than would be the case if one department assumed all responsibilities.

Taguchi does not prescribe a standard method of brainstorming as applicable to all situations. The nature and content of the brainstorming session will vary widely on the problem. For most studies a formal brainstorming session is highly effective. In many instances brainstorming can be completed in a few hours. In some instances the session may take a good part of the day.

One method of conducting brainstorming, or what is normally referred to as a workshop for the Taguchi experimental design, is presented in the text. The procedure has been found to be effective by the author, in his experience with various client industries. The procedure is not standard nor is it Taguchi's; it is the author's.

8-2 THE NATURE OF THE SESSION

The following guidelines determine the participants and the content of the brainstorming session:

Purpose of the Brainstorming Session

1. Identify factors, levels, and other pertinent information about the experiment, collectively with all departments and personnel concerned with a successful output from the experiment.
2. Develop team spirit and attitude to assure maximum participation of the team members.
3. Develop a consensus on the selection and the determination of those items which are objective and those which are subjective in nature.

Team Leader

For the successful completion of a Taguchi case study, the appointment of a team leader, from among the project team members, is necessary. The team leader must recognize the need for a brainstorming session and call for such a session. The leader should try to hold the session on neutral ground. The leader should ensure the participation of all departments with responsibilities for the product/process.

Session Advisor

The session should have in attendance someone with a good working knowledge of the Taguchi methodologies. Engineers or statisticians dedicated to helping others apply this tool often make better facilitators. They should offer advice and counsel but not lead the discussion.

Who Should Attend?

All those who have firsthand knowledge and/or a stake in the outcome should be included. For an engineering design or a manufacturing process, both the design and the manufacturing personnel should attend. If cost or supplier knowledge are likely factors, then persons with experience in these matters should be encouraged to attend (group size permitting). Marketing personnel should attend to provide customer viewpoints.

How Many Should Attend?

The more the better. However, the time involved is proportional to the number attending. The upper limit should be 15. It can be as low as 2. No matter the number of people involved, brainstorming will immensely benefit the whole process. A session with 15 people may take the whole day. For up to 8 people, half a day may suffice. More important than size is proper representation from all departments involved in design, development, production, marketing, sales, and service.

What is the Agenda for the Session?
Any brainstorming session, leading to a Taguchi experimental design, may use the topics presented in Section 8-3 for discussions. The emphasis and lenth of the discussion, however, will differ significantly for different problems.

Is Taguchi Training a Prerequisite?
No. Some exposure will help. Application experience on the part of some participants will be a plus. A facilitator with application experience can help the participants with brief overviews when needed.

8-3   TOPICS OF THE DISCUSSIONS

The following topics should be included in the agenda for the brainstorming session.

1. Objective of the Study

  A. What is the characteristic of quality? How can the characteristic be evaluated objectively?
  B. How can the quality characteristic be measured? What are the units of measurement?
  C. What are the criteria (attributes) for evaluation of the quality characteristic?
  D. When there are many criteria or several attributes of the quality characteristic, how can they be combined into a single Overall Evaluation Criterion (OEC)?
  E. How are the different quality criteria weighted?
  F. What is the sense of the quality characteristic? Lower is better, nominal is the best, etc.

2. Design Factors/Variables and Their Levels

  A. What are all the possible factors?
  B. Which ones are more important than others?
  C. How many factors should be included in the study?

   D. What level should be selected for the factors? How many levels?

   E. What is the trade-off between levels and factors?

   F. How urgent are the results? Should the design be aimed at a fast response with only a few factors, or is there time available to investigate more factors?

3. "Noise" Factors

   A. What factors are likely to influence the objective or outcome but can not be controlled in the experiment.

   B. How can the product under study be made insensitive to these noise factors, i.e., how can a robust solution be obtained?

   C. How are these factors included in the study?

4. Interaction Studies

   A. Which are the factors most likely to interact?

   B. How many interactions can be included?

   C. Should an interation be replaced by an additional factor?

   D. Do we need to study the interactions at all?

5. Task Assignments and Description

   A. What steps are to be followed in combining all the quality criteria into an OEC?

   B. What about the factors not included in the study?

   C. How well does the experiment simulate the customer/field applications?

   D. How many repetitions will be necessary, and in what order will the experiments be run?

   E. Who will do what and when? Who will analyze the data?

A brief outline of topics for discussion and their order is shown in Figure 8-1.

8-4 TYPICAL DISCUSSIONS IN THE SESSION

As indicated earlier the guidelines apply to most of the Taguchi application workshops but the specifics drawn will be unique to each situation. To demonstrate a brainstorming session, consider the cake baking process discussed in Chapter 3.

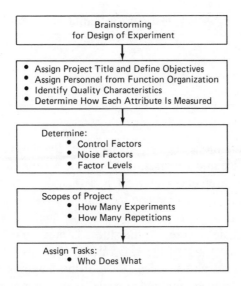

Figure 8-1. Agenda for a brainstorming session.

Suppose there are five participants at a meeting called specifically to discuss and plan a Taguchi experiment to determine the best recipe for the pound cake. The first question that comes up is, what are we after? Of course, everyone will agree that they are after the best cake. Obviously, the taste of the cake will be a criterion. But how can the taste be measured? How many will taste it? For a subjective evaluation like taste, evaluation by more than one person is desired. If more than one individual is involved, how can the net result be evaluated? A possible solution is to rate the cakes in terms of a numerical scale, say, on a scale of 0 to 10. Is 10 for the best taste? This needs to be defined. It can be anything agreed upon. But it is important that the matter be discussed, as this rule will dictate the sense of the quality characteristic. If 10 represents the best and 0 the worst, then the quality characteristic becomes "bigger is better." If five people were to taste the experimental cakes and the ratings vary, whom do we believe? All of them. Record the average of all five evaluations.

Is taste the only parameter to compare two cake samples? If two cakes have the same taste can a second parameter distinguish between them? What about the moistness? One may prefer a moister over a drier cake. How about shape, appearance, or shelf life? Perhaps moistness is somewhat less important than the taste. The idea of the brainstorming is to raise all questions, bring up all the issues, whether important or not. How

Table 8-1. Overall Evaluation Criteria

CRITERIA	VALUE	UNITS	WEIGHTING	MAXIMUM VALUE
Taste	5 (y_1)	none	68 (w_1)	10 (y_{1max})
Moistness	4.5 (y_2)	ounces	32 (w_2)	6 (y_{2max})

would one measure moistness? By appearance? Perhaps one would decide to take a fixed slice and weigh it, and note the weight in ounces. This is an objective measurement. But what is a "standard" slice? One would not necessarily need more than one measurement. Suppose that we agree to consider just these two criteria, i.e., taste and moistness. Taste is subjective on a scale of 0 to 10; moistness is measured in ounces. How sould one make sense out of the two values? How would we compare a cake rated 7 for taste and 4 ounces for moistness with another rated at 8 for taste and 3.5 ounces for moistness? What index can be devised to distinguish between the two samples? How can the data mix of subjective and objective values be combined and analyzed?

Are these criteria to be given equal weight or unequal weight? How important is moistness compared to taste? Is the moistness 1/4 as importnat as the taste? Is an assignment such as taste is 80% and the moistness is 20% reasonably correct? In other words, if one were to split a dollar among all the criteria, in accordance with the priority, how would one distribute the 100 cents? When such a question is asked of different groups, the responses are never the same. One group may feel taste is worth 80%, another group may say 60%. As a general rule, when confronted with subjective areas such as these, let consensus prevail. Let everyone participate. Let everyone offer their input. For each of the items, determine the group average.

Suppose that the consensus of the group has been that the weighting of the two quality criteria should be 68% for taste and 32% for moistness. With this knowledge one can proceed to combine the evaluations and produce a single quantified number (OEC). The evaluation parameters for the problem can be summarized as in Table 8-1.

The Overall Evaluation Criterion (OEC) can be defined as:

$$OEC = (y_1/y_{1max}) \times w_1 + (y_2/y_{2max}) \times w_2 + \ldots$$

$$= (5/10) \times 68/100 + (4.5/6) \times 32/100$$

$$= 0.34 + 0.24$$
$$= 0.58$$

where w_i = Weight of ith component
        y_i = Measurement of ith criterion
        y_{imax} = Maximum value of ith criterion

Observe that the evaluation (y) in each case is divided by the maximum value. This is done to get rid of its units (normalization). When multiplied by the weighting, a dimensionless number, the resulting values for each criterion are added to produce a net result in numerical dimensionless terms.

Suppose that an L_8 array is used to describe the eight trial conditions for the experiment. The eight cakes will have to be evaluated following the scheme given above. The OEC calculated above (OEC = 0.58) will represent the result for one trial. There will be seven other results like this. The eight values (OECs) will then form the result column in the OA. The process will have to be repeated if there were repetitions in each trial condition.

Discussions of factors and levels follow that of quality characteristics. The nature of these issues are based on common sense and some understanding of the problem under investigation. A leader or facilitator will often find it convenient to let their experience determine the flow of the discussions. The remaining portion of the brainstorming session is left up to the reader's imagination.

EXERCISES

8-1. In an experiment involving the study of an automobile door design, two criteria were used for evaluation purposes. Deflection at a fixed point in the door was measured to indicate the stiffness, and the door closing effort was subjectively recorded on a scale of 0 to 10.
   a. Develop a scheme to define an overall evaluation criterion.
   b. Explain why the overall evaluation may be useful.
8-2. During the brainstorming session for a Taguchi experiment, a large number of factors were initially identified. Discuss the type of information you need to consider to determine the number of factors for the experiment, and state how you will proceed to select these factors.

8-3. A group of manufacturing engineers identified the following process parameters for an experimental investigation:

- Fourteen 2 level factors (not all are considered important)
- One interaction between two factors (considered important)
- Three noise factors at two levels each (considered important)

If the total number of trial runs (samples) is not to exceed 32, design the experiment and indicate the sizes of the inner and outer arrays.

9

Examples of Taguchi Case Studies

9-1 APPLICATION BENCHMARKS

Experiments designed and carried out according to the Taguchi methodology, are generally referred to as case studies. Perhaps they are called case studies to indicate that they are well planned experiments and not simply a few tests to investigate the effects of varying one or more factors at a time. The term case study may also be used to signify that such planned experiments have been fruitfully carried out, that the results have been analyzed to determine the optimum combination of the factors under study, and that tests to confirm the optimum conditions have been conducted. But what does a case study look like? What are the steps to be followed in completing a case study?

In Chapters 5 and 6, the mechanics of the Taguchi design of experiments and the procedure for the analysis of the experimental data were discussed in detail. Those chapters included several application examples (case studies). The examples in this chapter are representative of practical problems the author has encountered during his associations with various industries and clients.

A typical application of the method will include the following five major steps (see also Figure B-1):

1. A brainstorming session
2. The designing of the experiment
3. The conducting of the experiments
4. Analyzing the results
5. The running of the confirmation test

Brainstorming for Taguchi experiments, is described in Chapter 8. It is an essential element of a Taguchi case study. When this step is completed, the planning is done. Each of the experimental situations may demand a unique quality objective. What are the attributes of the quality characteristics? In what manner should the results be monitored? How many factors should be included in the study? These and many other pertinent questions are answered in the brainstorming session. Brainstorming was discussed in detail in Chapter 8. In this chapter, the remaining four steps of the Taguchi methodology will be clarified by the following examples. In the solutions of these examples, extensive use is made of the software of Reference 11, which computes results following procedures described in Chapters 5 and 6.

9-2 APPLICATION EXAMPLES INCLUDING DESIGN AND ANALYSIS

Example 9-1
Engine Valve-Train Noise Study

An experiment is to be designed to study the influence of six factors, which were identified during brainstorming as influencing the noise emitted by the valve-train of a newly developed engine. Each factor is assigned two levels. The brainstorming session concluded that interaction effects were much less important than the main effects.

Solution
Since there are six 2 level factors, the smallest array is L_8. Since interactions are insignificant, the six factors can be assigned to the six of the seven columns in any order desired. The factors involved and their levels are shown in Table 9-1(a).

Assume that during the brainstorming session, the quality characteristics and the methods of measurement were also determined, in addition to the factors and levels. Based on these criteria certain key elements of the test plan are described in Table 9-1(a), using the principles of the design of experiment. These are shown under the headings. "Note", "Objective" and "Characteristic". For this experiment, the level of the noise was to be measured in terms of some noise index on a scale of 0 to 100. The index was so defined that its smaller value was always desirable.

The L_8 array is shown in Table 9-1(b). Note that only six columns define the test condition with the zeros in the unused column (column 7) showing that no condition is implied. The 2 level array L_8, describes

Table 9-1. Engine Valve-Train Noise Study (Design)

(a) Design Factors and Their Levels

COLUMN	FACTORS	LEVEL 1	LEVEL 2	LEVEL 3	LEVEL 4
1	Valve guide clearance	Low	High		
2	Upper guide length	Smaller	Larger		
3	Valve geometry	Type 1	Type 2		
4	Seat concentricity	Quality 1	Quality 2		
5	Lower guide length	Location 1	Location 2		
6	Valve face runout	Run out type 1	Run out type 2		
7	(Unused)				

Note: Six variables all at two levels studied.
Objective: Determine design configuration for least noise.
Characteristic: Smaller the better (measured in terms of noise index).

(b) The Experiment Uses the Following Array

TRIAL/COLUMN	1	2	3	4	5	6	7
Trial 1	1	1	1	1	1	1	0
Trial 2	1	1	1	2	2	2	0
Trial 3	1	2	2	1	1	2	0
Trial 4	1	2	2	2	2	1	0
Trial 5	2	1	2	1	2	1	0
Trial 6	2	1	2	2	1	2	0
Trial 7	2	2	1	1	2	2	0
Trial 8	2	2	1	2	1	1	0

eight trial conditions. The design may be created manually, but a computer program will perform such computations in a matter of seconds and without mathematical errors.

The results of the eight trial conditions, with one run per trial condition, are shown in Table 9-1-1(a). Examples in this chapter utilized the software of Reference 11 which displays up to 6 repetitions and their averages. These observed results are used to compute the main effects of the individual factors (Table 9-1-1(b)). Since the factors have only two levels, the main effects are shown under the two columns marked Level 1 and Level 2. The third column labeled ($L2-L1$) contains the difference between the main effects at Level 1 and Level 2. A minus sign (in the difference column) indicates a decrease in noise as the factor changes from Level 1 to Level 2. A positive value, on the other hand, indicates an increase

Table 9-1-1. Original Data and Their Averages (Results and Analysis)

(a) Original Observations and Their Averages

Quality Characteristic: Smaller is Better
Results: (Up to 6 Repetitions Shown)

TRIAL/ REPETITIONS	R_1	R_2	R_3	R_4	R_5	R_6	AVERAGE
1	45.00						45.00
2	34.00						34.00
3	56.00						56.00
4	45.00						45.00
5	46.00						46.00
6	34.00						34.00
7	39.00						39.00
8	43.00						43.00

(b) The Main Effects

COLUMN	FACTOR NAME	LEVEL 1	LEVEL 2	$(L_2 - L_1)$	LEVEL 3	LEVEL 4
1	Value guide clearance	45.00	40.50	−4.50	00.00	00.00
2	Upper guide length	39.75	45.75	6.00	00.00	00.00
3	Valve geometry	40.25	45.25	5.00	00.00	00.00
4	Seat concentricity	46.50	39.00	−7.50	00.00	00.00
5	Lower valve length	44.50	41.00	−3.50	00.00	00.00
6	Valve face run	44.75	40.75	−4.00	00.00	00.00

(c) ANOVA Table

COLUMN	FACTORS	DOF	SUM OF SQUARES	VARIANCE	F	PERCENT
1	Valve guide	(1)	(40.50)	Pooled		
2	Upper guide	1	72.00	72.00	2.011	9.96
3	Valve geometry	(1)	(50.00)	Pooled		
4	Seat concentricity	1	112.50	112.50	3.142	21.10
5	Lower guide	(1)	(24.50)	Pooled		
6	Valve face	(1)	(32.00)	Pooled		
All others/error		5	179.00	35.80		68.94
Total:		7	363.50			100.00

Note: Insignificant factorial effects are pooled as shown ( ).

in noise. A quick inspection of the difference column permits selection of the optimum combination, for example, the "smaller is better" characteristic. A negative sign in the column ($L2$-$L1$) indicates Level 2 of the factor is desirable while a positive value indicates Level 1 is the choice. This quick inspection is a sufficient test only when two levels are involved and all factors are considered significant.

If the desired characteristic was "bigger is better" then the level se-

Table 9-1-2. Engine Valve-Train Noise Study (Optimum and Confidence Interval)

(a) Estimate of the Optimum Condition of Design/Process: For Smaller the Better Characteristics

FACTOR DESCRIPTION	LEVEL DESCRIPTION	LEVEL	CONTRIBUTION
Upper guide length	Smaller	1	− 3.0000
Seat concentricity	Quality 2	2	− 3.7500
Contribution from all factors (total)			− 6.75
Current grand average of performance			42.75
Expected result at optimum condition			36.00

This estimate includes only those variables that have a significant contribution, i.e., pooled variables are excluded from the estimate. Estimates may also be made with variables of choice.

(b) Confidence Interval

Computing F function for 1 and 5 at 90% confidence level.
Confidence Interval (C.I.) is expressed as:

$$\text{C.I.} = \sqrt{\frac{F(1, n_2)V_e}{N_e}}$$

Where $F(n_1, n_2)$ = Computed value of F with $n_1 = 1$, n_2 = error DOF at a desired confidence level
   V_e = Error variance
   N_e = Effective number of replications

Based on: $F = 3.2999999$ $n_1 = 1$, $n_2 = 5$ $V_e = 35.8$ $N_e = 2.6667$

The confidence interval C.I. = ± 6.656011, which is the variation of the estimated result at the optimum condition, i.e., the mean of the result, m lies between (m + C.I.) and (m − C.I.) at 89.93% confidence level.

lection criteria will be the reverse of the scheme given above, positive values indicate Level 2, and all negative values will indicate choice of Level 1 for the optimum condition. In this example with all factors, the optimum condition for "smaller is better" is levels 2, 1, 1, 2, 2, and 2 for factors in columns 1 through 6 respectively. The sign ($\pm$) directs the selection of levels, while the magnitude suggests the strength of the influence of the factor. The quantitive measure of the influence of individual factors is obtained from ANOVA (Table 9-1-1(c)).

ANOVA follows procedures outlined in Chapter 6. No new data or decisions on the part of the experimenter are required. This is an ideal situation for standard computer routines. The results of ANOVA are shown in Table 9-1-1(c). A review of the percent column shows that Upper Guide (9.96%) and Seat Concentricity (21.10%) are significant. The other insignificant factors are pooled (combined) with the error term. Based on information from the ANOVA Table 9-1-1(c), the mean performance at optimum condition and the confidence interval are calculated as shown in Table 9-1-2(a) and Table 9-1-2(b), respectively.

The last step in the analysis is to estimate the performance at the optimum condition. Normally, only the significant factors are used to make this estimate. An examination of main effects indicates which levels will be included in the optimum condition. In addition, ANOVA indicates (by the percentage column in Table 9-1-1(c)) the relative influence of each factor. Thus all the necessary information for the determination of the optimum condition and the expected value of the response at this condition is available. No new information is necessary to calculate the performance at the optimum condition.

Example 9-2
Study of Crankshaft Surface Finishing Process

Recently, an engine was found to have an unusually high rate of crankshaft bearing failures. Engineers identified the crankshaft surface finishing as the root cause. A brainstorming session, with the engineers and the technicians involved in design and manufacturing activities, resulted in the selection of six factors which were considered to have a major influence on the quality of the surface finish. The Taguchi approach of experimental design was considered an effective way to optimize the process.

The brainstorming also identified two levels for each factor and a likely interaction between two of the factors. The group decided that the quality characteristic of the surface finish should be measured in terms of durability (life) under simulated laboratory tests.

Solution

With six factors and one interaction involved in this study, L_8 is suitable for the experimental design. The first step is to decide where to assign the interacting factors and which column to reserve for their interaction. The table of interaction (Table A-6) for 2 level orthogonal arrays shows that columns 1, 2, 3 form an interacting group. The two interacting factors

Table 9-2-1. Study of Crankshaft Surface-Finishing Process (Design)

(a) Design Factors and Their Levels

COLUMNS	FACTORS	LEVEL 1	LEVEL 2	LEVEL 3	LEVEL 4
1	Roundness (lobing)	700	1600		
2	Lay direction (cross)	Least	Most		
3	Interaction	N/A			
4	T_p (process index)	65%	90%		
5	Taper	.00025	.0005		
6	Wavines	Lower limit	Upper limit		
7	Shape factor	.0003	.0003		

Note: Interaction between roundness and lay direction.
Objective: Determine best grinding parameters.
Characteristic: Bigger the better (bearing durability life).

(b) Orthogonal Array Used for the Experiment

TRIAL/COLUMN	1	2	3	4	5	6	7
Trial 1	1	1	1	1	1	1	1
Trial 2	1	1	1	2	2	2	2
Trial 3	1	2	2	1	1	2	2
Trial 4	1	2	2	2	2	1	1
Trial 5	2	1	2	1	2	1	2
Trial 6	2	1	2	2	1	2	1
Trial 7	2	2	1	1	2	2	1
Trial 8	2	2	1	2	1	1	2

Table 9-2-2. Crankshaft Surface-Finishing Process
(Main Effect and ANOVA)

(a) Original Observations and Their Averages
  Quality Characteristic: Bigger is Better.
  Results: (Up to 6 Repetitions Shown)

TRIAL/ REPETITIONS	R_1	R_2	R_3	R_4	R_5	R_6	AVERAGE
1	34.00						34.00
2	56.00						56.00
3	45.00						45.00
4	35.00						35.00
5	46.00						46.00
6	53.00						53.00
7	43.00						43.00
8	41.00						41.00

(b) The Main Effects

COLUMN	FACTORS	LEVEL 1	LEVEL 2	$(L_2 - L_1)$	LEVEL 3	LEVEL 4
1	Roundness (lobing)	42.50	45.75	3.25	00.00	00.00
2	Lay direction	47.25	41.00	−6.25	00.00	00.00
3	Interaction	43.55	44.75	1.25	00.00	00.00
4	T_p (process index)	42.00	46.25	4.25	00.00	00.00
5	Taper	43.25	45.00	1.75	00.00	00.00
6	Waviness	39.00	49.25	10.25	00.00	00.00
7	Shape factor	41.25	47.00	5.75	00.00	00.00

(c) ANOVA Table

COLUMN	FACTORS	DOF	SUM OF SQUARES	VARIANCE	F	PERCENT
1	Roundedness	1	21.13	21.13		5.02
2	Lay direction	1	78.13	78.13		18.56
3	Interaction	1	3.13	3.13		0.74
4	T_p (process index)	1	36.13	36.13		8.58
5	Taper	1	6.13	6.13		1.46
6	Waviness	1	210.13	210.13		49.93
7	Shape factor	1	66.13	66.13		15.71
All others/error		0				
Total:		7	420.91			100.00

Table 9-2-3. Crankshaft Surface-Finishing Process
(Pooled ANOVA and Optimum)

(c) ANOVA Table

COLUMN	FACTORS	DOF	SUM OF SQUARES	VARIANCE	F	PERCENT
1	Roundedness	1	21.13	21.13	4.57	3.92
2	Lay direction	1	78.13	78.13	16.89	17.46
3	Interaction	(1)	(3.13)	Pooled		
4	T_p (process index)	1	36.13	36.13	7.81	7.48
5	Taper	(1)	(6.13)	Pooled		
6	Waviness	1	210.13	210.13	45.43	48.83
7	Shape factor	1	66.13	66.13	14.30	14.61
All others/error		2	9.25	4.63		7.69
Total:		7	420.91			100.00

Note: Insignificant factorial effects are pooled as shown ( ).

(b) Estimate of the Optimum Condition of Design/Process: For Bigger the Better
Characteristics

FACTOR DESCRIPTION	LEVEL DESCRIPTION	LEVEL	CONTRIBUTION
Roundness (lobing)	1600	2	1.6250
Lay direction (crosshatch)	Least	1	3.1250
T_p (process index)	90%	2	2.1250
Waviness	Upper limit	2	5.1250
Shape factor	.0003	2	2.8750
Contribution from all factors (total)			14.875
Current grand average of performance			44.125
Expected result at optimum condition			59.00

This estimate includes only those variables that have a significant contribution, i.e., pooled variables are excluded from the estimate. Estimates may also be made with variables of choice.

are therefore assigned to columns 1 and 2. Column 3 is kept aside for their interaction. The remaining four factors are then assigned to any of four remaining columns. The completed design, with descriptions of factors, their levels and the orthogonal array are shown in Table 9-2-1(a&b). Eight crankshafts were fabricated to the specifications described by the eight trial conditions. Each sample was tested for durability (life).

Since longer life was desirable, the quality characteristic applicable in this case was "bigger is better."

The observed durability, the main effects and the unpooled ANOVA are shown in Table 9-2-2. The study of the main effects indicates some interaction between the factors. This is shown by the magnitude 1.25 in the column labeled (L_2-L_1) in Table 9-2-2(b). This value is of the same order of magnitude as the values 3.25, -6.25, 4.25, etc. But is the interaction significant? The answer to this question can be obtained from the percentage column of the ANOVA table (Table 9-2-2(c)). The interaction under column 3 is only 0.74%. Contributions below 5 percent are generally not considered significant. The interaction and the factor in column 5 which has 1.46 in the percentage column, are pooled. The pooled ANOVA is shown in Table 9-2-3(a). Observe that upon pooling the percentage values the significant factors are adjusted slightly.

In estimating the performance at the optimum, only the significant factors are used. As shown in Table 9-2-3(b), the expected improvement in performance is 14.875 over the current average of performances (44.125). Since the interaction (Table 9-2-3(b)) has little significance, it is not considered in the selection of levels for the optimum condition.

Example 9-3
Automobile Generator Noise Study

Engineers identified one 4 level factor and four 2 level factors for experimental investigation to reduce the operating noise of a newly released generator. Taguchi methodologies were followed to lay out the experiments and analyze the test results.

Solution
The factors in this example present a mixed level situation. Although, experiment design is simplified if all factors have the same level, it is not always possible to compromise the factor level. For instance, if a factor influence is believed to be nonlinear, it should be assigned three or more levels. The factor and its influence are assumed to be continuous functions. If however, the factor assumes discrete levels such as design type 1, design type 2, etc., then the influence is a discrete function and each discrete step (level) must be incorporated in the design. The 4 level factor in the example, is discrete. Since the 4 level factor has 3 DOF,

and four 2 level factors each have 1 DOF, the total DOF for the experiment is 7. L_8 with seven 2 level columns and 7 DOF was selected for the design. The first step provides for the 4 level factor. Columns 1, 2, and 3 of L_8 are used to prepare a 4 level column. This new 4 level column now replaces column 1 and is assigned to the 4 level factor. As columns 2 and 3 were used to prepare column 1 as a 4 level column, they cannot be used for any other factor. Thus the four 2 level factors are assigned to the remaining columns 4, 5, 6, and 7. The design and the modified OA are shown in Tables 9-3-1(a) and (b).

One run at each trial condition was tested in the laboratory and the performance was measured in terms of a noise index. The index ranged between 0 (low noise) and 100 (loud noise). The lower value of this index was desirable. The data and calculated main effects are shown in

Table 9-3-1. Automobile Generator Noise (Design)

(a) Design Factors and Their Levels

COLUMNS	FACTORS	LEVEL 1	LEVEL 2	LEVEL 3	LEVEL 4
1	Casement structure	Present	Textured		
2	(Unused)				
3	(Unused)				
4	Air gap	Present	Increase		
5	Impregnation	Present type	Harder type		
6	Contact brush	Type 1	Type 2		
7	Stator structure	Present design	Epoxy coated		

Note: One 4 level and four 2 level factors are studied.
Objective: Determine generator design parameters for least noise.
Characteristic: Smaller is better (measured in predefined index).

(b) An L_8 Orthogonal Array Used in the Experiment

TRIAL/COLUMN	1	2	3	4	5	6	7
Trial 1	1	0	0	1	1	1	1
Trial 2	1	0	0	2	2	2	2
Trial 3	2	0	0	1	1	2	2
Trial 4	2	0	0	2	2	1	1
Trial 5	3	0	0	1	2	1	2
Trial 6	3	0	0	2	1	2	1
Trial 7	4	0	0	1	2	2	1
Trial 8	4	0	0	2	1	1	2

Table 9-3-2. Automobile Generator Noise (Main Effects)

(a) Original Observations and Their Averages
Quality Characteristic: Smaller is Better.
Results: (Up to 6 Repetitions Shown)

TRIAL/ REPETITIONS	R_1	R_2	R_3	R_4	R_5	R_6	AVERAGE
1	50.00						50.00
2	62.00						62.00
3	70.00						70.00
4	75.00						75.00
5	68.00						68.00
6	65.00						65.00
7	65.00						65.00
8	74.00						74.00

(b) Main Effects

COLUMN	FACTORS	LEVEL 1	LEVEL 2	$(L_2 - L_1)$	LEVEL 3	LEVEL 4
1	Casement structure	56.00	72.50	16.50	66.50	69.50
4	Air gap	63.25	69.00	5.75	00.00	00.00
5	Impregnation	64.75	67.50	2.75	00.00	00.00
6	Contact brush	66.75	65.50	−1.25	00.00	00.00
7	Stator structure	63.75	68.50	4.75	00.00	00.00

Tables 9-3-2(a) and (b), respectively. Note that the 4 level factor in column 1 (Casement Structure) has its main effects at the four levels. This factor has 3 DOF as noted in the ANOVA table (Table 9-3-3(a)) under the column marked DOF.

From the ANOVA table it is clear that the factor assigned to column 6 (Contact Brushes) has the smallest sum of squares and hence the least influence. This factor is pooled and the new ANOVA is shown in Table 9-3-3(a). Using the significant contributors, the estimated performance at the optimum condition was calculated to be 49.375. In this case the optimum condition is trial 1 (Levels 1 1 1 1 1). The result for trial 1 was 50 (Table 9-3-2(a)). The difference between the trial result and the estimated optimum performance (49.375) resulted from the dropping of the minor effect of the contact brush factor from the estimate.

Table 9-3-3. Automobile Generator Noise (ANOVA and Optimum)

(a) ANOVA Table

COLUMN	FACTORS	DOF	SUM OF SQUARES	VARIANCE	F	PERCENT
1	Casement structure	3	309.38	103.13	33.00	70.49
4	Air gap	1	66.13	66.13	21.16	15.07
5	Impregnation	1	15.13	15.13	4.84	3.45
6	Contact brushes	(1)	(3.13)	Pooled		
7	Stator structure	1	45.13	45.13	14.44	9.57
All others/error		1	3.13	3.12		4.98
Total:		7	438.88			100.00

Note: Insignificant factorial effects are pooled as shown ( ).

(b) Estimate of the Optimum Condition of Design/Process: For Smaller the Better
   Characteristic

FACTOR DESCRIPTION	LEVEL DESCRIPTION	LEVEL	CONTRIBUTION
Casement structure	Present design	1	− 10.1250
Air gap	Present gap	1	− 2.8750
Impregnation	Present type	1	− 1.3750
Stator structure	Present design	1	− 2.3750
Contribution from all factors (total)			− 16.750
Current grand average of performance			66.125
Expected result at optimum condition			49.375

This estimate includes only those variables that have significant contributions, i.e., pooled variables are excluded
from the estimate. Estimates may also be made with variables of choice.

Example 9-4
Engine Idle Stability Study

An engine development engineer identified three adjustment parameters
controlling the idle performance of an engine. Each of the factors is to
be studied at three levels to determine the best setting for the engine. A
Taguchi experiment design is to be utilized.

Solution

The smallest three level OA, L_9, has four 3 level columns. With three 3
level factors in this study, the L_9 is appropriate for the design. The factors
are placed in the first three columns, leaving the fourth column unused.

Table 9-4-1. Engine Idle Stability Study (Design)

(a) Design Factors and Their Levels

COLUMNS	FACTORS	LEVEL 1	LEVEL 2	LEVEL 3	LEVEL 4
1	Indexing	-5 Deg	0 Deg	$+5$ Deg	
2	Overlap area	0%	30%	60%	
3	Spark advance	25 Deg	30 Deg	35 Deg	
4	(Unused)				

Note: Three 3 level factors studied.
Objective: Determine best engine setting.
Characteristic: Smaller is better (Speed deviation).

(b) The Experiment Used an L_9 Orthogonal Array

TRIAL/COLUMN	1	2	3	4
Trial 1	1	1	1	0
Trial 2	1	2	2	0
Trial 3	1	3	3	0
Trial 4	2	1	3	0
Trial 5	2	2	1	0
Trial 6	2	3	2	0
Trial 7	3	1	2	0
Trial 8	3	2	3	0
Trial 9	3	3	1	0

The factors, their levels, and the modified OA are shown in Tables 9-4-1(a) and (b).

The performance of the engine tested under various trial conditions was measured in terms of the deviation of the speed from a nominal idle speed. A smaller deviation represented a more stable condition. Three separate observations were recorded for each trial condition as shown in Table 9-4-2(a). The signal to noise ratio (S/N) was used for the analysis of the results. The main effects, optimum condition, and ANOVA table are shown in Tables 9-4-2 and 9-4-3. Based on the error DOF and variance, the confidence interval of the estimated performance at optimum is also computed as shown in Table 9-4-3(b). The confidence interval (C.I.) value of $\pm.3341$ will mean that the estimated optimum performance (S/N ratio) will be $-25.878 \pm .3341$ at 90% confidence level (89.77% as a result of numerical solution by the computer software of Reference 11).

Table 9-4-2. Engine Idle Stability Studies (Main Effect and ANOVA)

(a) Original Observations and Their S/N Ratios
   Quality Characteristic: Smaller is Better.
   Results: (Up to 6 Repetitions Shown)

TRIAL/ REPETITIONS	P R_1	h R_2	c R_3	R_4	R_5	R_6	S/N
1	20.00	25.00	26.00				-27.54
2	34.00	36.00	26.00				-30.19
3	45.00	34.00	26.00				-31.10
4	13.00	23.00	22.00				-25.96
5	36.00	45.00	35.00				-31.81
6	23.00	25.00	34.00				-28.87
7	35.00	45.00	53.00				-33.06
8	56.00	46.00	75.00				-35.60
9	35.00	46.00	53.00				-33.12

(b) The Main Effects

COLUMN	FACTORS	LEVEL 1	LEVEL 2	$(L_2 - L_1)$	LEVEL 3	LEVEL 4
1	Indexing	-29.61	-28.88	0.73	-33.93	00.00
2	Overlap	-28.85	-32.53	-3.69	-31.03	00.00
3	Spark advance	-30.67	-29.76	0.91	-31.99	00.00

(c) ANOVA Table

COLUMN	FACTORS	DOF	SUM OF SQUARES	VARIANCE	F	PERCENT
1	Indexing	2	44.636	22.318	932.80	61.26
2	Overlap	2	20.541	10.271	429.27	28.15
3	Spark direction	2	7.565	3.783	158.10	10.33
All others/error		2	0.05	0.02		0.26
Total:		8	72.79			100.00

Example 9-5
Instrument Panel Structure Design Optimization

A group of analytical engineers undertaking the design of an instrument panel structure, are to study the influence of five critical structural modifications on the system. A finite element model of the total structure was available for a static stiffness analysis. The objective is

Table 9-4-3. Engine Idle Stability Studies
(Optimum and Confidence Interval)

(a) Estimate of the Optimum Condition of Design/Process: For Smaller the Better
Characteristic

FACTOR DESCRIPTION	LEVEL DESCRIPTION	LEVEL	CONTRIBUTION
Indexing	0 Deg	2	1.9256
Overlap	0%	1	1.9522
Spark direction	30 Deg	2	1.0489
Contribution from all factors (total)			4.92667
Current grand average of performance			− 30.80556
Expected result at optimum condition			− 25.87889

(b) Confidence Interval

Computing F function for 1 and 2 at 90% confidence level.
Confidence Interval (C.I.) is expressed as:

$$\text{C.I.} = \sqrt{\frac{F(1, n_2)V_e}{N_e}}$$

Where $F(n_1, n_2)$ = Computed value of F with $n_1 = 1$, n_2 = error DOF
at a desired confidence level
V_e = Error variance
V_e = Effective number of replications

Based on: $F = 5.999996$ $n_1 = 1$, $n_2 = 2$ $V_e = 2.392578E{-}2$
$N_e = 1.285714$

The confidence interval C.I. = ± 0.3341461

This is the variation of the estimated result at the optimum condition, i.e., the mean of
the result, m lies between $(m + \text{C.I.})$ and $(m - \text{C.I.})$ at 89.77% confidence level.

to determine the best combination of design alternatives. To reduce the
number of computer runs, a Taguchi experiment design was selected
to determine the number and conditions of the computer runs necessary
if each factor is to be studied at 2 levels. Two interactions are believed
to be important.

Solution

This investigation is an analytical simulation rather than a hardware experiment. The factors and levels shown in Table 9-5-1(a) are used in an L_9 OA to set up the simulation. Only one run per trial condition is necessary since the computer results should not change with repetition. The observation (stiffness values), the main effects and the optimum condition are shown in Tables 9-5-1(b), 9-5-2(a), and 9-5-2(b).

Table 9-5-1. Instrument Panel Structure Optimization (Design and Data)

(a) Design Factors and Their Levels

COLUMN	FACTORS	LEVEL 1	LEVEL 2	LEVEL 3	LEVEL 4
1	Front dash beam	Solid	Hollow		
2	Under structure	With	Without		
3	Interaction 1 × 2	N/A			
4	Forward panel	Current	New design		
5	Interaction 1 × 4	N/A			
6	Plenum structure	Steel	Plastic		
7	Surface structure	Baseline	New		

Note: Interactions 1 × 2 and 1 × 4 studied.
Objective: Determine structural parameters for maximum strength.
Characteristic: Bigger the better (measured in terms of stiffness).

(b) Original Observations and Their Averages
   Quality Characteristic: Bigger is Better.
   Results: (Up to 6 Repetitions Shown)

TRIAL/ REPETITIONS	R_1	R_2	R_3	R_4	R_5	R_6	AVERAGE
1	13.50						13.50
2	14.00						14.00
3	14.30						14.30
4	13.10						13.10
5	22.00						22.00
6	18.00						18.00
7	29.90						29.90
8	16.00						16.00

Table 9-5-2. Instrument Panel Structure Optimization
(Main Effect and Optimum)

(a) The Main Effects

COLUMN	FACTORS	LEVEL 1	LEVEL 2	$(L_2 - L_1)$	LEVEL 3	LEVEL 4
1	Front dash beam	13.73	21.48	7.75	00.00	00.00
2	Under structure	16.88	18.33	1.45	00.00	00.00
3	Interaction 1 × 2	18.35	16.85	−1.50	00.00	00.00
4	Forward panel	19.92	15.28	−4.65	00.00	00.00
5	Interaction 1 × 4	15.45	19.75	4.30	00.00	00.00
6	Plenum structure	16.15	19.05	2.89	00.00	00.00
7	Surface structure	18.63	16.58	−2.05	00.00	00.00

(b) Estimate of the Optimum Condition of Design/Process: For Bigger the Better
   Characteristic

FACTOR DESCRIPTION	LEVEL DESCRIPTION	LEVEL	CONTRIBUTION
Front dash beam	Hollow	2	3.8750
Forward panel	Current design	1	2.3250
Plenum structure	Plastic	2	1.4500
Contribution from all factors (total)			7.64999
Current grand average of performance			17.64000
Expected result at optimum condition			25.25000

This estimate includes only those variables that make a significant contribution, i.e., pooled variables are excluded
from the estimate. Estimates may also be made with variables of choice.

Example 9-6
Study Leading to the Selection of the
Worst Case Barrier Test Vehicle

   To assure that the design of a new vehicle complies with all the applicable Federal Motor Vehicle Safety Standards (FMVSS) requirements,
engineers involved in the crashworthiness development of a new vehicle
design, want to determine the worst combination of vehicle body style
and options. This vehicle is to be used as the test specimen for laboratory
validation tests instead of subjecting several prototype vehicles with all
available options and body styles to tests under all compliance conditions.
Four 2 level factors and one 4 level factor were considered to have major

Table 9-6-1. Selection of Worst Case Barrier Vehicle (Design)

(a) Study Leading to Selection of Worst Case Barrier Vehicle Design Factors and
Their Levels

COLUMNS	FACTORS	LEVEL 1	LEVEL 2	LEVEL 3	LEVEL 4
1	Test type	0 Deg-F	30 Deg-R	30 Deg-L	NCAP
2	(Unused)				
3	(Unused)				
4	Type of vehicle	Style 1	Style 2		
5	Power train	Light duty	Heavy duty		
6	Roof structure	Hard top	Sun-roof		
7	Seat structure	Standard	Reinforced		

Note: One 4 level and four 2 level factors studied.
Objective: Determine the worst vehicle/option combination.
Characteristic: Smaller is better (one or more injury criteria).

(b) The Experiment Used an L_8 Orthogonal Array

TRIAL/COLUMN	1	2	3	4	5	6	7
Trial 1	1	0	0	1	1	1	1
Trial 2	1	0	0	2	2	2	2
Trial 3	2	0	0	1	1	2	2
Trial 4	2	0	0	2	2	1	1
Trial 5	3	0	0	1	2	1	2
Trial 6	3	0	0	2	1	2	1
Trial 7	4	0	0	1	2	2	1
Trial 8	4	0	0	2	1	1	2

influence on the performance. A Taguchi experimental design approach
was followed.

Solution

The design involved modifying a 2 level column of an L_8 into a 4 level
one. The process is similar to that described in Example 7-3. The factors,
their levels, and the modified OA are shown in Tables 9-6-1(a) and (b).
The description of the trial conditions derived from the designed experiment served as the specifications for the test vehicle. For barrier tests,
the specimens are prototype vehicles built either in the production line,
or hand made, one of a kind, test vehicles. In either case the cost for

Table 9-6-2. Selection of Worst Case Barrier Vehicle
(Main Effect and ANOVA)

(a) Original Observations and Their Averages
Quality Characteristic: Smaller is Better.
Results: (Up to 6 Repetitions Shown)

TRIAL/ REPETITIONS	R_1	R_2	R_3	R_4	R_5	R_6	AVERAGE
1	45.00						45.00
2	65.00						65.00
3	38.00						38.00
4	48.00						48.00
5	59.00						59.00
6	32.00						32.00
7	36.00						36.00
8	38.00						38.00

(b) The Main Effects

COLUMN	FACTORS	LEVEL 1	LEVEL 2	$(L_2 - L_1)$	LEVEL 3	LEVEL 4
1	Test type	55.00	43.00	−12.00	00.00	00.00
2	Type of vehicle	44.50	45.75	1.25	00.00	00.00
5	Powertrain	38.25	52.00	−13.75	00.00	00.00
6	Roof structure	47.50	42.75	−4.75	00.00	00.00
7	Seat structure	40.25	50.00	9.75	00.00	00.00

(c) ANOVA Table

COLUMN	FACTORS	DOF	SUM OF SQUARES	VARIANCE	F	PERCENT
1	Test type	3	336.38	336.38	4.648	27.71
4	Type of vehicle	(1)	(3.13)	Pooled		
5	Powertrain	1	378.13	378.13	15.674	37.15
6	Roof structure	(1)	(45.13)	Pooled		
7	Seat structure	1	190.13	190.13	7.881	17.42
All others/error		2	48.25	24.13		17.72
Total:		7	952.88			100.00

Table 9-6-3. Selection of Worst Case Barrier Vehicle
(Optimum and Confidence Interval)

(a) Estimate of the Optimum Condition of Design/Process: For Smaller the Better
Characteristic

FACTOR DESCRIPTION	LEVEL DESCRIPTION	LEVEL	CONTRIBUTION
Test type	NCAP	4	-8.1250
Powertrain	Light duty	1	-6.8750
Seat structure	Standard	1	-4.8750
Contribution from all factors (total)			-19.8750
Current grand average of performance			45.1250
Expected result at optimum condition			25.2500

This estimate includes only those variables that make a significant contribution, i.e., pooled variables are excluded
from the estimate. Estimates may also be made with variables of choice.

(b) Confidence Interval

Computing F function for 1 and 2 at 90% confidence level.
Confidence Interval (C.I.) is expressed as:

$$C.I. = \sqrt{\frac{F(1, n_2)V_e}{N_e}}$$

Where $F(n_1, n_2)$ = Computed value of F with $n_1 = 1$, n_2 = error DOF
at a desired confidence level
V_e = Error variance
N_e = Effective number of replications

Based on: $F = 5.999996$ $n_1 = 1$, $n_2 = 2$ $V_e = 24.125$ $N_e = 1.333333$

The confidence interval C.I. $\cong \pm 10.4$

preparing the test vehicles could easily run in the hundreds of thousands
of dollars. Proper specification, in a timely manner, is crucial to the cost
effectiveness of the total vehicle development program. For the purposes
of the tests, eight vehicles were built in the production line following the
specifications which correspond to the eight trial conditions. These vehicles were barrier tested and the results recorded in terms of a predefined
occupant injury index. The results and the analyses are shown in Tables
9-6-2 and 9-6-3. By using eight test vehicles, the engineers were able to

Table 9-7-1. Air Bag Design Study (Design)

(a) Design Factors and Their Levels

COLUMN	FACTOR NAME	LEVEL 1	LEVEL 2	LEVEL 3	LEVEL 4
1	(Unused)				
2	Steering column rotation	Rot 1	Rot 2	Rot 3	Rot 4
3	Steering column crash stiffness	300	350	400	500
4	Knee bolster stiffness	S1	S2	S3	S4
5	Knee bolster location	100 mm	115 mm	150 mm	175 mm
6	Inflation rate	Rate 1	Rate 2	Rate 3	Rate 4
7	Development time	14 ms	18 ms	24 ms	32 ms
8	Vent size	650 mm	970 mm	1300 mm	1625 mm
9	Bag size (E-7 mm)	5.0	5.8	6.5	7.2
10	Maximum bag pressure	P1	P2	P3	P4

(b) Orthogonal Array

TRIAL/ COLUMN	1	2	3	4	5	6	7	8	9	10	R1
Trial 1	0	1	1	1	1	1	1	1	1	1	8.00
Trial 2	0	1	2	2	2	2	2	2	2	2	5.50
Trial 3	0	1	3	3	3	3	3	3	3	3	5.00
Trial 4	0	1	4	4	4	4	4	4	4	4	7.00
Trial 5	0	2	1	1	2	2	3	3	4	4	8.00
Trial 6	0	2	2	2	1	1	4	4	3	3	4.00
Trial 7	0	2	3	3	4	4	1	1	2	2	5.00
Trial 8	0	2	4	4	3	3	2	2	1	1	7.00
Trial 9	0	3	1	2	3	4	1	2	3	4	8.00
Trial 10	0	3	2	1	4	3	2	1	4	3	3.00
Trial 11	0	3	3	4	1	2	3	4	1	2	5.00
Trial 12	0	3	4	3	2	1	4	3	2	1	4.00
Trial 13	0	4	1	2	4	3	3	4	2	1	6.00
Trial 14	0	4	2	1	3	4	4	3	1	2	4.00
Trial 15	0	4	3	4	2	1	1	2	4	3	7.00
Trial 16	0	4	4	3	1	2	2	1	3	4	5.00
Trial 17	0	1	1	4	1	4	2	3	2	4	3.00
Trial 18	0	1	2	3	2	3	1	4	1	4	5.00
Trial 19	0	1	3	2	3	2	4	1	4	1	7.00
Trial 20	0	1	4	1	4	1	3	2	3	2	9.00
Trial 21	0	2	1	4	2	3	4	1	3	2	5.00
Trial 22	0	2	2	3	1	4	3	2	4	1	6.00

Table 9-7-1. *Continued*

TRIAL/ COLUMN	1	2	3	4	5	6	7	8	9	10	R1
Trial 23	0	2	3	2	4	1	2	3	1	4	7.00
Trial 24	0	2	4	1	3	2	1	4	2	3	7.00
Trial 25	0	3	1	3	3	1	2	4	4	2	6.00
Trial 26	0	3	2	4	4	2	1	3	3	1	5.00
Trial 27	0	3	3	1	1	3	4	2	2	4	4.00
Trial 28	0	3	4	2	2	4	3	1	1	3	5.00
Trial 29	0	4	1	3	4	2	4	2	1	3	6.00
Trial 30	0	4	2	4	3	1	3	1	2	4	7.00
Trial 31	0	4	3	1	2	4	2	4	3	1	8.00
Trial 32	0	4	4	2	1	3	1	3	4	2	4.50

learn the worst vehicle configuration. This information was then used to adhere to several of the compliance regulations.

Example 9-7
Airbag Design Study

Engineers involved in the development of an impact sensitive inflatable airbag for automobiles, identified nine 4 level factors as the major influences on performance. Using this information the Taguchi experimental design approach was used to determine the optimum design.

Solution

Since the experiment involves nine 4 level factors, L_{32} with the nine 4 level columns and one 2 level column was selected for the design. Since there is no 2 level factor in this design, the 2 level column (column 1) of the OA shown in Table 9-7-1(b) is set to zero. The factors, their levels, and the analyses are shown in Tables 9-7-1(a) through 9-7-3(b). The study was done using a theoretical simulation of the system. The trial conditions were used to set up the input conditions for the computer runs. The results of the computer runs at each of the trial conditions were recorded on a scale of 1 to 10 and are as shown with the OA (right most column) in Table 9-7-1(b). The main effects and ANOVA are presented

Table 9-7-2. Air Bag Design Study (Main Effect and ANOVA)

(a) The Main Effects

COLUMN	FACTOR NAME	LEVEL 1	LEVEL 2	$(L_2 - L_1)$	LEVEL 3	LEVEL 4
2	Steering column rotation	6.19	6.13	−0.07	5.00	5.94
3	Steering column crush stiffness	6.25	4.94	−1.32	6.00	6.06
4	Knee bolster stiffness	6.38	5.88	−0.50	5.25	5.75
5	Knee bloster location	4.94	5.94	1.00	6.38	6.00
6	Inflation rate	6.50	6.06	−0.44	4.94	5.75
7	Development time	6.19	5.56	−0.63	6.38	5.13
8	Vent size	5.63	6.56	0.93	5.06	6.00
9	Bag size (E-7 mm)	5.88	5.19	−0.69	6.13	6.06
10	Maximum bag pressure	6.63	5.50	−0.88	5.00	6.38

(c) ANOVA Table

COLUMN	FACTORS	DOF	SUM OF SQUARES	VARIANCE	F	PERCENT
2	Steering column rotation	(3)	(7.313)	Pooled		
3	Steering column crush stiffness	(3)	(8.438)	Pooled		
4	Knee bolster stiffness	(3)	(5.125)	Pooled		
5	Knee bolster location	3	9.063	3.021	1.631	4.65
6	Inflation rate	3	10.438	3.479	1.879	6.48
7	Development time	(3)	(7.938)	Pooled		
8	Vent size	3	9.563	3.188	1.721	5.32
9	Bag size (E-7 mm)	(3)	(4.438)	Pooled		
10	Maximum bag pressure	3	11.125	3.708	2.002	7.39
All others/error		19	35.19	1.85		76.17
Total:		31	75.38			100.00

in Tables 9-7-2(a) and (b). The optimum vehicle option combination and confidence level of the design appear in Table 9-7-3(a) and (b).

Example 9-8
Transmission Control Cable Adjustment Parameters

A Taguchi experiment was conducted to determine the best parameters for the design of a transmission control cable. The engineers identified one 4 level factor and five 2 level factors as well as three interactions among three of the five 2 level factors.

Table 9-7-3. Air Bag Design Study (Optimum and Confidence)

(a) Estimate of the Optimum Condition of Design/Process: For Smaller the Better
Characteristic

FACTOR DESCRIPTION	LEVEL DESCRIPTION	LEVEL	CONTRIBUTION
Knee bolster location	100	1	−0.8750
Inflation rate	Rate 4	4	−0.0625
Vent size	1300 mm	3	−0.7500
Max bag pressure	P3	3	−0.8125
Contribution from all factors (total)			−2.5000
Current grand average of performance			5.8125
Expected result at optimum condition			3.3125

This estimate includes only those variables that have a significant contribution, i.e., pooled variables are excluded
from the estimate. Estimates may also be made with variables of choice.

(b) Confidence Interval

Computing F-functions for 1 and 19 at 90% confidence level.
Confidence Interval (C.I.) is expressed as:

$$C.I. = \sqrt{\frac{F(1, n_2) \cdot V_e}{N_e}}$$

Where $F(n_1, n_2)$ = Computed value of F with $n_1 = 1$, n_2 = error DOF,
at a desired confidence level
V_e = Error variance
N_e = Effective number of replications.

Based on: $F = 2.600$ $n_1 = 1$, $n_2 = 19$ $V_e = 1.851974$ $N_e = 2.461539$

The confidence interval   C.I. $\cong \pm 1.3$

Solution
This experiment required both level of modification and interaction study.
The total DOF for the experiment was 11 $[(4 - 1) + 5 \times (2 - 1) + 3 \times (1 \times 1)]$. L_{12} has 11 DOF. But it requires a special OA which
cannot be used for interaction studies. L_{16} is selected for the design. The
factors and their levels are described in Table 9-8-1(a). For a 4 level
column and for the three interaction, four groups of natural interaction
columns are first selected. The sets selected are 1, 2, 3; 7, 8, 15; 11, 4,

Table 9-8-1. Study of Transmission Control Cable Adjustment
(Design and Modified OA)

(a) Study of Transmission Control Cable Adjustment Design Factors and Their Levels

COLUMN	FACTOR NAME	LEVEL 1	LEVEL 2	LEVEL 3	LEVEL 4
1	Adjuster type/source	Type 1	Type 2	Type 3	Type 4
2	(Used with column 1)				
3	(Used with column 1)				
4	Bracket deflection	Low	High		
5	Adjuster load	Low	High		
6	Cable elasticity	1×19	7×7		
7	Interaction 8×15	N/A			
8	Speed of adjuster	Low	High		
9	(Unused)				
10	(Unused)				
11	Interaction 4×15	N/A			
12	Interaction 4×15	N/A			
13	(Unused)				
14	(Unused)				
15	Adjusting torque	Low	High		

Note: A four levels factor and three interactions.
Objective: Determine best setting/adjustment.
Characteristic: Nominal the best (deviation from nominal measured).

(b) Orthogonal Array Used for the Experiment

TRIAL/ COLUMN	1	2	3	4	5	6	7	8	9	10	11	12	13	14	15
Trial 1	1	0	0	1	1	1	1	1	0	0	1	1	0	0	1
Trial 2	1	0	0	1	1	1	1	2	0	0	2	2	0	0	2
Trial 3	1	0	0	2	2	2	2	1	0	0	1	2	0	0	2
Trial 4	1	0	0	2	2	2	2	2	0	0	2	1	0	0	1
Trial 5	2	0	0	1	1	2	2	1	0	0	2	1	0	0	2
Trial 6	2	0	0	1	1	2	2	2	0	0	1	2	0	0	1
Trial 7	2	0	0	2	2	1	1	1	0	0	2	2	0	0	1
Trial 8	2	0	0	2	2	1	1	2	0	0	1	1	0	0	2
Trial 9	3	0	0	1	2	1	2	1	0	0	2	1	0	0	2
Trial 10	3	0	0	1	2	1	2	2	0	0	1	2	0	0	1
Trial 11	3	0	0	2	1	2	1	1	0	0	2	2	0	0	1
Trial 12	3	0	0	2	1	2	1	2	0	0	1	1	0	0	2
Trial 13	4	0	0	1	2	2	1	1	0	0	1	1	0	0	1
Trial 14	4	0	0	1	2	2	1	2	0	0	2	2	0	0	2
Trial 15	4	0	0	2	1	1	2	1	0	0	2	2	0	0	2
Trial 16	4	0	0	2	1	1	2	2	0	0	1	1	0	0	1

Table 9-9-1. Front Structure Crush Characteristics (Design and Data)

(a) Design Factors and Their Levels

COLUMN	FACTOR NAME	LEVEL 1	LEVEL 2	LEVEL 3	LEVEL 4
1	Lower rail section	Current	Proposed		
2	Upper rail geometry	Open section	Closed section		
3	Cross member	Present	Reinforced		

Note: Three 2 level factors studied.
Objective: Determine best design for barrier crush.
Characteristic: Nominal the best (impact deformation).

(b) This Experiment Uses an L_4

TRIAL/COLUMNS	1	2	3
Trial 1	1	1	1
Trial 2	1	2	2
Trial 3	2	1	2
Trial 4	2	2	1

(c) Original Observations and Their S/N Ratios
   Quality Characteristic: Nominal is Best

TRIAL/ REPETITIONS	R_1	R_2	R_3	R_4	R_5	R_6	S/N
1	12.00	14.00	11.00				−6.37
2	18.00	16.00	15.00				−8.46
3	14.00	15.00	15.00				−1.76
4	19.00	18.00	15.00				−11.47

15; and 12, 4, 8. Columns 1, 2, 3 are used to upgrade column 1 into a 4 level column. The other three sets are reserved for the interactions among the three factors assigned to columns 4, 8, and 15 such that the interaction between 4 × 15 is shown in column 11, the interaction between 4 × 8 in column 12, and the interaction between 8 × 15 in column 7. The factor with 4 levels is assigned to column 1 which is now a 4 level column. The remaining two 2 level columns are assigned to the columns 5 and 6 . The columns 9, 10, 13, and 14 remain unused. The modified L_{16} and the factors assigned to the appropriate columns are shown in Table 9-8-1(a).

Table 9-9-2. Front Structure Crush Characteristics
(Main Effect, ANOVA and Optima)

(a) The Main Effects

COLUMN	FACTOR NAME	LEVEL 1	LEVEL 2	$(L_2 - L_1)$	LEVEL 3	LEVEL 4
1	Lower rail section	−7.42	−4.86	2.56	00.00	00.00
2	Upper rail section	−2.30	−9.97	−7.66	00.00	00.00
3	Cross member	−8.92	−3.35	5.57	00.00	00.00

(b) ANOVA Table

COLUMN	FACTORS	DOF	SUM OF SQUARES	VARIANCE	F	PERCENT
1	Lower rail section	1	6.554	6.554		6.81
2	Upper rail section	1	58.676	58.676		60.96
3	Cross member	1	31.025	31.025		32.23
All others/error		0				
Total:		3	96.250			100.00

(c) Estimate of the Optimum Condition of Design/Process:

FACTOR DESCRIPTION	LEVEL DESCRIPTION	LEVEL	CONTRIBUTION
Lower rail section	Proposed design	2	1.2800
Upper rail section	Open section	1	3.8300
Cross member	Reinforced design	2	2.7850
Contribution from all factors (total)			7.8950
Current grand average of performance			−6.1350
Expected result at optimum condition			1.7600

This estimate includes only those variables that have a significant contribution, i.e., pooled variables are excluded from the estimate. Estimates may also be made with variables of choice.

Example 9-9
Front Structure Crush Characteristics

The Taguchi design of experiment methodology was used to optimize the design of the basic load carrying members of an automobile front structure. The development engineers were interested in determining the best combination of designs, with three factors, each of which had two alternatives. The performance of the structure was measured in terms of the deformation under a drop silo test. For the test variability, three samples at each configuration were tested.

Solution
The factor descriptions and the analyses are shown in Tables 9-9-1 and 9-9-2. The design and the analysis is straightforward. The analysis utilizes a *S/N* ratio with "nominal is best" quality characteristic.

References

1. Patrick M. Burgman. "Design of Experiments—The Taguchi Way." *Manufacturing Engineering*. May 1985, pp. 44–46.
2. Yuin Wu and Willie Hobbs Moore. 1986. *Quality Engineering—Product and Process Optimization*. Dearborn, Michigan: American Supplier Institute.
3. Ronald L. Iman and W. J. Conover. 1983. *A Modern Approach to Statistics*. New York: John Wiley & Sons.
4. Yuin Wu. 1986. *Orthogonal Arrays and Linear Graphs*. Dearborn, Michigan: American Supplier Institute.
5. Burton Gunter. 1987. *A Perspective on the Taguchi Methods*. Quality Progress. American Society for Quality Control, Milwaukee, WI.
6. Lawrence P. Sullivan. June 1987. *The Power of the Taguchi Methods*. Quality Progress. American Society for Quality Control, Milwaukee, WI.
7. Philip J. Ross. 1988. *Taguchi Techniques for Quality Engineering*. New York: McGraw Hill Book Company.
8. Thomas B. Baker and Don P. Causing. *Quality Engineering by Design—The Taguchi Method*. 40th Annual ASQC Conference, March 1984.
9. Jim Quinlan. 1985. *Product Improvement By Application of Taguchi Methods*. Midvale, Ohio: Flex Products, Inc.
10. Genichi Taguchi. 1987. *System of Experimental Design*. New York: UNIPUB, Kraus International Publications.
11. Ranjit K. Roy. QUALITEK-3:IBM PC Software for Design and Analysis of Taguchi Experiments. NUTEK Inc. 30400 Telegraph, Suite 380, Birmingham, MI 48010. (Ph. 313-642-4560).
12. R. A. Fisher. 1951. *Design of Experiments*. Edinburgh: Oliver & Boyd.
13. W. G. Cochran and G. M. Cox. 1957. *Experimental Designs*. Second edition. New York: John Wiley & Sons.
14. Diane M. Byrne and Shin Taguchi. 1987. "The Taguchi Approach to Parameter Design." 40th Annual Quality Congress Transactions. Milwaukee, Wisconsin: American Society for Quality Control.
15. G. Taguchi and S. Konishi. 1987. *Orthogonal Arrays and Linear Graphs—Tools for Quality Engineering*. Dearborn, Michigan: American Supplier Institute, Inc.
16. Third Supplier Symposium on Taguchi Method. American Supplier Institute, Inc. Dearborn, Michigan. October 8, 1985.

APPENDIX A

Orthogonal arrays, triangular tables and linear graphs

Table A-1. Common Orthogonal Arrays**

ARRAY	NUMBER OF FACTORS	NUMBER OF LEVELS
$L_4(2^3)$	3	2
$L_8(2^7)$	7	2
$L_{12}(2^{11})$	11	2
$L_{16}(2^{15})$	15	2
$L_{32}(2^{31})$	31	2
$L_9(3^4)$	4	3
*$L_{18}(2^1,3^7)$	1	2
	and 7	3
$L_{27}(3^{13})$	13	3
$L_{16}(4^5)$	5	4
*$L_{32}(2^1,4^9)$	1	2
	and 9	4
$L_{64}(4^{21})$	21	4

*Mixed level arrays
**Orthogonal arrays from G. Taguchi and S. Konishi, *Orthogonal Arrays and Linear Graphs*. Dearborn, Michigan: American Supplier Institute, Inc. 1987.

Table A-2. Orthogonal Arrays L_4 and L_8 (2-Level)*

(a)

COLUMN	$L_4(2^3)$		
CONDITION	1	2	3
1	1	1	1
2	1	2	2
3	2	1	2
4	2	2	1

(b)

COLUMN	$L_8(2^7)$						
CONDITION	1	2	3	4	5	6	7
1	1	1	1	1	1	1	1
2	1	1	1	2	2	2	2
3	1	2	2	1	1	2	2
4	1	2	2	2	2	1	1
5	2	1	2	1	2	1	2
6	2	1	2	2	1	2	1
7	2	2	1	1	2	2	1
8	2	2	1	2	1	1	2

*Reprinted with permission of the American Supplier Institute, Inc.

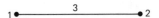

Figure A-1. Linear graph for L_4.

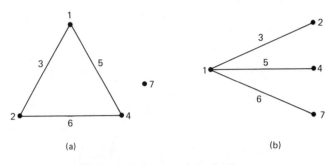

(a)

(b)

Figure A-2. Linear graphs for L_8.

Table A-3. Orthogonal Arrays L_{12} and L_{16} (2 Level)*

$L_{12}(2^{11})$

NO.	1	2	3	4	5	6	7	8	9	10	11
1	1	1	1	1	1	1	1	1	1	1	1
2	1	1	1	1	1	2	2	2	2	2	2
3	1	1	2	2	2	1	1	1	2	2	2
4	1	2	1	2	2	1	2	2	1	1	2
5	1	2	2	1	2	2	1	2	1	2	1
6	1	2	2	2	1	2	2	1	2	1	1
7	2	1	2	2	1	1	2	2	1	2	1
8	2	1	2	1	2	2	2	1	1	1	2
9	2	1	1	2	2	2	1	2	2	1	1
10	2	2	2	1	1	1	1	2	2	1	2
11	2	2	1	2	1	2	1	1	1	2	2
12	2	2	1	1	2	1	1	2	2	2	1

The $L_{12}(2^{11})$ is a specially designed array, in that interactions are distributed more or less uniformly to all columns. There is no linear graph for this array. If should not be used to analyze interactions. The advantage of this design is its capability to investigate 11 main effects, making it a highly recommended array.

$L_{16}(2^{15})$

NO.	1	2	3	4	5	6	7	8	9	10	11	12	13	14	15
1	1	1	1	1	1	1	1	1	1	1	1	1	1	1	1
2	1	1	1	1	1	1	1	2	2	2	2	2	2	2	2
3	1	1	1	2	2	2	2	1	1	1	1	2	2	2	2
4	1	1	1	2	2	2	2	2	2	2	2	1	1	1	1
5	1	2	2	1	1	2	2	1	1	2	2	1	1	2	2
6	1	2	2	1	1	2	2	2	2	1	1	2	2	1	1
7	1	2	2	2	2	1	1	1	1	2	2	2	2	1	1
8	1	2	2	2	2	1	1	2	2	1	1	1	1	2	2
9	2	1	2	1	2	1	2	1	2	1	2	1	2	1	2
10	2	1	2	1	2	1	2	2	1	2	1	2	1	2	1
11	2	1	2	2	1	2	1	1	2	1	2	2	1	2	1
12	2	1	2	2	1	2	1	2	1	2	1	1	2	1	2
13	2	2	1	1	2	2	1	1	2	2	1	1	2	2	1
14	2	2	1	1	2	2	1	2	1	1	2	2	1	1	2
15	2	2	1	2	1	1	2	1	2	2	1	2	1	1	2
16	2	2	1	2	1	1	2	2	1	1	2	1	2	2	1

*Reprinted with permission of the American Supplier Institute, Inc.

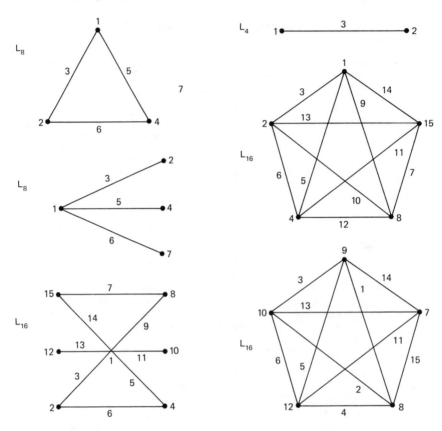

Figure A-3. Linear graphs for 2 level orthogonal arrays.

Table A–4. Orthogonal Arrays L_{32} (2 Level, 31 Factors)*

L_{32} (2^{31})

CONDITION \ COLUMN	1	2	3	4	5	6	7	8	9	10	11	12	13	14	15	16	17	18	19	20	21	22	23	24	25	26	27	28	29	30	31
1	1	1	1	1	1	1	1	1	1	1	1	1	1	1	1	1	1	1	1	1	1	1	1	1	1	1	1	1	1	1	1
2	1	1	1	1	1	1	1	1	1	1	1	1	1	1	1	2	2	2	2	2	2	2	2	2	2	2	2	2	2	2	2
3	1	1	1	1	1	1	1	2	2	2	2	2	2	2	2	1	1	1	1	1	1	1	1	2	2	2	2	2	2	2	2
4	1	1	1	1	1	1	1	2	2	2	2	2	2	2	2	2	2	2	2	2	2	2	2	1	1	1	1	1	1	1	1
5	1	1	1	2	2	2	2	1	1	1	1	2	2	2	2	1	1	1	1	2	2	2	2	1	1	1	1	2	2	2	2
6	1	1	1	2	2	2	2	1	1	1	1	2	2	2	2	2	2	2	2	1	1	1	1	2	2	2	2	1	1	1	1
7	1	1	1	2	2	2	2	2	2	2	2	1	1	1	1	1	1	1	1	2	2	2	2	2	2	2	2	1	1	1	1
8	1	1	1	2	2	2	2	2	2	2	2	1	1	1	1	2	2	2	2	1	1	1	1	1	1	1	1	2	2	2	2
9	1	2	2	1	1	2	2	1	1	2	2	1	1	2	2	1	1	2	2	1	1	2	2	1	1	2	2	1	1	2	2
10	1	2	2	1	1	2	2	1	1	2	2	1	1	2	2	2	2	1	1	2	2	1	1	2	2	1	1	2	2	1	1
11	1	2	2	1	1	2	2	2	2	1	1	2	2	1	1	1	1	2	2	1	1	2	2	2	2	1	1	2	2	1	1
12	1	2	2	1	1	2	2	2	2	1	1	2	2	1	1	2	2	1	1	2	2	1	1	1	1	2	2	1	1	2	2
13	1	2	2	2	2	1	1	1	1	2	2	2	2	1	1	1	1	2	2	2	2	1	1	1	1	2	2	2	2	1	1
14	1	2	2	2	2	1	1	1	1	2	2	2	2	1	1	2	2	1	1	1	1	2	2	2	2	1	1	1	1	2	2
15	1	2	2	2	2	1	1	2	2	1	1	1	1	2	2	1	1	2	2	2	2	1	1	2	2	1	1	1	1	2	2

(continued)

Table A–4. Orthogonal Arrays L_{32} (2 Level, 31 Factors) (Continued)

L_{32} (2^{31})

CONDITION \ COLUMN	1	2	3	4	5	6	7	8	9	10	11	12	13	14	15	16	17	18	19	20	21	22	23	24	25	26	27	28	29	30	31
16	1	2	2	2	2	1	1	2	2	1	1	1	1	2	2	2	2	1	1	1	1	2	2	1	1	2	2	2	2	1	1
17	2	1	2	1	2	1	2	1	2	1	2	1	2	1	2	1	2	1	2	1	2	1	2	1	2	1	2	1	2	1	2
18	2	1	2	1	2	1	2	1	2	1	2	1	2	1	2	2	1	2	1	2	1	2	1	2	1	2	1	2	1	2	1
19	2	1	2	1	2	1	2	2	1	2	1	2	1	2	1	1	2	1	2	1	2	1	2	2	1	2	1	2	1	2	1
20	2	1	2	1	2	1	2	2	1	2	1	2	1	2	1	2	1	2	1	2	1	2	1	1	2	1	2	1	2	1	2
21	2	1	2	2	1	2	1	1	2	1	2	2	1	2	1	1	2	1	2	2	1	2	1	1	2	1	2	2	1	2	1
22	2	1	2	2	1	2	1	1	2	1	2	2	1	2	1	2	1	2	1	1	2	1	2	2	1	2	1	1	2	1	2
23	2	1	2	2	1	2	1	2	1	2	1	1	2	1	2	1	2	1	2	2	1	2	1	2	1	2	1	1	2	1	2
24	2	1	2	2	1	2	1	2	1	2	1	1	2	1	2	2	1	2	1	1	2	1	2	1	2	1	2	2	1	2	1
25	2	2	1	1	2	2	1	1	2	2	1	1	2	2	1	1	2	2	1	1	2	2	1	1	2	2	1	1	2	2	1
26	2	2	1	1	2	2	1	1	2	2	1	1	2	2	1	2	1	1	2	2	1	1	2	2	1	1	2	2	1	1	2
27	2	2	1	1	2	2	1	2	1	1	2	2	1	1	2	1	2	2	1	1	2	2	1	2	1	1	2	2	1	1	2
28	2	2	1	1	2	2	1	2	1	1	2	2	1	1	2	2	1	1	2	2	1	1	2	1	2	2	1	1	2	2	1
29	2	2	1	2	1	1	2	1	2	2	1	2	1	1	2	1	2	2	1	2	1	1	2	1	2	2	1	2	1	1	2
30	2	2	1	2	1	1	2	1	2	2	1	2	1	1	2	2	1	1	2	1	2	2	1	2	1	1	2	1	2	2	1
31	2	2	1	2	1	1	2	2	1	1	2	1	2	2	1	1	2	2	1	2	1	1	2	2	1	1	2	1	2	2	1
32	2	2	1	2	1	1	2	2	1	1	2	1	2	2	1	2	1	1	2	1	2	2	1	1	2	2	1	2	1	1	2

216

Table A-5-1. Orthogonal Arrays L_{64} (2 Level)*

L_{64} (2^{63})

No.	1	2	3	4	5	6	7	8	9	10	11	12	13	14	15	16	17	18	19	20	21	22	23	24	25	26	27	28	29	30	31
1	1	1	1	1	1	1	1	1	1	1	1	1	1	1	1	1	1	1	1	1	1	1	1	1	1	1	1	1	1	1	1
2	1	1	1	1	1	1	1	1	1	1	1	1	1	1	1	1	1	1	1	1	1	1	1	1	1	1	1	1	1	1	1
3	1	1	1	1	1	1	1	1	1	1	1	1	1	1	1	2	2	2	2	2	2	2	2	2	2	2	2	2	2	2	2
4	1	1	1	1	1	1	1	1	1	1	1	1	1	1	1	2	2	2	2	2	2	2	2	2	2	2	2	2	2	2	2
5	1	1	1	1	1	1	1	2	2	2	2	2	2	2	2	1	1	1	1	1	1	1	1	2	2	2	2	2	2	2	2
6	1	1	1	1	1	1	1	2	2	2	2	2	2	2	2	1	1	1	1	1	1	1	1	2	2	2	2	2	2	2	2
7	1	1	1	1	1	1	1	2	2	2	2	2	2	2	2	2	2	2	2	2	2	2	2	1	1	1	1	1	1	1	1
8	1	1	1	1	1	1	1	2	2	2	2	2	2	2	2	2	2	2	2	2	2	2	2	1	1	1	1	1	1	1	1
9	1	1	1	2	2	2	2	1	1	1	1	2	2	2	2	1	1	1	1	2	2	2	2	1	1	1	1	2	2	2	2
10	1	1	1	2	2	2	2	1	1	1	1	2	2	2	2	1	1	1	1	2	2	2	2	1	1	1	1	2	2	2	2
11	1	1	1	2	2	2	2	1	1	1	1	2	2	2	2	2	2	2	2	1	1	1	1	2	2	2	2	1	1	1	1
12	1	1	1	2	2	2	2	1	1	1	1	2	2	2	2	2	2	2	2	1	1	1	1	2	2	2	2	1	1	1	1
13	1	1	1	2	2	2	2	2	2	2	2	1	1	1	1	1	1	1	1	2	2	2	2	2	2	2	2	1	1	1	1
14	1	1	1	2	2	2	2	2	2	2	2	1	1	1	1	1	1	1	1	2	2	2	2	2	2	2	2	1	1	1	1
15	1	1	1	2	2	2	2	2	2	2	2	1	1	1	1	2	2	2	2	1	1	1	1	1	1	1	1	2	2	2	2
16	1	1	1	2	2	2	2	2	2	2	2	1	1	1	1	2	2	2	2	1	1	1	1	1	1	1	1	2	2	2	2
17	1	2	2	1	1	2	2	1	1	2	2	1	1	2	2	1	1	2	2	1	1	2	2	1	1	2	2	1	1	2	2
18	1	2	2	1	1	2	2	1	1	2	2	1	1	2	2	1	1	2	2	1	1	2	2	1	1	2	2	1	1	2	2
19	1	2	2	1	1	2	2	1	1	2	2	1	1	2	2	2	2	1	1	2	2	1	1	2	2	1	1	2	2	1	1
20	1	2	2	1	1	2	2	1	1	2	2	1	1	2	2	2	2	1	1	2	2	1	1	2	2	1	1	2	2	1	1
21	1	2	2	1	1	2	2	2	2	1	1	2	2	1	1	1	1	2	2	1	1	2	2	2	2	1	1	2	2	1	1
22	1	2	2	1	1	2	2	2	2	1	1	2	2	1	1	1	1	2	2	1	1	2	2	2	2	1	1	2	2	1	1
23	1	2	2	1	1	2	2	2	2	1	1	2	2	1	1	2	2	1	1	2	2	1	1	1	1	2	2	1	1	2	2

(continued)

217

Table A-5-1. Orthogonal Arrays L_{64} (2 Level) (Continued)

L_{64} (2^{63})

No.	1	2	3	4	5	6	7	8	9	10	11	12	13	14	15	16	17	18	19	20	21	22	23	24	25	26	27	28	29	30	31
24	1	2	2	1	1	2	2	2	2	1	1	2	2	1	1	2	2	1	1	2	2	1	1	1	1	2	2	1	1	2	2
25	1	2	2	2	2	1	1	1	1	2	2	2	2	1	1	1	1	2	2	2	2	1	1	2	2	1	1	2	2	1	1
26	1	2	2	2	2	1	1	1	1	2	2	2	2	1	1	1	1	2	2	2	2	1	1	2	2	1	1	2	2	1	1
27	1	2	2	2	2	1	1	1	1	2	2	2	2	1	1	2	2	1	1	1	1	2	2	1	1	2	2	2	2	1	1
28	1	2	2	2	2	1	1	1	1	2	2	2	2	1	1	2	2	1	1	1	1	2	2	2	2	1	1	1	1	2	2
29	1	2	2	2	2	1	1	2	2	1	1	2	2	2	2	1	1	2	2	1	1	2	2	2	2	1	1	2	2	1	1
30	1	2	2	2	2	1	1	2	2	1	1	1	1	2	2	2	2	1	1	2	2	1	1	1	1	2	2	2	2	1	1
31	1	2	2	2	2	1	1	2	2	1	1	1	1	2	2	2	2	1	1	1	1	2	2	2	2	1	1	2	2	1	1
32	1	2	2	2	2	1	1	2	2	1	1	1	1	2	2	2	2	1	1	1	1	2	2	2	2	1	1	1	1	2	2
33	2	1	2	1	2	1	2	1	2	1	2	2	2	1	1	1	2	2	1	2	1	2	1	1	2	2	1	1	2	2	1
34	2	1	1	2	1	2	1	1	2	2	1	2	2	1	2	1	2	2	2	2	2	1	2	1	1	2	2	1	2	2	1
35	2	1	2	1	2	1	2	1	2	1	2	1	1	2	2	2	1	1	2	1	2	2	1	2	1	2	1	1	2	2	1
36	2	1	1	2	1	2	1	1	2	2	1	2	2	1	2	1	2	1	1	2	1	2	2	2	1	2	1	2	2	2	1
37	2	1	2	1	2	1	2	2	1	1	2	2	2	1	1	2	1	2	1	2	1	1	2	1	2	2	1	2	1	2	1
38	2	1	1	2	1	2	1	2	1	2	1	2	2	1	2	1	2	1	2	2	2	1	2	1	1	2	1	2	2	1	1
39	2	1	2	1	2	1	2	2	1	1	2	1	1	2	2	1	2	2	1	2	1	2	1	1	2	2	1	2	1	2	1
40	2	1	1	2	1	2	1	2	1	2	1	2	2	2	2	2	1	1	1	1	1	1	1	2	2	1	1	1	1	2	2
41	2	1	2	2	2	2	1	2	2	2	2	2	2	2	2	2	2	2	2	2	2	2	1	1	2	2	2	2	1	2	1
42	2	1	2	2	1	2	1	1	2	2	2	2	1	2	1	2	2	2	2	2	1	1	1	1	2	1	2	2	2	1	2
43	2	1	2	2	1	1	1	1	2	2	2	2	1	2	2	2	1	2	1	1	2	2	2	2	2	2	1	1	2	1	2

44	2	2	2	2	2	1	2	2	1	2	1	2	1	1	2	1	2	1	2	1	2	2	1	2	2	1	1	2	1	2	2
45	2	1	2	2	2	1	2	2	1	1	2	1	2	2	1	2	1	2	1	2	1	1	2	1	1	2	2	1	2	1	2
46	2	1	2	2	2	1	2	2	1	1	2	2	1	1	2	2	1	1	2	2	1	1	2	2	1	1	2	2	1	2	2
47	2	1	2	2	2	1	1	1	2	2	2	1	1	1	2	2	2	2	1	1	1	2	2	2	2	1	1	1	2	1	1
48	2	1	2	2	2	1	1	1	2	2	2	2	2	2	1	1	1	1	2	2	2	2	1	1	1	2	2	2	1	2	1
49	2	2	2	1	1	2	2	1	2	2	1	2	1	1	2	2	1	2	1	1	2	1	2	1	1	2	2	1	1	2	2
50	2	2	2	1	1	2	2	1	2	2	1	1	2	2	1	1	2	1	2	2	1	1	2	2	2	1	1	2	1	1	2
51	2	2	2	1	1	2	2	1	1	1	2	1	2	2	1	2	1	1	2	2	1	2	1	1	2	2	1	2	1	2	1
52	2	2	2	1	1	2	2	1	1	1	2	2	1	1	2	1	2	2	1	1	2	2	1	2	1	1	2	1	2	2	1
53	2	2	2	1	1	2	1	2	2	1	1	2	1	2	1	2	1	1	2	1	2	2	1	2	1	1	2	1	2	1	2
54	2	2	2	1	1	1	1	2	2	1	1	1	2	1	2	1	2	2	1	2	1	1	2	1	2	2	1	2	1	2	2
55	2	2	2	1	1	1	1	2	1	2	2	2	1	2	1	1	2	1	2	1	2	2	1	1	2	2	1	1	2	1	2
56	2	2	2	1	1	1	1	2	1	2	2	1	2	1	2	2	1	2	1	2	1	1	2	2	1	1	2	2	1	2	2
57	2	2	2	1	2	2	2	1	2	2	1	2	2	1	1	2	2	1	1	2	2	1	1	2	1	1	2	2	1	2	2
58	2	2	2	1	2	2	2	1	2	2	1	1	1	2	2	1	1	2	2	1	1	2	2	1	2	2	1	1	2	1	2
59	2	2	2	1	2	2	2	1	1	1	2	2	2	1	1	2	2	1	1	2	2	1	1	2	2	1	1	2	1	2	1
60	2	2	2	1	2	2	2	1	1	1	2	1	2	2	1	1	2	2	2	1	1	2	2	1	1	2	2	1	2	1	1
61	2	2	2	1	2	1	1	2	2	1	1	2	2	1	2	1	1	2	2	1	1	2	2	1	2	2	1	1	2	2	2
62	2	2	2	1	2	1	1	2	2	1	1	1	1	2	1	2	2	1	1	2	2	1	1	2	1	1	2	2	1	2	2
63	2	2	2	1	2	1	1	2	1	2	2	2	1	1	2	1	1	2	2	1	1	2	2	1	1	1	2	2	1	1	2
64	2	2	2	1	2	1	1	2	1	2	2	1	2	2	1	2	2	1	1	2	2	1	1	2	2	2	1	1	2	2	2

Table A-5-2. Orthogonal Array L_{64} (Continues Table A-5-1) (2 Level)

*Reprinted with permission of the American Supplier Institute, Inc.

Table A–6 Triangular Table for 2 Level Orthogonal Arrays

1	2	3	4	5	6	7	8	9	10	11	12	13	14	15	16	17	18	19	20	21	22	23	24	25	26	27	28	29	30	31
(1)	3	2	5	4	7	6	9	8	11	10	13	12	15	14	17	16	19	18	21	20	23	22	25	24	27	26	29	28	31	30
	(2)	1	6	7	4	5	10	11	8	9	14	15	12	13	18	19	16	17	22	23	20	21	26	27	24	25	30	31	28	29
		(3)	7	6	5	4	11	10	9	8	15	14	13	12	19	18	17	16	23	22	21	20	27	26	25	24	31	30	29	28
			(4)	1	2	3	12	13	14	15	8	9	10	11	20	21	22	23	16	17	18	19	28	29	30	31	24	25	26	27
				(5)	3	2	13	12	15	14	9	8	11	10	21	20	23	22	17	16	19	18	29	28	31	30	25	24	27	26
					(6)	1	14	15	12	13	10	11	8	9	22	23	20	21	18	19	16	17	30	31	28	29	26	27	24	25
						(7)	15	14	13	12	11	10	9	8	23	22	21	20	19	18	17	16	31	30	29	28	27	26	25	24
							(8)	1	2	3	4	5	6	7	24	25	26	27	28	29	30	31	16	17	18	19	20	21	22	23
								(9)	3	2	5	4	7	6	25	24	27	26	29	28	31	30	17	16	19	18	21	20	23	22
									(10)	1	6	7	4	5	26	27	24	25	30	31	28	29	18	19	16	17	22	23	20	21
										(11)	7	6	5	4	27	26	25	24	31	30	29	28	19	18	17	16	23	22	21	20
											(12)	1	2	3	28	29	30	31	24	25	26	27	20	21	22	23	16	17	18	19
												(13)	3	2	29	28	31	30	25	24	27	26	21	20	23	22	17	16	19	18

	(15)	(16)	(17)	(18)	(19)	(20)	(21)	(22)	(23)	(24)	(25)	(26)	(27)	(28)	(29)	(30)	(31)
(14)	1	30	31	28	29	26	27	24	25	22	23	20	21	18	19	16	17
(15)		31	30	29	28	27	26	25	24	23	22	21	20	19	18	17	16
(16)			1	2	3	4	5	6	7	8	9	10	11	12	13	14	15
(17)				3	2	5	4	7	6	9	8	11	10	13	12	15	14
(18)					1	6	7	4	5	10	11	8	9	14	15	12	13
(19)						7	6	5	4	11	10	9	8	15	14	13	12
(20)							1	2	3	12	13	14	15	8	9	10	11
(21)								3	2	13	12	15	14	9	8	11	10
(22)									1	14	15	12	13	10	11	8	9
(23)										15	14	13	12	11	10	9	8
(24)											1	2	3	4	5	6	7
(25)												3	2	5	4	7	6
(26)													1	6	7	4	5
(27)														7	6	5	4
(28)															1	2	3
(29)																3	2
(30)																	1

Table A-7. Orthogonal Arrays (3 Level, L_9 and L_{18})*

(a)

COLUMN CONDITION	$L_9(3^4)$			
	1	2	3	4
1	1	1	1	1
2	1	2	2	2
3	1	3	3	3
4	2	1	2	3
5	2	2	3	1
6	2	3	1	2
7	3	1	3	2
8	3	2	1	3
9	3	3	2	1

(b)

NO.	$L_{18}(2^1 \times 3^7)$							
	1	2	3	4	5	6	7	8
1	1	1	1	1	1	1	1	1
2	1	1	2	2	2	2	2	2
3	1	1	3	3	3	3	3	3
4	1	2	1	1	2	2	3	3
5	1	2	2	2	3	3	1	1
6	1	2	3	3	1	1	2	2
7	1	3	1	2	1	3	2	3
8	1	3	2	3	2	1	3	1
9	1	3	3	1	3	2	1	2
10	2	1	1	3	3	2	2	1
11	2	1	2	1	1	3	3	2
12	2	1	3	2	2	1	1	3
13	2	2	1	2	3	1	3	2
14	2	2	2	3	1	2	1	3
15	2	2	3	1	2	3	2	1
16	2	3	1	3	2	3	1	2
17	2	3	2	1	3	1	2	3
18	2	3	3	2	1	2	3	1

Note: Like the L_{12} (2^{11}), this is a specially designed array. An interaction is builit in between the first two columns. This interaction information can be obtained without sacrificing any other column. Interactions between three-level columns are distributed more or less uniformly to all the other three-level columns, which permits investigation of main effects. Thus, it is a highly recommended array for experiments.
*Reprinted with permission of the American Supplier Institute, Inc.

Table A-8. Orthogonal Arrays (3 Level, L_{27})*

COLUMN CONDITION	L_{27} (3^{13})												
	1	2	3	4	5	6	7	8	9	10	11	12	13
1	1	1	1	1	1	1	1	1	1	1	1	1	1
2	1	1	1	1	2	2	2	2	2	2	2	2	2
3	1	1	1	1	3	3	3	3	3	3	3	3	3
4	1	2	2	2	1	1	1	2	2	2	3	3	3
5	1	2	2	2	2	2	2	3	3	3	1	1	1
6	1	2	2	2	3	3	3	1	1	1	2	2	2
7	1	3	3	3	1	1	1	3	3	3	2	2	2
8	1	3	3	3	2	2	2	1	1	1	3	3	3
9	1	3	3	3	3	3	3	2	2	2	1	1	1
10	2	1	2	3	1	2	3	1	2	3	1	2	3
11	2	1	2	3	2	3	1	2	3	1	2	3	1
12	2	1	2	3	3	1	2	3	1	2	3	1	2
13	2	2	3	1	1	2	3	2	3	1	3	1	2
14	2	2	3	1	2	3	1	3	1	2	1	2	3
15	2	2	3	1	3	1	2	1	2	3	2	3	1
16	2	3	1	2	1	2	3	3	1	2	2	3	1
17	2	3	1	2	2	3	1	1	2	3	3	1	2
18	2	3	1	2	3	1	2	2	3	1	1	2	3
19	3	1	3	2	1	3	2	1	3	2	1	3	2
20	3	1	3	2	2	1	3	2	1	3	2	1	3
21	3	1	3	2	3	2	1	3	2	1	3	2	1
22	3	2	1	3	1	3	2	2	1	3	3	2	1
23	3	2	1	3	2	1	3	3	2	1	1	3	2
24	3	2	1	3	3	2	1	1	3	2	2	1	3
25	3	3	2	1	1	3	2	3	2	1	2	1	3
26	3	3	2	1	2	1	3	1	3	2	3	2	1
27	3	3	2	1	3	2	1	2	1	3	1	3	2

*Reprinted with permission of the American Supplier Institute, Inc.

Table A-9. Triangular Table for 3 Level Orthogonal Arrays*

1	2	3	4	5	6	7	8	9	10	11	12	13
(1)	3	2	2	6	5	5	9	8	8	12	11	11
	4	4	3	7	7	6	10	10	9	13	13	12
	(2)	1	1	8	9	10	5	6	7	5	6	7
		4	3	11	12	13	11	12	13	8	9	10
		(3)	1	9	10	8	7	5	6	6	7	5
			2	13	11	12	12	13	11	10	8	9
			(4)	10	8	9	6	7	5	7	5	6
				12	13	11	13	11	12	9	10	8
				(5)	1	1	2	3	4	2	4	3
					7	6	11	13	12	8	10	9
					(6)	1	4	2	3	3	2	4
						5	13	12	11	10	9	8
						(7)	3	4	2	4	3	2
							12	11	13	9	8	10
							(8)	1	1	2	3	4
								10	9	5	7	6
								(9)	1	4	2	3
									8	7	6	5
									(10)	3	4	2
										6	5	7
										(11)	1	1
											13	12
											(12)	1
												11

*Reprinted with permission of the American Supplier Institute, Inc.

Table A-10. Orthogonal Arrays (2 Level and 4 Level)*

No.	1	2	3	4	5	6	7	8	9	10
1	1	1	1	1	1	1	1	1	1	1
1	1	1	2	2	2	2	2	2	2	2
3	1	1	3	3	3	3	3	3	3	3
4	1	1	4	4	4	4	4	4	4	4
5	1	2	1	1	2	2	3	3	4	4
6	1	2	2	2	1	1	4	4	3	3
7	1	2	3	3	4	4	1	1	2	2
8	1	2	4	4	3	3	2	2	1	1
9	1	3	1	2	3	4	1	2	3	4
10	1	3	2	1	4	3	2	1	4	3
11	1	3	3	4	1	2	3	4	1	2
12	1	3	4	3	2	1	4	3	2	1
13	1	4	1	2	4	3	3	4	2	1
14	1	4	2	1	3	4	4	3	1	2
15	1	4	3	4	2	1	1	2	4	3
16	1	4	4	3	1	2	2	1	3	4
17	2	1	1	4	1	4	2	3	2	3
18	2	1	2	3	2	3	1	4	1	4
19	2	1	3	2	3	2	4	1	4	1
20	2	1	4	1	4	1	3	2	3	2
21	2	2	1	4	2	3	4	1	3	2
22	2	2	2	3	1	4	3	2	4	1
23	2	2	3	2	4	1	2	3	1	4
24	2	2	4	1	3	2	1	4	2	3
25	2	3	1	3	3	1	2	4	4	2
26	2	3	2	4	4	2	1	3	3	1
27	2	3	3	1	1	3	4	2	2	4
28	2	3	4	2	2	4	3	1	1	3
29	2	4	1	3	4	2	4	2	1	3
30	2	4	2	4	3	1	3	1	2	4
31	2	4	3	1	2	4	2	4	3	1
32	2	4	4	2	1	3	1	3	4	2

*Reprinted with permission of the American Supplier Institute, Inc.

Table A-11. Triangular Table for 4 Level Orthogonal Arrays*

	2	3	4	5	6	7	8	9	10	11	12	13	14	15	16	17	18	19	20	21
1	3 4 5	2 4 5	2 3 5	2 3 4	7 8 9	6 8 9	6 7 9	6 7 8	11 12 13	10 12 13	10 11 13	10 11 12	15 16 17	14 16 17	14 15 17	14 15 16	19 20 21	18 20 21	18 19 21	18 19 20
2	(2)	1 4 5	1 3 5	1 3 4	10 14 18	11 15 19	12 16 20	13 17 21	6 14 18	7 15 19	8 16 20	9 17 21	6 10 18	7 11 19	8 12 20	9 13 21	6 10 14	7 11 15	8 12 16	9 13 17
3		(3)	1 2 5	1 2 4	11 16 21	10 17 20	13 14 19	12 15 18	7 17 20	6 16 21	9 15 18	8 14 19	8 13 19	9 12 18	6 11 21	7 10 20	9 12 15	8 13 14	7 10 17	6 11 16
4			(4)	1 2 3	12 17 19	13 16 18	10 15 21	11 14 20	8 15 21	9 14 20	6 17 19	7 16 18	9 11 20	8 10 21	7 13 18	6 12 19	7 13 16	6 12 17	9 11 14	8 10 15
5				(5)	13 15 20	12 14 21	11 17 18	10 16 19	9 16 19	8 17 18	7 14 21	6 15 20	7 12 21	6 13 20	9 10 19	8 11 18	8 11 17	9 10 16	6 13 15	7 12 14
6					(6)	1 8 9	1 7 9	1 7 8	2 14 18	3 16 21	4 17 19	5 15 20	2 10 18	5 13 20	3 11 21	4 12 19	2 10 14	4 12 17	5 13 15	3 11 16
7						(7)	1 6 9	1 6 8	3 17 20	2 15 19	5 14 21	4 16 18	5 12 21	2 11 19	4 13 18	3 10 20	4 13 16	2 11 15	3 10 17	5 12 14
8							(8)	1 6 7	4 15 21	5 17 18	2 16 20	3 14 19	3 13 19	4 10 21	2 12 20	5 11 18	5 11 17	3 13 14	2 12 16	4 10 15
9								(9)	5 16 19	4 14 20	3 15 18	2 17 21	4 11 20	3 12 18	5 10 19	2 13 21	3 12 15	5 10 16	4 11 14	2 13 17
10									(10)	1 12 13	1 11 13	1 11 12	2 6 18	4 8 21	5 9 19	3 7 20	2 6 14	5 9 16	3 7 17	4 8 15
11										(11)	1 10 13	1 10 12	4 9 20	2 7 19	3 6 21	5 8 18	5 8 17	2 7 15	4 9 14	3 6 16
12											(12)	1 10 11	5 7 21	3 9 18	2 8 20	4 6 19	3 9 15	4 6 17	2 8 16	5 7 14
13												(13)	3 8 19	5 6 20	4 7 18	2 9 21	4 7 16	3 8 14	5 6 15	2 9 17
14													(14)	1 16 17	1 15 17	1 15 16	2 6 10	3 8 13	4 9 11	5 7 12
15														(15)	1 14 17	1 14 16	3 9 12	2 7 11	5 6 13	4 8 10
16															(16)	1 14 15	4 7 13	5 9 10	2 8 12	3 6 11
17																(17)	5 8 11	4 6 12	3 7 10	2 9 13
18																	(18)	1 20 21	1 19 21	1 19 20
19																		(19)	1 18 21	1 18 20
20																			(20)	1 18 19
21																				(21)

3 6 16	5 7 14	2 9 17	5 7 12	4 8 10	3 8 11	2 9 13	1 19 20	1 18 20	1 18 19
4 9 14	2 8 16	5 6 15	4 9 11	5 8 13	2 9 12	3 7 10	1 19 21	1 18 21	(20)
2 7 15	4 6 17	3 8 14	3 8 13	2 7 11	5 9 10	4 8 12	1 20 21	(19)	
5 9 17	3 9 15	4 7 16	2 6 10	3 9 12	4 7 13	5 8 11	(18)		
5 8 18	4 6 19	2 9 21	1 15 16	1 14 18	1 14 15	(17)			
3 6 21	2 9 20	4 7 18	1 15 17	1 14 17	(16)				
2 7 19	3 9 18	5 6 20	1 16 17	(15)					
4 9 20	5 7 21	3 9 19	(14)						
1 10 12	1 10 11	(13)							
1 10 13	(12)								
(11)									

APPENDIX B

F–Tables

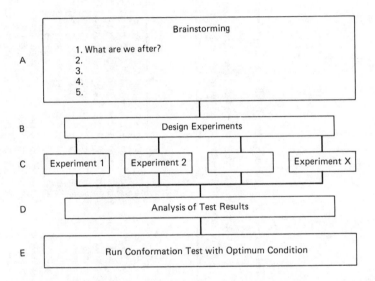

Figure B-1. A Taguchi experiment flow diagram.

Table B-1. F Table $F_{.10}(f_1, f_2)$, 90% Confidence

f_1 = Number of degrees of freedom of numerator
f_2 = Number of degrees of freedom of denominator

f_2 \ f_1	1	2	3	4	5	6	7	8	9	10	12	15	20	24	30	40	60	120	∞
1	39.864	49.500	53.593	55.833	57.241	58.204	58.906	59.439	59.858	60.195	60.705	61.220	61.740	62.002	62.265	62.529	62.794	63.061	63.328
2	8.5263	9.0000	9.1618	9.2434	9.2926	9.3255	9.3491	9.3668	9.3805	9.3916	9.4081	9.4247	9.4413	9.4496	9.4579	9.4663	9.4746	9.4829	9.4913
3	5.5383	5.4624	5.3908	5.3427	5.3092	5.2847	5.2662	5.2517	5.2400	5.2304	5.2156	5.2003	5.1845	5.1764	5.1681	5.1597	5.1512	5.1425	5.1337
4	4.5448	4.3246	4.1908	4.1073	4.0506	4.0098	3.9790	3.9549	3.9357	3.9199	3.8955	3.8689	3.8443	3.8310	3.8174	3.8036	3.7986	3.7753	3.7607
5	4.0604	3.7797	3.6195	3.5202	3.4530	3.4045	3.3679	3.3393	3.3163	3.2974	3.2682	3.2380	3.2067	3.1905	3.1741	3.1573	3.1402	3.1228	3.1050
6	3.7760	3.4633	3.2888	3.1808	3.1075	3.0546	3.0145	2.9830	2.9577	2.9369	2.9047	2.8712	2.8363	2.8183	2.8000	2.7812	2.7620	2.7423	2.7222
7	3.5894	3.2574	3.0741	2.9605	2.8833	2.8274	2.7849	2.7516	2.7247	2.7025	2.6681	2.6322	2.5947	2.5723	2.5555	2.5351	2.5142	2.4928	2.4708
8	3.4579	3.1131	2.9238	2.8064	2.7265	2.6683	2.6241	2.5893	2.5612	2.5380	2.5020	2.4642	2.4246	2.4041	2.3830	2.3614	2.3391	2.3162	2.2926
9	3.3603	3.0065	2.8129	2.6927	2.6106	2.5509	2.5053	2.4594	2.4403	2.4163	2.3789	2.3396	2.2983	2.2768	2.2547	2.2320	2.2085	2.1843	2.1592
10	3.2850	2.9245	2.7277	2.6053	2.5216	2.4606	2.4140	2.3772	2.3473	2.3226	2.2841	2.2435	2.2007	2.1784	2.1554	2.1317	2.1072	2.0818	2.0554
11	3.2252	2.8595	2.6602	2.5362	2.4512	2.3981	2.3416	2.3040	2.2735	2.2482	2.2087	2.1671	2.1230	2.1000	2.0762	2.0516	2.0261	1.9997	1.9721
12	3.1765	2.8068	2.6055	2.4801	2.3940	2.3310	2.2828	2.2446	2.2135	2.1878	2.1474	2.1049	2.0597	2.0360	2.0115	1.9861	1.9597	1.9323	1.9036
13	3.1362	2.7632	2.5603	2.4337	2.3467	2.2830	2.2341	2.1953	2.1638	2.1376	2.0966	2.0532	2.0070	1.9827	1.9576	1.9315	1.9043	1.8759	1.8462

ν																			
14	3.1022	2.7265	2.5222	2.3947	2.3059	2.2426	2.1931	2.1539	2.1220	2.0954	2.0537	2.0095	1.9625	1.9377	1.9119	1.8852	1.8572	1.8280	1.7973
15	3.0732	2.6952	2.4898	2.3614	2.2730	2.2081	2.1582	2.1185	2.0862	2.0593	2.0171	1.9722	1.9243	1.8890	1.8728	1.8454	1.8168	1.7867	1.7551
16	3.0481	2.6682	2.4618	2.3327	2.2438	2.1783	2.1280	2.0880	2.0553	2.0281	1.9854	1.9399	1.8913	1.8656	1.8388	1.8108	1.7816	1.7507	1.7182
17	3.0262	2.6446	2.4374	2.3077	2.2183	2.1524	2.1017	2.0613	2.0284	2.0009	1.9577	1.9117	1.8624	1.8362	1.8090	1.7805	1.7506	1.7191	1.6856
18	3.0070	2.6239	2.4160	2.2858	2.1958	2.1296	2.0785	2.0379	2.0047	1.9770	1.9333	1.8868	1.8368	1.8103	1.7827	1.7537	1.7232	1.6910	1.6567
19	2.9899	2.6056	2.3970	2.2663	2.1760	2.1094	2.0580	2.0171	1.9836	1.9557	1.9117	1.8647	1.8142	1.7873	1.7592	1.7298	1.6988	1.6659	1.6308
20	2.9747	2.5893	2.3801	2.2489	2.1582	2.0913	2.0397	1.9985	1.9649	1.9367	1.8924	1.8449	1.7938	1.7667	1.7382	1.7083	1.6769	1.6433	1.6074
21	2.9609	2.5746	2.3649	2.2333	2.1423	2.0751	2.0232	1.9819	1.9480	1.9197	1.8750	1.8272	1.7756	1.7481	1.7193	1.6890	1.6569	1.6228	1.5862
22	2.9486	2.5613	2.3512	2.2193	2.1279	2.0605	2.0084	1.9668	1.9327	1.9043	1.8593	1.8111	1.7590	1.7312	1.7021	1.6714	1.6389	1.6042	1.5668
23	2.9374	2.5493	2.3387	2.2065	2.1149	2.0472	1.9949	1.9531	1.9189	1.8903	1.8450	1.7964	1.7439	1.7159	1.6864	1.6554	1.6224	1.5871	1.5490
24	2.9271	2.5383	2.3274	2.1949	2.1030	2.0351	1.9826	1.9407	1.9063	1.8775	1.8319	1.7831	1.7302	1.7019	1.6721	1.6407	1.6073	1.5715	1.5327
25	2.9177	2.5283	2.3170	2.1843	2.0922	2.0241	1.9714	1.9292	1.8947	1.8658	1.8200	1.7708	1.7175	1.6890	1.6589	1.6272	1.5934	1.5570	1.5176
26	2.9091	2.5191	2.3075	2.1745	2.0822	2.0139	1.9610	1.9188	1.8841	1.8550	1.8090	1.7596	1.7059	1.6771	1.6468	1.6147	1.5805	1.5437	1.5036
27	2.9012	2.5106	2.2987	2.1655	2.0730	2.0045	1.9515	1.9091	1.8743	1.8451	1.7989	1.7492	1.6951	1.6662	1.6356	1.6032	1.5687	1.5313	1.4906
28	2.8939	2.5028	2.2906	2.1571	2.0645	1.9959	1.9427	1.9001	1.8652	1.8359	1.7895	1.7395	1.6852	1.6560	1.6252	1.5925	1.5575	1.5198	1.4784
29	2.8871	2.4955	2.2831	2.1494	2.0566	1.9880	1.9345	1.8918	1.8560	1.8274	1.7808	1.7306	1.6759	1.6465	1.6155	1.5825	1.5472	1.5090	1.4670
30	2.8807	2.4887	2.2761	2.1422	2.0492	1.9803	1.9269	1.8841	1.8498	1.8195	1.7727	1.7223	1.6673	1.6377	1.6065	1.5732	1.5376	1.4989	1.4564
40	2.8354	2.4404	2.2261	2.0909	1.9968	1.9269	1.8725	1.8289	1.7929	1.7627	1.7146	1.6624	1.6052	1.5741	1.5411	1.5056	1.4572	1.4248	1.3769
60	2.7914	2.3932	2.1774	2.0410	1.9457	1.8747	1.8194	1.7748	1.7380	1.7070	1.6574	1.6034	1.5435	1.5107	1.4755	1.4373	1.3952	1.3476	1.2915
120	2.7478	2.3473	2.1300	1.9923	1.8959	1.8238	1.7675	1.7220	1.6843	1.6524	1.6012	1.5450	1.4821	1.4472	1.4094	1.3676	1.3203	1.2646	1.1926
∞	2.7055	2.3026	2.0638	1.9449	1.8473	1.7741	1.7167	1.6702	1.6315	1.5987	1.5458	1.4871	1.4206	1.3832	1.3410	1.2951	1.2400	1.1686	1.0000

Table B-2. F Table $F_{.05,(f_1, f_2)}$, 95% Confidence

f_1 = Number of degrees of freedom of numerator
f_2 = Number of degrees of freedom of denominator

f_2 \ f_1	1	2	3	4	5	6	7	8	9	10	12	15	20	24	30	40	60	120	∞
1	161.45	199.50	215.71	224.58	230.16	233.99	236.77	238.88	240.54	241.88	243.91	245.95	248.01	249.05	250.09	251.14	252.20	253.25	254.32
2	18.513	19.000	19.614	19.247	19.296	19.330	19.353	19.371	19.385	19.396	19.413	19.429	19.446	19.454	19.462	19.471	19.479	19.487	19.496
3	10.128	9.5521	9.2766	9.1172	9.0135	8.9406	8.8868	8.8452	8.8123	8.7855	8.7446	8.7029	8.6602	8.6385	8.6166	8.5944	8.5720	8.5494	8.5265
4	7.7086	6.9443	6.5914	6.3883	6.2560	6.1631	6.0942	6.0410	5.9988	5.9644	5.9117	5.8578	5.8025	5.7744	5.7459	5.7170	5.6878	5.6581	5.6281
5	6.6079	5.7861	5.4095	5.1922	5.0503	4.9503	4.8759	4.8183	4.7725	4.7351	4.6777	4.6188	4.5581	4.5272	4.4957	4.4638	4.4314	4.3984	4.3650
6	5.9874	5.1433	4.7571	4.5337	4.3874	4.2830	4.2066	4.1468	4.0990	4.0600	3.9999	3.9381	3.8742	3.8415	3.8082	3.7743	3.7398	3.7047	3.6688
7	5.5914	4.7374	4.3468	4.1203	3.9715	3.8660	3.7870	3.7257	3.6767	3.6365	3.5747	3.5108	3.4445	3.4105	3.3758	3.3404	3.3043	3.2674	3.2298
8	5.3177	4.4590	4.0662	3.8378	3.6875	3.5806	3.5005	3.4381	3.3881	3.3472	3.2840	3.2184	3.1503	3.1152	3.0794	3.0428	3.0053	2.9669	2.9276
9	5.1174	4.2565	3.8626	3.6331	3.4817	3.3738	3.2927	3.2296	3.1789	3.1373	3.0729	3.0061	2.9365	2.9005	2.8637	2.8259	2.7872	2.7475	2.7067
10	4.9646	4.1028	3.7083	3.4780	3.3258	3.2172	3.1355	3.0717	3.0204	2.9782	2.9130	2.8450	2.7740	2.7372	2.6996	2.6609	2.6211	2.5801	2.5379
11	4.8443	3.9823	3.5874	3.3567	3.2039	3.0946	3.0123	2.9480	2.8962	2.8536	2.7876	2.7186	2.6464	2.6090	2.5705	2.5309	2.4901	2.4480	2.4045
12	4.7472	3.8853	3.4903	3.2592	3.1059	2.9961	2.9134	2.8486	2.7964	2.7534	2.6866	2.6169	2.5436	2.5055	2.4663	2.4259	2.3842	2.3410	2.2962
13	4.6672	3.8056	3.4105	3.1791	3.0254	2.9153	2.8321	2.7669	2.7144	2.6710	2.6037	2.5331	2.4589	2.4202	2.3803	2.3392	2.2966	2.2524	2.2064

14	4.6001	3.7389	3.3439	3.1122	2.9582	2.8477	2.7642	2.6987	2.6458	2.6021	2.5342	2.4630	2.3879	2.3487	2.3082	2.2664	2.2230	2.1778	2.1307
15	4.5431	3.6823	3.2874	3.0556	2.9013	2.7905	2.7066	2.6408	2.5876	2.5437	2.4753	2.4035	2.3275	2.2878	2.2468	2.2043	2.1601	2.1141	2.0658
16	4.4940	3.6337	3.2389	3.0069	2.8524	2.7413	2.6572	2.5911	2.5377	2.4935	2.4247	2.3522	2.2756	2.2354	2.1938	2.1507	2.1058	2.0589	2.0096
17	4.4513	3.5915	3.1968	2.9647	2.8100	2.6987	2.6143	2.5480	2.4943	2.4499	2.3807	2.3077	2.2304	2.1898	2.1477	2.1040	2.0584	2.0107	1.9604
18	4.4139	3.5546	3.1599	2.9277	2.7729	2.6613	2.5767	2.5102	2.4563	2.4117	2.3421	2.2686	2.1906	2.1497	2.1071	2.0629	2.0166	1.9681	1.9168
19	4.3808	3.5219	3.1274	2.8951	2.7401	2.6283	2.5435	2.4768	2.4227	2.3779	2.3080	2.2341	2.1555	2.1141	2.0712	2.0264	1.9796	1.9302	1.8780
20	4.3513	3.4928	3.0984	2.8661	2.7109	2.5990	2.5140	2.4471	2.3928	2.3479	2.2776	2.2033	2.1242	2.0825	2.0391	1.9938	1.9464	1.8963	1.8432
21	4.3248	3.4668	3.0725	2.8401	2.6848	2.5727	2.4876	2.4205	2.3661	2.3210	2.2504	2.1757	2.0960	2.0540	2.0102	1.9645	1.9165	1.8657	1.8117
22	4.3009	3.4434	3.0491	2.8167	2.6613	2.5491	2.4638	2.3965	2.3419	2.2967	2.2258	2.1508	2.0707	2.0283	1.9842	1.9380	1.8895	1.8380	1.7831
23	4.2793	3.4221	3.0280	2.7955	2.6400	2.5277	2.4422	2.3748	2.3201	2.2747	2.2036	2.1282	2.0476	2.0050	1.9605	1.9139	1.8649	1.8128	1.7570
24	4.2597	3.4026	3.0088	2.7763	2.6207	2.5082	2.4226	2.3551	2.3002	2.2547	2.1834	2.1077	2.0267	1.9838	1.9390	1.8920	1.8424	1.7897	1.7331
25	4.2417	3.3852	2.9912	2.7587	2.6030	2.4904	2.4047	2.3371	2.2821	2.2365	2.1649	2.0889	2.0075	1.9643	1.9192	1.8718	1.8217	1.7684	1.7110
26	4.2252	3.3690	2.9751	2.7426	2.5868	2.4741	2.3883	2.3205	2.2655	2.2197	2.1479	2.0716	1.9898	1.9464	1.9010	1.8533	1.8027	1.7488	1.6906
27	4.2100	3.3541	2.9604	2.7278	2.5719	2.4591	2.3732	2.3053	2.2501	2.2043	2.1323	2.0558	1.9736	1.9299	1.8842	1.8361	1.7851	1.7307	1.6717
28	4.1960	3.3404	2.9467	2.7141	2.5581	2.4453	2.3593	2.2913	2.2360	2.1900	2.1179	2.0411	1.9586	1.9147	1.8687	1.8203	1.7689	1.7138	1.6541
29	4.1830	3.3277	2.9340	2.7014	2.5454	2.4324	2.3463	2.2782	2.2229	2.1768	2.1045	2.0275	1.9446	1.9005	1.8543	1.8055	1.7537	1.6981	1.6377
30	4.1709	3.3158	2.9223	2.6896	2.5336	2.4205	2.3343	2.2662	2.2107	2.1646	2.0921	2.0148	1.9317	1.8874	1.8409	1.7918	1.7396	1.6835	1.6223
40	4.0848	3.2317	2.8387	2.6060	2.4495	2.3359	2.2490	2.1802	2.1240	2.0772	2.0035	1.9245	1.8389	1.7929	1.7444	1.6928	1.6373	1.5766	1.5089
60	4.0012	3.1504	2.7581	2.5252	2.3683	2.2540	2.1665	1.0970	2.0401	1.9926	1.9174	1.8364	1.7480	1.7001	1.6491	1.5943	1.5343	1.4673	1.3893
120	3.9201	3.0718	2.6802	2.4472	2.2900	2.1750	2.0867	2.0164	1.9588	1.9105	1.8337	1.7505	1.6587	1.6084	1.5543	1.4952	1.4290	1.3519	1.2539
∞	3.8415	2.9957	2.6049	2.3719	2.2141	2.0986	2.0096	1.9384	1.8799	1.8307	1.7522	1.6664	1.5705	1.5173	1.4591	1.3940	1.3180	1.2214	1.0000

Table B-3. F Table $F_{.025}(f_1, f_2)$, 97.5% Confidence

f_1 = Number of degrees of freedom of numerator
f_2 = Number of degrees of freedom of denominator

f_2 \ f_1	1	2	3	4	5	6	7	8	9	10	12	15	20	24	30	40	60	120	∞
1	647.79	799.50	864.16	899.58	921.85	937.11	948.22	956.66	963.28	968.63	976.71	984.87	993.10	997.25	1001.4	1005.6	1009.8	1014.0	1018.3
2	38.506	39.000	39.165	39.248	39.298	39.331	39.355	39.373	39.387	39.398	39.415	39.431	39.448	39.456	39.465	39.473	39.481	39.490	39.498
3	17.443	16.044	15.439	15.101	14.885	14.735	14.624	14.540	14.473	14.419	14.337	14.253	14.167	14.124	14.081	14.037	13.992	13.947	13.902
4	12.218	10.649	9.9792	9.6045	9.3645	9.1973	9.0741	8.9796	8.9047	8.8439	8.7512	8.6565	8.5599	8.5109	8.4613	8.4111	8.3604	8.3092	8.2573
5	10.007	8.4336	7.7636	7.3879	7.1464	6.9777	6.8531	6.7572	6.6810	6.6192	6.5246	6.4277	6.3285	6.2780	6.2269	6.1751	6.1225	6.0693	6.0153
6	8.8131	7.2598	6.5988	6.2272	5.9876	5.8197	5.6955	5.5996	5.5234	5.4613	5.3662	5.2687	5.1684	5.1172	5.0652	5.0125	4.9589	4.9045	4.8491
7	8.0727	6.5415	5.8898	5.5226	5.2852	5.1186	4.9949	4.8994	4.8232	4.7611	4.6658	4.5678	4.4667	4.4150	4.3624	4.3089	4.2544	4.1989	4.1423
8	7.5709	6.0595	5.4160	5.0526	4.8173	4.6517	4.5286	4.4332	4.3572	4.2951	4.1997	4.1012	3.9995	3.9472	3.8940	3.8398	3.7844	3.7279	3.6702
9	7.2093	5.7147	5.0781	4.7181	4.4844	4.3107	4.1971	4.1020	4.0260	3.9639	3.8682	3.7694	3.6669	3.6142	3.5604	3.5055	3.4493	3.3918	3.3329
10	6.9367	5.4564	4.8256	4.4683	4.2361	4.0721	3.9498	3.8549	3.7790	3.7168	3.6209	3.5217	3.4186	3.3654	3.3110	3.2554	3.1984	3.1399	3.0798
11	6.7241	5.2559	4.6300	4.2751	4.0440	3.8807	3.7586	3.6638	3.5879	3.5257	3.4296	3.3299	3.2261	3.1725	3.1176	3.0613	3.0035	2.9441	2.8828
12	6.5538	5.0959	4.4742	4.1212	3.8911	3.7293	3.6065	3.5118	3.4358	3.3736	3.2773	3.1772	3.0728	3.0187	2.9633	2.9063	2.8478	2.7874	2.7249
13	6.4143	4.9653	4.3472	3.9959	3.7667	3.6043	3.4827	3.3880	3.3120	3.2497	3.1532	3.0527	2.9477	2.8932	2.8373	2.7797	2.7204	2.6590	2.5955

14	6.2979	4.8567	4.2417	3.8919	3.6634	3.5014	3.3799	3.2853	3.2093	3.1469	3.0501	2.9493	2.8437	2.7888	2.7324	2.6742	2.6142	2.5519	2.4872
15	6.1995	4.7650	4.1528	3.8043	3.5764	3.4147	3.2934	3.1987	3.1227	3.0602	2.9633	2.8621	2.7559	2.7006	2.6437	2.5850	2.5242	2.4611	2.3953
16	6.1151	4.6867	4.0768	3.7294	3.5021	3.3406	3.2194	3.1248	3.0488	2.9862	2.8890	2.7875	2.6808	2.6252	2.5678	2.5085	2.4471	2.3831	2.3163
17	6.0420	4.6189	4.0112	3.6648	3.4379	3.2767	3.1556	3.0610	2.9849	2.9222	2.8249	2.7230	2.6158	2.5598	2.5021	2.4422	2.3801	2.3153	2.2474
18	5.9781	4.5597	3.9539	3.6083	3.3820	3.2209	3.0999	3.0053	2.9291	2.8664	2.7689	2.6667	2.5590	2.5027	2.4445	2.3842	2.3214	2.2558	2.1869
19	5.9216	4.5075	3.9034	3.5587	3.3327	3.1718	3.0509	2.9563	2.8800	2.8173	2.7196	2.6171	2.5089	2.4523	2.3937	2.3329	2.2695	2.2032	2.1333
20	5.8715	4.4613	3.8587	3.5147	3.2891	3.1283	3.0074	2.9128	2.8365	2.7737	2.6758	2.5731	2.4645	2.4076	2.3486	2.2873	2.2234	2.1562	2.0853
21	5.8266	4.4199	3.8188	3.4754	3.2501	3.0895	2.9686	2.8740	2.7977	2.7348	2.6368	2.5338	2.4247	2.3675	2.3082	2.2465	2.1819	2.1141	2.0422
22	5.7863	4.3828	3.7829	3.4401	3.2151	3.0546	2.9338	2.8392	2.7628	2.6998	2.6017	2.4984	2.3890	2.3315	2.2718	2.2097	2.1446	2.0760	2.0032
23	5.7498	4.3492	3.7505	3.4083	3.1835	3.0232	2.9024	2.8077	2.7313	2.6682	2.5699	2.4665	2.3567	2.2989	2.2389	2.1763	2.1107	2.0415	1.9677
24	5.7167	4.3187	3.7211	3.3794	3.1548	2.9946	2.8738	2.7791	2.7027	2.6396	2.5412	2.4374	2.3273	2.2693	2.2090	2.1460	2.0799	2.0099	1.9353
25	5.6864	4.2909	3.6943	3.3530	3.1287	2.9685	2.8478	2.7531	2.6766	2.6135	2.5149	2.4110	2.3005	2.2422	2.1816	2.1183	2.0517	1.9811	1.9055
26	5.6586	4.2655	3.6697	3.3289	3.1048	2.9447	2.8240	2.7293	2.6528	2.5895	2.4909	2.3867	2.2759	2.2174	2.1565	2.0928	2.0257	1.9545	1.8781
27	5.6331	4.2421	3.6472	3.3067	3.0828	2.9228	2.8021	2.7074	2.6309	2.5675	2.4688	2.3644	2.2533	2.1946	2.1334	2.0693	2.0018	1.9299	1.8527
28	5.6096	4.2205	3.6264	3.2863	3.0625	2.9027	2.7820	2.6872	2.6106	2.5473	2.4484	2.3438	2.2324	2.1735	2.1121	2.0477	1.9796	1.9072	1.8291
29	5.5878	4.2006	3.6072	3.2674	3.0438	2.8840	2.7633	2.6686	2.5919	2.5286	2.4295	2.3248	2.2131	2.1540	2.0923	2.0276	1.9591	1.8861	1.8072
30	5.5675	4.1821	3.5894	3.2499	3.0265	2.8667	2.7460	2.6513	2.5746	2.5112	2.4120	2.3072	2.1952	2.1359	2.0739	2.0089	1.9400	1.8664	1.7867
40	5.4239	4.0510	3.4633	3.1261	2.9037	2.7444	2.6238	2.5289	2.4519	2.3882	2.2882	2.1819	2.0677	2.0069	1.9429	1.8752	1.8028	1.7242	1.6371
60	5.2857	3.9253	3.3425	3.0077	2.7863	2.6274	2.5068	2.4117	2.3344	2.2702	2.1692	2.0613	1.9445	1.8817	1.8152	1.7440	1.6668	1.5810	1.4822
120	5.1524	3.8046	3.2270	2.8943	2.6740	2.5154	2.3948	2.2994	2.2217	2.1570	2.0548	1.9450	1.8249	1.7597	1.6899	1.6141	1.5299	1.4327	1.3104
∞	5.0239	3.6889	3.1161	2.7858	2.5665	2.4082	2.2875	2.1918	2.1136	2.0493	1.9447	1.8326	1.7085	1.6402	1.5660	1.4835	1.3883	1.2684	1.0000

Table B-4. F Table $F_{.01}(f_1, f_2)$, 99% Confidence

f_1 = Number of degrees of freedom of numerator
f_2 = Number of degrees of freedom of denominator

f_2 \ f_1	1	2	3	4	5	6	7	8	9	10	12	15	20	24	30	40	80	120	∞
1	4052.2	4999.5	5403.3	5624.6	5763.7	5859.0	5928.3	5981.6	6022.5	6055.8	6106.3	6157.3	6208.7	6234.6	6260.7	6286.8	6313.0	6339.4	6366.0
2	98.503	99.000	99.166	99.249	99.299	99.332	99.356	99.374	99.388	99.399	99.415	99.432	99.449	99.458	99.466	99.474	99.483	99.491	99.501
3	34.116	30.817	29.457	28.710	28.237	27.911	27.672	27.489	27.345	27.229	27.052	26.872	26.690	26.598	26.505	26.411	26.316	26.221	26.125
4	21.198	18.000	16.694	15.977	15.522	15.207	14.986	14.799	14.659	14.546	14.374	14.198	14.020	13.929	13.838	13.745	13.652	13.558	13.463
5	16.258	13.274	12.060	11.392	10.967	10.672	10.456	10.289	10.158	10.051	9.8883	9.7222	9.5527	9.4665	9.3793	9.2912	9.2020	9.1118	9.0204
6	13.745	10.925	9.7795	9.1483	8.7459	8.4661	8.2600	8.1016	7.9761	7.8741	7.7183	7.5590	7.3958	7.3127	7.2285	7.1432	7.0568	6.9690	6.8801
7	12.246	9.5466	8.4513	7.8467	7.4604	7.1914	6.9928	6.8401	6.7188	6.6201	6.4691	6.3143	6.1554	6.0743	5.9921	5.9084	5.8236	5.7372	5.6495
8	11.259	8.6491	7.5910	7.0060	6.6318	6.3707	6.1776	6.0289	5.9106	5.8143	5.6668	5.5151	5.3591	5.2793	5.1981	5.1156	5.0316	4.9460	4.8588
9	10.561	8.0215	6.9919	6.4221	6.0569	5.8018	5.6129	5.4671	5.3511	5.2565	5.1114	4.9621	4.8080	4.7290	4.6486	4.5667	4.4831	4.3978	4.3105
10	10.044	7.5584	6.5523	5.9943	5.6363	5.3858	5.2001	5.0567	4.9424	4.8402	4.7059	4.5582	4.4054	4.3269	4.2469	4.1653	4.0619	3.9965	3.9090
11	9.6460	7.2057	6.2167	5.6683	5.3160	5.0692	4.8861	4.7445	4.6315	4.5393	4.3974	4.2509	4.0990	4.0209	3.9411	3.8596	3.7761	3.6904	3.6025
12	9.3302	6.9266	5.9526	5.4119	5.0643	4.8206	4.6395	4.4994	4.3875	4.2961	4.1553	4.0096	3.8584	3.7805	3.7008	3.6192	3.5355	3.4494	3.3608
13	9.0738	6.7010	5.7394	5.2053	4.8616	4.6204	4.4410	4.3021	4.1911	4.1003	3.9603	3.8154	3.6646	3.5868	3.5070	3.4253	3.3413	3.2548	3.1654

14	8.8616	6.5149	5.5639	5.0354	4.6950	4.4558	4.2779	4.1399	4.0297	3.9394	3.8001	3.6557	3.5052	3.4274	3.3476	3.2656	3.1813	3.0942	3.0040
15	8.6831	6.3589	5.4170	4.8932	4.5556	4.3183	4.1415	4.0045	3.8948	3.8049	3.6662	3.5222	3.3719	3.2940	3.2141	3.1319	3.0471	2.9595	2.8684
16	8.5310	6.2262	5.2922	4.7726	4.4374	4.2016	4.0259	3.8896	3.7804	3.6909	3.5527	3.4089	3.2588	3.1808	3.1007	3.0182	2.9330	2.8447	2.7528
17	8.3997	6.1121	5.1850	4.6590	4.3359	4.1015	3.9267	3.7910	3.6822	3.5931	3.4552	3.3117	3.1615	3.0835	3.0032	2.9205	2.8348	2.7459	2.6530
18	8.2854	6.0129	5.0919	4.5790	4.2479	4.0146	3.8406	3.7054	3.5971	3.5082	3.3706	3.2273	3.0771	2.9990	2.9185	2.8354	2.7493	2.6597	2.5660
19	8.1850	5.9259	5.0103	4.5003	4.1708	3.9386	3.7653	3.6305	3.5225	3.4338	3.2965	3.1533	3.0031	2.9249	2.8442	2.7608	2.6742	2.5839	2.4893
20	8.0960	5.8489	4.9382	4.4307	4.1027	3.8714	3.6987	3.5644	3.4567	3.3682	3.2311	3.0880	2.9377	2.8594	2.7785	2.6947	2.6077	2.5168	2.4212
21	8.0166	5.7804	4.8740	4.3688	4.0421	3.8117	3.6396	3.5056	3.3981	3.3098	3.1729	3.0299	2.8976	2.8011	2.7200	2.6359	2.5484	2.4568	2.3603
22	7.9454	5.7190	4.8166	4.3134	3.9880	3.7583	3.5867	3.4530	3.3458	3.2576	3.1209	2.9780	2.8274	2.7488	2.6675	2.5831	2.4951	2.4029	2.3055
23	7.8811	5.6637	4.7649	4.2635	3.9392	3.7102	3.5390	3.4057	3.2986	3.2106	3.0740	2.9311	2.7805	2.7017	2.6202	2.5355	2.4471	2.3542	2.2559
24	7.8229	5.6136	4.7181	4.2184	3.8951	3.6667	3.4959	3.3629	3.2560	3.1681	3.0316	2.8887	2.7380	2.6591	2.5773	2.4923	2.4035	2.3099	2.2107
25	7.7698	5.5680	4.6755	4.1774	3.8550	3.6272	3.4568	3.3239	3.2172	3.1294	2.9931	2.8502	2.6993	2.6203	2.5383	2.4530	2.3637	2.2695	2.1694
26	7.7213	5.5263	4.6366	4.1400	3.8183	3.5911	3.4210	3.2884	3.1818	3.0941	2.9579	2.8150	2.6640	2.5848	2.5026	2.4170	2.3273	2.2325	2.1315
27	7.6767	5.4881	4.6009	4.1056	3.7848	3.5580	3.3882	3.2558	3.1494	3.0618	2.9256	2.7827	2.6316	2.5522	2.4699	2.3840	2.2938	2.1984	2.0965
28	7.6356	5.4529	4.5681	4.0740	3.7539	3.5276	3.3581	3.2259	3.1195	3.0320	2.8959	2.7530	2.6017	2.5223	2.4397	2.3535	2.2629	2.1670	2.0642
29	7.5976	5.4205	4.5378	4.0449	3.7254	3.4995	3.3302	3.1982	3.0920	3.0045	2.8685	2.7256	2.5742	2.4946	2.4118	2.3253	2.2344	2.1378	2.0342
30	7.5625	5.3904	4.5097	4.0179	3.6990	3.4735	3.3045	3.1726	3.0665	2.9791	2.8431	2.7002	2.5487	2.4689	2.3860	2.2992	2.2079	2.1107	2.0062
40	7.3141	5.1785	4.3126	3.8283	3.5138	3.2910	3.1238	2.9930	2.8876	2.8005	2.6649	2.5216	2.3689	2.2880	2.2034	2.1142	2.0194	1.9172	1.8047
60	7.0771	4.9774	4.1259	3.6591	3.3389	3.1187	2.9530	2.8233	2.7185	2.6318	2.4961	2.3523	2.1978	2.1154	2.0285	1.9360	1.8363	1.7263	1.6006
120	6.8510	4.7865	3.9493	3.4796	3.1735	2.9559	2.7918	2.6629	2.5586	2.4721	2.3363	2.1915	2.0346	1.9500	1.8600	1.7629	1.6557	1.5330	1.3805
8	6.6349	4.6052	3.7816	3.3192	3.0173	2.8020	2.6393	2.5113	2.4073	2.3209	2.1848	2.0385	1.8783	1.7908	1.6964	1.5923	1.4730	1.3246	1.0000

Table B-5. F Table $F_{.005}(f_1, f_2)$, 99.5% Confidence

f_1 = Number of degrees of freedom of numerator
f_2 = Number of degrees of freedom of denominator

f_2 \ f_1	1	2	3	4	5	6	7	8	9	10	12	15	20	24	30	40	80	120	∞
1	16211	20000	21615	22500	23056	23437	23715	23925	24091	24224	24426	24630	24836	24940	25044	25148	25253	25359	25465
2	198.50	199.00	199.17	199.25	199.30	199.33	199.36	199.37	199.39	199.40	199.42	199.43	199.45	199.46	199.47	199.47	199.48	199.49	199.51
3	55.552	49.799	47.467	46.195	45.392	44.838	44.434	44.126	43.882	43.686	43.387	43.085	42.778	42.622	42.466	42.308	42.149	41.989	41.829
4	31.333	26.284	24.259	23.155	22.456	21.975	21.622	21.352	21.139	20.967	20.705	20.438	20.167	20.030	19.892	19.752	19.611	19.468	19.325
5	22.785	18.314	16.530	15.556	14.940	14.513	14.200	13.961	13.772	13.618	13.384	13.146	12.903	12.780	12.656	12.530	12.402	12.274	12.144
6	18.635	14.544	12.917	12.028	11.464	11.073	10.786	10.566	10.391	10.250	10.034	9.8140	9.5888	9.4741	9.3583	9.2408	9.1219	9.0015	8.8793
7	16.236	12.404	10.882	10.050	9.5221	9.1554	8.8854	8.6781	8.5138	8.3803	8.1764	7.9578	7.7540	7.6450	7.5345	7.4225	7.3088	7.1933	7.0760
8	14.688	11.042	9.5965	8.8061	8.3018	7.9520	7.6952	7.4960	7.3386	7.2107	7.0149	6.8143	6.6082	6.5029	6.3961	6.2875	6.1772	6.0649	5.9505
9	13.614	10.107	8.7171	7.9559	7.4711	7.1338	6.8849	6.6933	6.5411	6.4171	6.2274	6.0325	5.8318	5.7292	5.6248	5.5186	5.4104	5.3001	5.1875
10	12.826	9.4270	8.0807	7.3428	6.8723	6.5446	6.3025	6.1159	5.9676	5.8467	5.6613	5.4707	5.2740	5.1732	5.0705	4.9659	4.8592	4.7501	4.6385
11	12.226	8.9122	7.6004	6.8809	6.4217	6.1015	5.8648	5.6821	5.5368	5.4182	5.2363	5.0489	4.8552	4.7557	4.6543	4.5508	4.4450	4.3367	4.2256
12	11.754	8.5096	7.2258	6.5211	6.0711	5.7570	5.5245	5.3451	5.2021	5.0855	4.9063	4.7214	4.5299	4.4315	4.3309	4.2282	4.1229	4.0149	3.9039
13	11.374	8.1865	6.9257	6.2335	5.7910	5.4819	5.2529	5.0761	4.9351	4.8199	4.6429	4.4600	4.2703	4.1726	4.0727	3.9704	3.8655	3.7577	3.6465

14	11.060	7.9217	6.6803	5.9984	5.5623	5.2574	5.0313	4.8566	4.7173	4.6034	4.4281	4.2468	4.0585	3.9614	3.8619	3.7600	3.6553	3.5473	3.4359
15	10.798	7.7008	6.4760	5.8029	5.3721	5.0708	4.8473	4.6743	4.5364	4.4236	4.2498	4.0698	3.8826	3.7859	3.6867	3.5850	3.4803	3.3722	3.2602
16	10.575	7.5138	6.3034	5.6378	5.2117	4.9134	4.6920	4.5207	4.3838	4.2719	4.0994	3.9205	3.7342	3.6378	3.5388	3.4372	3.3324	3.2240	3.1115
17	10.384	7.3536	6.1556	5.4967	5.0746	4.7789	4.5594	4.3893	4.2535	4.1423	3.9709	3.7929	3.6073	3.5112	3.4124	3.3107	3.2058	3.0971	2.9839
18	10.218	7.2148	6.0277	5.3746	4.9560	4.6627	4.4448	4.2759	4.1410	4.0305	3.8599	3.6827	3.4977	3.4017	3.3030	3.2014	3.0962	2.9871	2.8732
19	10.073	7.0935	5.9161	5.2681	4.8526	4.5614	4.3448	4.1770	4.0428	3.9329	3.7631	3.5866	3.4020	3.3062	3.2075	3.1058	3.0004	2.8906	2.7762
20	9.9439	6.9865	5.8177	5.1743	4.7616	4.4721	4.2569	4.0900	3.9564	3.8470	3.6779	3.5020	3.3178	3.2220	3.1234	3.0215	2.9159	2.8058	2.6904
21	9.8295	6.8914	5.7304	5.0911	4.6808	4.3931	4.1789	4.0128	3.8799	3.7709	3.6024	3.4270	3.2431	3.1474	3.0488	2.9467	2.8408	2.7302	2.6140
22	9.7271	6.8064	5.6524	5.0168	4.6088	4.3225	4.1094	3.9440	3.8116	3.7030	3.5350	3.3600	3.1764	3.0807	2.9821	2.8799	2.7736	2.6625	2.5455
23	9.6348	6.7300	5.5823	4.9500	4.5441	4.2591	4.0469	3.8822	3.7502	3.6420	3.4745	3.2999	3.1165	3.0208	2.9221	2.8198	2.7132	2.6016	2.4837
24	9.5513	6.6610	5.5190	4.8898	4.4857	4.2019	3.9905	3.8264	3.6949	3.5870	3.4199	3.2456	3.0624	2.9667	2.8679	2.7654	2.6585	2.5463	2.4276
25	9.4753	6.5982	5.4615	4.8351	4.4327	4.1500	3.9394	3.7758	3.6447	3.5370	3.3704	3.1953	3.0133	2.9176	2.8187	2.7160	2.6099	2.4960	2.3765
26	9.4059	6.5409	5.4091	4.7852	4.3844	4.1027	3.8929	3.7297	3.5989	3.4916	3.3252	3.1515	2.9685	2.8728	2.7738	2.6709	2.5633	2.4501	2.3297
27	9.3423	6.4885	5.3611	4.7396	4.3402	4.0594	3.8501	3.6875	3.5571	3.4499	3.2839	3.1104	2.9275	2.8318	2.7327	2.6296	2.5217	2.4078	2.2867
28	9.2838	6.4403	5.3170	4.6977	4.2996	4.0197	3.8110	3.6487	3.5186	3.4117	3.2460	3.0727	2.8899	2.7941	2.6949	2.5916	2.4834	2.3689	2.2469
29	9.2297	6.3958	5.2764	4.6591	4.2622	3.9830	3.7749	3.6130	3.4832	3.3765	3.2111	3.0379	2.8551	2.7594	2.6601	2.5565	2.4479	2.3330	2.2102
30	9.1797	6.3547	5.2388	4.6233	4.2276	3.9492	3.7416	3.5801	3.4505	3.3440	3.1787	3.0057	2.8230	2.7272	2.6278	2.5241	2.4151	2.2997	2.1760
40	8.8278	6.0664	4.9759	4.3738	3.9860	3.7129	3.5088	3.3498	3.2220	3.1167	2.9531	2.7811	2.5984	2.5020	2.4015	2.2958	2.1838	2.0635	1.9318
60	8.4946	5.7950	4.7290	4.1399	3.7600	3.4918	3.2911	3.1344	3.0083	2.9042	2.7419	2.5705	2.3872	2.2989	2.1874	2.0789	1.9622	1.8341	1.6885
120	8.1790	5.5393	4.4973	3.9207	3.5482	3.2849	3.0874	2.9330	2.8083	2.7052	2.5439	2.3727	2.1881	2.0890	1.9839	1.8709	1.7459	1.6055	1.4311
∞	7.8794	5.2983	4.2794	3.7151	3.3499	3.0913	2.8968	2.7444	2.6210	2.5188	2.3583	2.1868	1.9998	1.8983	1.7891	1.6691	1.5325	1.3637	1.0000

APPENDIX C

Glossary

ANOVA: An analysis of variance is a table of information that displays the contributions of each factor.

Controllable factor: A design variable that is considered to influence the response and is included in the experiment. Its level can be controlled by the experimenters.

Design of experiment: A systematic procedure to lay out the factors and conditions of an experiment. Taguchi employs specific partial factorial arrangements (orthogonal arrays) to determine the optimum design.

Factorial Experiment: A systematic procedure in which all controllable factors except one are held constant as the variable factor is altered discretely or continuously.

Error: The amount of variation in the response caused by factors other than controllable factors included in the experiment.

Interaction: Two factors are said to have interaction with each other if the influence of one on the response function is dependent on the value of the other.

Linear Graph: A graphical representation of relative column locations of factors and their interactions. These were development by Dr. Taguchi to assist in assigning different factors to columns of the orthogonal array.

Loss Function: A mathematical expression proposed by Dr. Taguchi to quantitatively determine the additional cost to society caused by the lack of quality in a product. This additional cost is viewed as a loss to society and is expressed as a direct function of the mean square deviation from the target value.

Noise Factors: Noise factors are those factors that have an influence over a response but cannot be controlled in actual applications. They are of three kinds.

  Outer Noise: Consists of environmental conditions such as humidity temperature, operators, etc.

  Inner Noise: The deterioration of machines, tools and parts.

  Between Product Noise: The variation from piece to piece.

Off-Line Quality Control: Refers to the quality enhancement efforts in activities before production. These are activities such as upstream planning, R & D, systems design, parametric design, tolerance design and loss function, etc.

Orthogonal Array: A set of tables used to determine the least number of experiments and their conditions. The word orthogonal means balanced.

Outer Array: An orthogonal array used to define the conditions for the repetitions of the inner array design to measure the effects of various noise factors. An experiment with outer arrays will reduce the product variability and sensitivity to the influence of noise factors.

Parameter Design: Parameter design is used to design a product by selecting the optimum condition of the parameter levels so that the product is least sensitive to noise factors.

Quality Characteristic: The yardstick which measures the performance of a product or a process under study. For a plastic molding process this could be the strength of the molded piece. For a cake, this could be a combination of taste, shape and moistness.

Response: A quantitative value of the measured quality characteristic. e.g, stiffness, weight, flatness.

Variation Reduction: The variation in the output of a process produces nonuniformity in the product and is perceived as quality. Reduced variation increases customer satisfaction and reduces warranty cost arising from variation. To achieve better quality, a product must perform optimally and should have less variation around the optimum performance.

Robustness: Describes a condition in which a product or process is least influenced by the variation of individual factors. To become robust is to become less sensitive to variations.

S/N **Ratio:** Stands for the signal to noise ratio, i.e., the ratio of the power of a signal to the power of the noise (error). A high *S/N* ratio will mean that there is high sensitivity with the least error of measurement. In Taguchi analysis using *S/N* ratios, a higher value is always desirable regardless of the quality characteristic.

Signal Factor: A factor that influences the average value, but not the variability in response.

System Design: The design of a product or a process using special Taguchi techniques.

Taguchi Design: A methodology to increase quality by optimizing system design, parameter design, and tolerance design. This text deals with system design.

Target Value: A value that a product is expected to posses. Most often this value is different from what a single unit actually does exhibit. For a 9 volt transistor battery the target value is 9 volts.

Tolerance Design: This is a sophisticated version of parametric design used to optimize tolerance, reduce costs, and increase customer satisfaction.

Variables, Factors, or Parameters: These words are used synonymously to indicate the controllable factors in an experiment. In the case of a plastic molding experiment, molding temperature, injection pressure, set time, etc., are factors.

Index

Accuracy, 4
Agricultural condition, 1
Air bag design, 202, 203
Allied forces, 7
Analysis of results, 16, 65
  signal/noise, 18
Analysis of variance (ANOVA), 3, 16, 32,
    100, 115, 117, 130, 143, 144, 152, 153,
    170, 188, 189, 191, 193, 194, 199, 200,
    204, 208
Analytical simulation, 17
Application example, 182
Array notation, 85, 184
Automobile generator, 190
Average effects, 2, 3, 48, 49, 67, 69
Average factor effects, 99
Average performance, 48
Average value, 33

Baking process, 24
  experiment, 62
Barrier test vehicle, 198
Bell Laboratories, 7
Best combinations, 2
Brainstorming, 17, 29, 31, 44, 173
  major steps of, 181
  session, 173, 175

Casting process, 83, 161
Characteristic effect, 173
Chemical and pharmaceutical industries, 1
Chocolate chip cookie, 2
Classical technique, 18
Column modification, 76
Column preparation, 79
Combination design, 90
Combinations, 2
Competitive position, 1
Conclusions, 47
Confidence interval, 116, 138, 139, 140, 141,
    185, 196, 201, 205

Confirmation test, 56
Conformance to specifications, 13
Consistency in experimental design, 17
Controllable factors, 27, 45, 90
Corrections factors, 50, 113
Cost of rejections, 39
  variation, 22
Crank shaft surface, 186
Critical dimension, 11
Customer satisfaction, 12, 14
Customer preference, 2

Degrees of freedom (DOF), 50, 51, 52, 62,
    101, 105, 115, 120, 132, 144, 150
Degrees of interaction, 3
Deming, W. E., 8
Design of experiment, 2
Design factors, 175, 187, 191, 194, 197, 206,
    207. *See also* Factor
Dryer motor belt, 166
Dummy treatment, 76, 82, 83, 84
Dummy level, 84, 85

Effective number of replications, 140
Electrical communication laboratories (ECL), 7
Engine valve train, 182, 183, 185
Engine idle stability, 193
Engineering, 2
  communication, 44
Evaluation criteria, 175
Error sum of squares, 104
  DOF, 136
  variance, 136
Estimated results, 139
Examination of customer response, 2
Experimental efficiency, 31, 32, 42
  data, 59
  errors, 5

Factorial design of experiment, 1, 27, 30, 42
Factor, 2
  description, 189, 193, 208

Fish finder, 32
Fisher, R. A., 1, 27, 40
Fractional factorial design, 27
Frequency distribution, 12
Front structure crush, 207, 208
Fuel pump noise, 169
Full factorial experiment, 31, 55
    design, 41
Fundamental concepts, 9

General variance, 102
Grand total, 55
Graphical method, 59

Ingredients, 2
Inner array, 28, 91, 95
Instrument panel structure, 195
Interacting pair, 60
Interaction, 3, 40, 58, 59, 60, 81, 128
    effects, 70, 90
    pair, 69
    studies, 176
Intersecting lines, 69

Japanese telephone system, 7

Latin squares, 14
Levels, 2
Life expectancy, 9
Linear combination, 44
Linear graph, 61, 63, 71, 74, 77, 82
Loss function, 10, 11, 13, 18, 33, 156, 157,
    160, 163, 164, 171

Main effects, 3, 30, 44, 49, 82, 86, 93, 94,
    143, 152, 176, 184, 188, 192, 195, 198,
    200, 204, 208
Manufacturing process control, 32
Manufacturing tolerance, 39, 161, 167, 168
Market survey, 2, 3
Mean squared deviation (MSD), 33, 36, 92,
    146, 149, 162
Mean squares, 50
Mixed levels, 40, 58
Molding process, 45, 75
Monthly savings, 165
Multiple runs, 142

Noise condition, 94

factor, 9, 30, 90, 92, 94, 95, 176
    experiment, 95
Nonparallel, 3

Objective evaluation, 19
Off-line strategy, 8
    quality improvement, 8
One way ANOVA, 106, 112
Operating condition, 16
Optimization, 1, 29
Optimum combination, 55, 86
    condition, 10, 16, 29, 33, 44, 48, 49, 94,
        96
    performance, 55
    treatment, 1
Orthogonal arrays (OA), 14, 93, 187, 202,
    206
Outer array, 28, 91, 95
Out-of-tolerance, 12
Overall evaluation criteria (OEC), 19, 178,
    179

Pace maker, 1
Parallel, 3
Parameter design, 10, 24
Partial factorial experiment, 40, 41
Percent characteristics, 13
Percent contribution, 50, 51, 110, 115, 123
Percent influence, 55
Pooled effects, 54
Pooling, 124, 134
Pound cake, 26
Price and performance, 1
Problem solving, 18
Product parameter, 8
Product warranty, 18
Profitability, 1
Pure sum of squares, 50, 51, 109, 111, 123,
    133

QUALITEK-3 software, 125
Quality characteristic, 19, 20, 156, 158
Quality strategy, 23

Random order, 46, 47
Relative influence, 30
    contribution, 50
    significance, 72

Repetition, 47, 91
Replication, 47, 121
Reproducibility, 41
Response
  customer, 2
  mean, 2
Robust condition, 9, 17, 91

Second World War, 7, 14
Session advisor, 174
Signal to noise ratio (S/N), 28, 31, 33, 36,
    92, 96, 145, 148, 150, 153, 154
Simulation studies, 18
Snack food, 2
Societal loss, 11, 14
Sony, 12
Specification limit, 11
Standard analysis, 126
  approach, 16
  arrays, 30, 58
  deviation, 33, 105, 163, 164
Statistical process control (SPC), 32, 103
Subjective evaluation, 19
Sugar, 2, 3
Sums of squares, 50, 115
Supplier tolerance, 161, 168
System design, 10

Taguchi philosophy, 8
Target value, 9, 158
  properties, 11
Team approach, 17, 18
Team leader, 174
Technique, 1
Total degrees of freedom, 50
Tolerance
  design, 10
  levels, 37
  limits, 167, 168
Traditional practices, 7
Transmission control cable, 204
Treatment, 2
Trial condition, 14, 89, 98
Trial run, 89
Triangular table, 60, 61, 71, 72
Two way ANOVA, 117

Uncontrollable factors, 27
Up-front thinking, 31

Variability, 100
Variance, 102
  ratio, 50, 53, 109, 115, 120, 133
  data, 163, 164
Variation, 9, 20, 115

ORDER FORM

QUALITEK-3, Version 3.1 $795
IBM PC SOFTWARE FOR DESIGN AND ANALYSIS OF TAGUCHI EXPERIMENTS

Name _____

Company _____

Address _____

_____

Phone Number (   )_____-_____

PO Number _____

MasterCard or Visa _____

Expiration Date _____

Number of Copies _____

Diskette size: _____ 3 1/2" _____ 5 1/4"

Send order form or call for information:

NUTEK, INC.
30400 Telegraph Rd., #380
BIRMINGHAM, MI 48010
(313)642-4560